THE GLOOMY DEAN

the thought of
William Ralph Inge

The Thought of William Ralph Inge

THE
GLOOMY
DEAN

by

ROBERT M. HELM

JOHN F. BLAIR, *Publisher* Winston-Salem 1962

TO MY MOTHER

in grateful recognition
of her assistance
and encouragement

FOREWORD

This book is not intended primarily as a work of biography, for only the first chapter is biographical. Nor is it a critique in the usual sense, although I have not refrained entirely from critical comment. It is, rather, an account of the roles played by the late W. R. Inge as scholar, clergyman, critic, and moralist.

I am indebted to the Carnegie Foundation for a generous grant which made possible much of the travel and research on which this work is based. I am also grateful to Wake Forest College for making funds available for preparation of the manuscript.

Among the many individuals who have helped me in one way or another, I want particularly to thank Alban G. Widgery, Professor Emeritus of Philosophy at Duke University, for advice and assistance dating from a time long before the actual writing was begun. Others who contributed generously of their time and advice and hospitality were Clement C. J. Webb, sometime Professor of the Philosophy of the Christian Religion in the University of Oxford, and the Very Reverend W. R. Matthews, Dean of St. Paul's.

Finally, I wish to acknowledge my indebtedness to Dr. Inge himself. His sympathetic interest in my work, his invaluable suggestions, and the courtesy he showed me when I visited him at Brightwell Manor enabled me to view his thought in a perspective which would not otherwise have been possible.

CONTENTS

THE GLOOMY DEAN

the thought of
William Ralph Inge

I THE MAN
AND HIS
WRITINGS

Wᴵᴸᴸᴵᴬᴹ ʀᴬᴸᴾʜ ᴵᴺɢᴇ was recognized during his lifetime, not merely as a prominent clergyman, but as one of his country's outstanding literary figures. In the present century his reputation has extended beyond the bounds of his native country, for Continental writers have brought his views to the attention of Europeans, and his works have been widely circulated in America.

Inge himself was somewhat skeptical concerning the extent of his popularity. "If I'm so well known in America," he once asked, "why don't Americans buy more of my books?" However, whether or not his writings were commercial successes in the New World, his name—or at least his sobriquet, "The Gloomy Dean"—was quite familiar to a generation of Americans, many of whom had no notion what he might be dean of or of the reason for his alleged gloom. Furthermore, many of his books are read and appreciated by persons who have little knowledge of or interest in the philosophical Neoplatonism which is at the core of his thinking. This fact is in part due to the charm and wit with which he presents his views and in part to a clarity of vision which made him capable of rendering essentially sound criticisms in certain areas of contemporary life simply because he saw the modern world in the sort of perspective provided by a considerable knowledge of history, a lifetime of thought, and a \conspicuous/ability to avoid entanglement with the "spirits of the age." Although many of the battles in which he engaged have now already been won or lost, his writings are, nevertheless, still worth the attention of any thoughtful person, for Inge was the best-known exponent in his day of a tradition which has been held to be a central one in Anglican Christianity. Inge was, to be sure, interested in the world, but his thoughts invariably led him beyond history to that Ground of all change which he regarded as beyond change. This consistent and devoted preoccupation with the Divine Nature commands the respect of many persons whose metaphysics are at wide variance with Inge's. To appreciate him is not necessarily to agree with him.

For a long time Inge was reluctant to publish information about his personal affairs. He thought most biographies of celebrities to be psychologically worthless, for he believed that the ambitious man deliberately creates his own biographical data for public consumption. Concerning such a public figure, he says:

Whether he is writing a letter of condolence, or his first impressions of the Lake of Lucerne, he thinks subconsciously, "How will this read in my *Life and Letters?*" He decides early that he will be a judge, or a bishop, or a cabinet minister, and drills himself always to behave, and if possible to look, like that kind of person. Habit soon becomes second nature—and, for that matter, nature is only first habit. By the time he is a bishop, it is no effort to him to be dignified, fatherly, and cautious. By the time he is a judge, he looks, even in his bath, as wise as a stuffed owl. By the time he is a cabinet minister, he looks as if he had been born in a frock-coat, and has acquired the art of fulminating for an hour without saying anything at all. Such lives lack psychological interest, being entirely directed outwards; but unquestionably this kind of honourable ambition inhibits a crowd of temptations, and produces very useful citizens.[1]

Inge had no early intention of being a dean. He did not in his youth consciously create material for biographers. His reticence concerning his personal life was hardly cracked when, on his retirement as Dean of St. Paul's, he gave the public his *Vale,* in which he revealed as much as he thought suitable of the influences shaping his thought. However, his *Diary of a Dean,* published in 1949, gives a more intimate account of a portion of his private life. From his earliest years, ideas played a large part in the formation of his character, and a discussion of his personality based on his writings would not be inconsistent with that afforded by available biographical materials.

Inge was born in the North Riding of Yorkshire, on June 6, 1860, the son of the Rev. William Inge, D.D., Curate of Crayke, and his wife, Susan Mary. The religious upbringing which he might have been expected to receive in the home of a nineteenth-century clergyman was further insured by the relative isolation of his early life. His family had few neighbors and his home was far from any railway. His parents, who supervised his childhood education, had him learn many passages of the Bible by heart and thus very early cast his thoughts in a scriptural mold frequently evident in his writings. His classicism was foreshadowed by his ready response to the able tuition given him by his father and mother, "scholarly and admirable teachers," who included in the curriculum for their children such excellent and now almost extinct exercises as reading aloud. Inge never proved false to the values inculcated by his quiet and secluded country rearing. Throughout his life he remained a careful and independent thinker, with a strong revulsion to being made a victim of crowd psychology or transient concerns. He thoroughly appreciated the restraint imposed upon him by his early training. "The habit of rushing about from place to place," he wrote, "and of craving for amusements, was unknown to us as to very many of our contemporaries. I do not think that the change has been altogether for the better."[2]

Although Inge was destined to become known as a theological liberal, there can be little doubt that his attitude toward ecclesiastical matters was tempered by the fact that he was brought up in a home permeated by the atmosphere of the early days of the Oxford Movement.

It was not the dominant religious climate of Inge's own generation. At the time of his birth, twenty-seven years had passed since John Keble had preached his famous sermon at Oxford on "National Apostasy," upholding the authority of the Church of England against the secular power of Parliament in ecclesiastical matters. The movement thus begun was given form and direction through a series of ninety tracts written by Keble, John Henry Newman, Edward Bouverie Pusey, and Richard Hurrell Froude. These writings, published under the title *Tracts for the Times,* gave the movement its alternate name of "Tractarian." In them a theory of the Church was formulated which was to become generally known as "Anglo-

Catholic." The Church of England, with its associated churches in the Anglican Communion, is held to be a legitimate branch of the "one Holy, Catholic, and Apostolic Church of Christ," bound together with the Roman and Eastern churches by common origin, by creed, and by the apostolic succession, but separated from them by the circumstances of history. By implication, the Anglican tradition is held to represent the purest form of Catholicism, providing a middle way between Rome, whose doctrines go beyond revealed truth, and the Evangelicals, whose beliefs fall short of it. Though the Bishop of Rome is recognized as occupying a position of great dignity within the Church, his claim as Pope to authority over the other bishops is denied.

But if Anglo-Catholicism rejected an infallible papacy, it came to be equally firm in its denial that the whole truth is to be found in a literal interpretation of Scripture. A part of Christian truth is only implied in the Gospels and is developed more explicitly only in the living history of the Church. It was this position which later in the movement made possible a certain hospitality to liberal thought, consistent with the Anglican view of the nature of the Church.

It is not to be supposed that Inge was, as a boy, directly aware of the shifting currents in the Tractarian attitude toward Christianity which were to affect his thinking. Theological liberalism, although already present in the movement at large, was not conspicuously evident in his home. His parents were products of the earlier days of Tractarianism and apparently even less hospitable to textual criticism than the founders of the movement. More-

over, they were little affected by the development among
High-churchmen of an increased regard for ritual and
ceremony. Young Inge was exposed to this aspect of the
movement only after his family moved to Oxford, where
he was impressed by the beauty of the services at St.
Barnabas but found the preaching and teaching distasteful.
All in all, he seems to have remained virtually unaffected
by the growth of ritualism, a circumstance due in part
to his indifference to the attitudes toward the Eucharist
which gave rise to some of the more "Roman" practices
of the Anglo-Catholic clergy and in part to a totally un-
musical ear. His real dislike of music was not altered by
time or training. At the age of ninety-one, he confessed
his lack of enthusiasm for the ability demonstrated by
one of his sons as a pianist and stoutly proclaimed, "If I
knew that I had to spend eternity listening to the music of
celestial choirs, I shouldn't be nearly so keen on living the
good life."

Life in Inge's childhood home was strongly influenced
by his maternal grandfather, Edward Churton, Archdeacon
of Cleveland and Rector of Crayke. It was from him that
many of the influences growing out of the early Oxford
Movement were transmitted to the family, for young Inge's
father, though a scholarly man in his own right, appears to have ordered his home according to the pattern
set at the Rectory. Conservatism and piety were strongly
emphasized. Fasting during Lent was customary but un-
spectacular, consisting largely in abstention from sugar in
tea and consumption of rice pudding. Sunday observance
was rigid, and the theatre, though not condemned, was not
patronized. Novel-reading was confined to older works,

and "Low Churchmen," "Broad Churchmen," and theological liberals were regarded with varying degrees of pity,
contempt, or horror.

It is evident that Inge had some admiration for the early
Tractarians and was not unsympathetic to certain of their
aims. Their very real devotion continued to attract him as
much as the bigotry of some of their followers came to
repel him. As the medieval simplicity which characterized
the earlier history of the Anglo-Catholic party gave way to
the ritualism and pretentiousness which Inge thought to be
all too often present in the later attitudes of its members,
he was to find himself engaged in battle with them on
more than one occasion. Charles Gore, Bishop of Birming-
ham, drew Inge's fire in 1908 for his militant High-
churchmanship. The increasingly Latin tone of the movement, which seemed to make it reasonable for the less
Protestant of its followers to follow Newman, Ward, and
Manning into the arms of Rome, was a source of continuing alarm. The Oxford Movement had, in Inge's view,
become a threat to the English Church as nothing else had
been since the Wesleyan secession—a greater threat, in
fact, for he feared that a victorious High-Church party
would alter the whole character of the Established Church
rather than merely weaken its numbers.

In Inge's position with regard to Tractarianism, as indeed in his whole outlook, the influences of his early life
at Crayke are clearly evident. The Church of his youth
was solidly English and generally Tory. Inge remained essentially conservative in his political convictions, and,
despite certain critical attitudes which caused the Abbé
Nédoncelle to describe him as "a Christian who does not

love the Church, or at least the visible Church,"[3] he was, throughout his life, loyal to the Church of England as the organization which in inimitable fashion represents the religious convictions and practices of the English people. The threat of disestablishment was one which he viewed with dismay, and he felt that if the Anglo-Catholics were to prevail, disestablishment or surrender to Rome would be a not unlikely result.

He also became alarmed at the involvement of leaders of the High-Church movement in progressive political and economic movements during the early part of the twentieth century. From the Anglo-Catholic viewpoint, an interest in social and economic betterment was the natural out-growth of a conception of the mission of the Church as embracing every facet of human life. Even during the nineteenth century the movement numbered priests and laymen who devoted themselves to ministry among the poor, particularly in the slums of the industrialized cities which were rapidly spreading their blight over large sections of England. The conservatism of the early Tractarians gave way to an active desire on the part of many Anglo-Catholics to build a society on a foundation of Christian concern for human welfare. Their concern was one of the major factors which led to the founding in 1889 of the Christian Social Union.

The Union was the first of many Anglican responses to the challenge of the secular Socialists, whose concern for social betterment was often combined with an indifference to religion. Rightly or wrongly, Inge felt that in appropriating to the Church the social programs of the reformers,

some Anglo-Catholic leaders had sold out to the Socialists. Although his remarks about Socialism sometimes
seem to exhibit the weary resignation of a man facing
the inevitable, the conservatism of his upbringing made
it impossible for him to see in the various proletarian
movements anything other than a direct threat to the basic
values of English life. Though he felt some sympathy for
the humanitarian motives which led some church leaders
into the political and economic arena, he prophesied
grimly that a church which lent its support to Socialism
would be used for political purposes and then cynically
cast aside. An unrepentant advocate of an aristocratic
ethos, he never recognized the claim of the underprivileged
or their self-appointed representatives to be the possessors
of a superior moral code.

In 1874, after the death of Inge's maternal grandfather,
his parents moved to Alrewas, near Lichfield, where his
father was given the benefice. This move reinstated the
family in its ancestral county but gave young Inge's father
the duty of restoring his newly-acquired church, largely
out of his own funds. He accomplished this labor in six
years and was then appointed by Lord Salisbury as Provost
of Worcester College at Oxford, where he had been a
Scholar and Fellow. He was later offered the bishopric of
Salisbury but, convinced that he was not qualified for the
post, immediately declined it. His son later felt that he was
possibly justified in his refusal. He was, according to the
Dean, "a slow worker and not an impressive preacher."[4]
At any rate, the family continued to live happily at
Worcester College until the death of the elder Inge in

1903. Inge's mother, in fact, remained a resident of Oxford until her death during the First World War at the age of eighty-three.

Despite the sobriquet given him by the press, Inge gave very little evidence throughout his later life of any tendency toward pessimism or morbidity. However, he reports that his early years, from a time before he was seven years old until his marriage, were troubled by a persistent melancholia. He attributed a portion of his difficulty to overwork in school and at the university, where he was in continuous and fierce competition with other ambitious and scholarly young men, but the early occurrence of these fits of depression make it impossible for all of them to be ascribed to overwork. Inge wisely recognized that it is generally futile to attempt to specify the cause of such conditions. The effort to do so usually results in a good deal of rationalization while the real source remains hidden from the sufferer. One clue, however, we are given. The onslaughts of melancholy disappeared with his happy marriage to the woman for whom he entertained the utmost respect and affection for the rest of his life. "I have no doubt," he writes, "that when a man suffers from these troubles, and the *acedia* to which they lead, the blessed realization that he loves and is loved is the best of all remedies."[5] One suspects that he felt a certain sense of isolation during his childhood. His parents, he confesses, failed to understand him, and his father, who apparently suffered from no complexities of temperament, could contribute no more helpful advice than the admonition, "Remember good Bishop Hacket's motto—Serve God and be cheerful." "Alas!" Inge says. "How could I be, with a legion of devils waiting for me in my unoccupied moments?"[6]

Dean Matthews, his successor at St. Paul's, ascribes some of Inge's difficulty to his awareness that the liberal tendencies of his theology were a source of grief to his mother. Inge himself, in the published version of his diary, discusses his mother's Tractarian intolerance of his views:

This was a real tragedy for me; my mother never really forgave me for not being an Anglo-Catholic. When a friend wrote to congratulate her on my appointment to St. Paul's, he was startled to find that my promotion had given her no pleasure. It was bad enough to be a 'Low Churchman'; but a 'Broad Churchman' was damned below Judas. But I think in the last years of her life, thanks partly to Kitty's good offices, she was able to feel rather differently towards me.[7]

In the light of his own experience with these moods, Inge advises parents of children faced with similar situations to bring their troubles into the open. Such a cathartic process generally reveals the absurdity of the condition, and the insight gained helps the sufferer to take a healthy and objective view of the situation which, if it does not cure, at least minimizes the difficulty. "Nothing helped me more," Inge reports, "than the discovery that if I woke up in the night, I could tell the time within an hour by the state of my spirits. A mental temperature of below zero meant that it was between three and five!"[8] Looking back on his youth, Inge acknowledges that his depressed moods probably did not occupy as much of his time as they seemed to in retrospect. Their traumatic character made them much clearer to memory in his later life than the more frequent times when he was happy or not critically concerned with his mood.

After three months at a preparatory school, young Inge, then fourteen years old, stood for a scholarship at Eton and was elected second on the list. His father, after trying unsuccessfully to place him under two of the younger masters, whose lists were full, selected as a tutor for his son a cousin of the novelist Thackeray, an enthusiastic student of the classics who was, according to Inge, "the best tutor at Eton for boys who wished to work, and perhaps the worst for those who did not."[9] Inge had no aversion to work, and his devotion to classical thought was given direction and clear purpose at Eton.

A scholarly young man of nineteen, he entered King's College, Cambridge, in 1879. Interested in cricket, and serving his college team occasionally as a player, he nevertheless devoted most of his efforts to his studies, with notable success. His undergraduate career, as he himself records, was largely "a record of scholarships and prizes."[10] He was Bell Scholar and Porson Prizeman in 1880; Porson Scholar in 1881; Craven Scholar and Browne Medallist in 1882; Senior Chancellor's Medallist in 1883; and Hare Prizeman in 1885. In 1882 and 1883, he took first-class honors in the classics. At the university he had full scope for that exploration of ancient thought which he had learned to love as a boy, and he tells us that the most enjoyable period of his work came when he was reading for the ancient history section of the second part of the Classical Tripos.

It seems that, in spite of his churchly upbringing, no thought crossed his mind during his college days that he might be destined for an ecclesiastical career. Certainly no premonition prepared him for the day, still thirty-odd

years in the future, when he would find himself responsible
for the liturgical and choral activities of St. Paul's Cathedral. "It amuses me," he writes, "to remember that I
obtained leave from the college authorities to absent myself from the elaborate choral services on Sunday after-
noons in King's Chapel, on the understanding that I went
to a parochial service in the evening. I little knew what
the fates had in store for me."[11]

In 1884, Inge returned to Eton as an Assistant Master and
served there until 1888. During the last two years of this
period, he was also a Fellow at King's College. He wrote a
series of Greek and Latin texts for Eton and produced the
essay entitled *Society in Rome under the Caesars,* which
won him the Hare Prize at Cambridge and gained for him
critical acclaim for his ability to capture the essence of a
remote period of history. After three years at Eton he began
to think seriously of ordination. Deacon's orders were given
him by Bishop King of the diocese of Lincoln, by virtue
of Inge's position at King's College, which fell within that
diocese. The young deacon was still unsure of his clerical
vocation and was remarkably slow in pursuing it further.
In fact, it was not until four years later that he accepted
priest's orders and not until 1905 that he accepted a parish.

In 1889, shortly after his ordination, Inge was appointed
Fellow and Tutor at Hertford College, Oxford, where he
remained until 1904.

The fact that during his student days in Cambridge Inge
had concentrated upon the study of Greek literature accounts in great measure for the sharp contrast between the
tenor of his thought and the traditional spirit of Cambridge philosophy, a spirit characterized by close attention

to science, mathematics, and modern rather than ancient thought. In Oxford he found himself in a more congenial intellectual atmosphere and began to read widely in philosophy. It does not seem incorrect to say that he never really had a philosophical training. As a result of his classical background, he was strongly attracted by Greek philosophy and was particularly influenced by the more idealistic traditions in ancient thought. Characteristically, he used his studies in philosophy to search for a firm intellectual ground for his religious convictions, and this effort provided him with the idiom in which he was to speak for the remainder of his life. In the writings of St. Paul and St. John, Scotus Erigena and Meister Eckhart, the Cambridge Platonists and Bishop Westcott, he found a tradition of "mysticism based on a foundation of reason," which seemed to him to constitute an independent line of Christian thought quite different from the traditions of authority of Church or Bible found respectively in Catholicism and Protestantism. Many years later, he was to express succinctly the conclusions he had formed at Oxford, when, in 1926, he wrote in his preface to *The Platonic Tradition in English Religious Thought:*

This short course of Lectures . . . must be taken for what it is, a plea for the recognition of a third type of Christian thought and belief, by the side of the two great types which, for want of better names, are usually called Catholic and Protestant. The three types are happily not mutually exclusive. Just as there is a strong Evangelical element in the best Catholics, and just as many devout Protestants are earnest sacramentalists, so mysticism, and the Christian Platonism which is the philosophy of mysticism, are at home in all branches of Christendom. But I have claimed that the history of Christian Platonism, and the fruits which it has borne, justify its recognition as a legitimate and independent type of Christian theology and practice.[12]

The son and grandson of Anglican clergymen, an habitué of ecclesiastical circles, and a conscientious Christian clergyman, Inge endeavored to expound his views so as to conform as closely as possible to traditional Christian thought and phraseology. The voice was the voice of Christendom, but the hands were the hands of Plato.

Inge found such a position much better suited to his temperament than any of the more militant varieties of Catholicism or Protestantism would have been. The view that an institutional church could rightly be regarded as infallible he regarded as outrageous. "Nothing can be more fantastic," he felt, "than the Tractarian theory that the General Councils were infallibly guided, but that the gift of infallibility went into abeyance when the Church was divided, like an old English peerage when there is more than one daughter but no son."[13] Just as he could not align himself with any set of institutionalists professing authority over the individual, so he could not agree with those who regarded the Bible as an inerrant document constituting "the religion of Protestants." The claim of verbal inspiration is not made in the Scriptures. Inge saw quite clearly that if such a claim is to be made at all, it must rest upon the conviction that the church which drew up the Canon could not err, for it had to determine which of many books were inspired and which were not. But to admit such infallibility would have brought him back to a position which he had already had to reject. At any rate, he felt, modern Biblical criticism had dealt a death blow to the traditional views about the Christian Scriptures, and an educated man could no longer be a literalist. Insistence upon regarding the Old and New Testaments as a continuous book had, he felt, made the forms of Anglican worship more Jewish than was necessary. It was from this atmosphere that he fled to the more congenial realm of Greek thought and the inner life of the spirit. He felt that he had no choice.

At the time of his retirement from St. Paul's he wrote that he had never had what are commonly called mystical experiences. Nevertheless, he turned to Christian mysticism because of his confidence in the Platonic philosophy which has so often been associated with it. After all, he concluded, prayer is the fundamental mystical experience, and if most of us do not progress as far in the life of the spirit as the saints who have given up much that they may gain more, we have no right to regard their testimony as invalid on that account. They are entitled to the same confidence that we accord to experts in other fields. The uniformity of their testimony with regard to the things of the spirit is remarkable and is most reasonably explained by the assumption that their experiences are experiences of reality. "I was convinced very early," Inge writes, "and I have never wavered in my conviction, that this testimony of the saints and mystics has far greater evidential value than is usually supposed, and that it may properly take the place of those traditional 'evidences' which for one reason or another have lost their cogency."[14]

While still at Oxford, Inge was asked to deliver the Bampton Lectures. According to the will of Canon Bampton of Salisbury, founder of the series, the heads of Colleges at the University, proceeding according to an unvarying ritual, were required each year to select a Lecturer for the following year to deliver eight Divinity Lecture Sermons at St. Mary's in Oxford. The Lecturer was required to have at least the Master of Arts degree from either Oxford or Cambridge. The will further stipulated:

Also I direct and appoint, that the eight Divinity Lecture Sermons shall be preached upon either of the following Subjects— to confirm and establish the Christian Faith, and to confute all heretics and schismatics—upon the Divine authority of the Holy Scriptures—upon the authority of the writings of the primitive Fathers, as to the faith and practice of the primitive Church— upon the Divinity of our Lord and Saviour Jesus Christ—upon the Divinity of the Holy Ghost—upon the Articles of the Christain Faith, as comprehended in the Apostles' and Nicene Creeds.[15]

It must have been obvious to Inge that the only one of these subjects which could possibly serve as a vehicle for an exposition of the philosophy which he had by that time adopted was the first. Even so, it is possible that Canon Bampton might have been somewhat surprised at the form which the confirmation and establishment of the Christian faith took in the lectures delivered in that last year of the nineteenth century. Inge himself admits to some hesitation in his decision to develop the lectures in the framework of a historical treatment of Christian mysticism, but for him it was that or nothing. Admitting that "this arrangement may cause my object to be misunderstood," he nevertheless stoutly maintained that he wished his work to be judged "as a contribution to apologetics, rather than as a historical sketch of Christian Mysticism."[16] Actually, once he had decided that Platonism represented the real central core of Christian theology, Inge honestly regarded himself as engaged in a defense of the Christian faith in his careful and scholarly treatment of those men whom he viewed as the bearers of the great tradition. The "heretics and schismatics" whom he set about to confute appear to have been the Roman Catholics, with their "debased mysticism," the rigidly Biblical Protestants, the occultists, the positivists, and a host of other opponents whom he found to be foes or corrupters of Platonism. His criticism of a work by Ribet (*La Mystique Divine distinguée des Contrefaçons diaboliques*) appeared, even to him, to be such strong meat that he eliminated it from the published lectures, where he had intended it to form an appendix. In his preface to the lectures, he explains his motive for this action.

It would have opened the eyes of some of my readers to the irreconcilable antagonism between the Roman Church and science; but though I translated and summarised my author faithfully, the result had all the appearance of a malicious travesty. I have therefore suppressed this Appendix; but with regard to Roman Catholic "Mysticism" there is no use in mincing matters. Those who find edification in signs and wonders of this kind, and think that such "supernatural phenomena," even if they were well authenticated instead of being ridiculous fables, could possibly establish spiritual truths, will find little or nothing to please or interest them in these pages. But those who reverence Nature and Reason, and have no wish to hear of either of them being "overruled" or "suspended," will, I hope, agree with me in valuing highly the later developments of mystical thought in Northern Europe.[17]

Through the publication of the Bampton Lectures, Inge, already well known among English scholars, gained a wider recognition for himself and for the place in British religious thought of mysticism and Platonism.

It was while he was at Oxford also that Inge became interested in the work of Plotinus, the Egyptian philosopher and mystic who taught in Rome in the third century A.D. Although Plotinus was not a member of the Christian Church and recognized Plato as his master, Inge found in him the fullest flowering of the approach to reality which he regarded as most distinctively Christian. Plotinus became his guide to the religious life, and Inge began that work on the Egyptian's philosophy which, written little by little over a long period of time, was to become his *magnum opus*. "Plotinus," he was to write years later, "is the greatest of all truly religious philosophers. His is a deep spiritual religion resting partly on philosophic thought and partly on intimate personal experience. It stands free of any historical events in past or future. For this reason, he has a message for us today. To speak for myself, I have lived with him for nearly thirty years, and I have not sought him in vain, in prosperity or adversity."[18]

As his days at Oxford drew toward their close, Inge, now an ordained priest of the Church of England, came to be in wide demand as a guest preacher. He collected a group of his sermons in 1904 and published them under the title of *Faith and Knowledge*. A university sermon preached at St. Mary's, Oxford, in March of 1904, on the subject of "Liberal Catholicism" is probably the most noteworthy in the volume. In it, he began a feud with the Catholic Modernists which he was destined to wage with considerable energy for nearly half a century, and which was to diminish in intensity only during his tenth decade, when, living in retirement at Brightwell Manor, he finally

admitted that he had changed his mind to some extent on
the subject and had come to agree with Loisy and his followers that we lay too much stress in Christianity on what
happened two thousand years ago. "The significant thing,"
he at last decided, "is what Christ means for us today."

In 1904, however, no such temperate mood was evident
in the attack delivered against the Roman Catholic heresy.
His chief target was Alfred Firmin Loisy, a French cleric
some three years Inge's senior. Loisy had for some years
fought a battle with his conscience over his inability to accept as factually true the accounts in the Gospels on which
the doctrines of the Church are based. As early as 1893
views originating with him had been condemned in an
encyclical issued by Pope Leo XIII, and less than a year before Inge's sermon five of Loisy's books were placed on the
Index. However, his works had aroused a good deal of
favorable attention among Roman and non-Roman churchmen alike for his contention that the principle of development must be recognized as central in the philosophy of
the Church if dogmatic theology is to be preserved in the
face of scientific onslaughts and critical analysis. In Loisy,
the recognition of this principle took a rather startlingly
pragmatic form. We may, he held, give an unhesitating
assent to the dogmas of the Church, but not because they
are true in any literal sense. He showed, in fact, a marked
enthusiasm for any evidence which would tend to make it
impossible to accept them as literally true. Jesus of Nazareth, he maintained, is not the Lord Christ of the Church.
He was a peasant of "limited intelligence," who wrongly
believed that certain apocalyptic events were at hand and
wasted his energies in urging men to prepare for them.

Across the gulf of the centuries, Loisy apparently believed, this figure has nothing to say to our intellects. As a matter of fact, in our devotion to the Church, we must not rely upon the intellect. The will and the moral sense are the source of our acceptance of theological propositions arrived at by the Church. And it is in the Church, not in history, that we find the "Christ of Faith," who is, in fact, a product of the long history of the Catholic Church. This view also found support in the writings of the Irish Jesuit scholar, George Tyrrell.

Ironically, but inevitably, Loisy and Tyrrell were excommunicated by the body which they had sought to defend as the true repository of Christian revelation. They would have fared no better in a church in which Inge might have wielded Papal authority, for he regarded their offense as a triple one. In the first place, he saw their exaltation of will at the expense of intelligence as intolerable. He also reacted with alarm to the claim to absolute authority implicit in Loisy's bland acceptance of anything which a growing and developing organism like the Roman Church may see fit to define as a matter of faith. However, at that time, Inge also found himself in agreement with the Pope, who in condemning modernism as a heresy, recognized its deep-seated incompatibility with what Christians have historically believed and what they must believe if they are to remain Christian.

When Jesus Christ was on earth [Inge writes], He promised His disciples that the Holy Spirit should abide for ever in the Church, bringing to our remembrance all that He had said unto them, and teaching us some things which they were still unable to bear. Are we to see in the statutory, historical Church the fulfilment of this promise? Is Catholicism, in all its later develop-

ments, the true image of the body of Christ? Is it here, and not in
the Gospels, that we are to study the character and life of our
Redeemer? St. Paul, who is often invoked by this school, made
it his hope and aim that the Church might grow up *into* Him in
all things, which is the head, even Christ. We are now told that
we must be content to grow up *out of* Him. Our historical pattern has been taken away from us. We are forbidden to look
back. Any new developments which may be necessary for the
survival of the statutory Church are justified, nay consecrated,
by being necessary.

It is a monstrous delusion to suppose that this was St. Paul's
theology, or St. Augustine's.[19]

In 1905 Inge followed up the material presented in the
Bampton Lectures with a series of lectures on the same
subject delivered in the Church of St. Margaret's, Westminster. In these discussions, published in 1906 under
the title *Studies of English Mystics,* he reaffirmed his faith
in rational mysticism as a foundation for belief independent of history and authority and resting solely on human
experience. Mystics, he concluded, "are the only thoroughgoing empiricists."[20]

It was in 1905 also that Inge again changed his employ-
ment. Ravenscroft Stewart, Vicar of All Saints' Church,
Ennismore Gardens in London, was appointed Archdeacon of Bristol, and Inge was offered Stewart's former living.
He accepted without hesitation, feeling that the change
would be good for his work. A quiet bachelor life in college rooms was pleasant to one of his scholarly temperament, but he confesses that he had begun to wish for a
home of his own. Furthermore, his study of the classics
had led him to a broader interest in philosophical and theological problems than could be satisfied by the linguistic
approach to the classics which his teaching duties required.

All Saints', one of the parishes formed from the once large parish of St. Margaret's, Westminster, was fashionable, aristocratic, and rich, containing, as it did, a large number of retired business and professional men who were, apparently, not ungenerous. Inge made the church richer. He remarks with some self-satisfaction that "though the golden age of the West End incumbents was already coming to an end, I kept my congregation together, and rather characteristically (for I have always been unnecessarily careful about money) piled up a large balance on the parish funds, of which my successor reaped the benefit."[21]

As a practicing clergyman, Inge was undeniably confronted with situations demanding greater breadth of thinking and more skill in social relations than had been required in his somewhat sheltered university life. He adapted himself, apparently without too much difficulty, to a society and a way of life different from what he had previously known. London's West End had not in those years prior to the First World War lost the aura of Victorian splendor developed during the nineteenth century. In the homes of his parishioners, some from the aristocracy and some newly rich, he was regaled with long and splendid dinners, surrounded by hordes of servants, and indoctrinated with social views which he recognized as belonging to a dying age, but which were always thereafter to color his thinking. The demands of his congregation placed some limits upon his preaching, for in addition to the necessity of meeting the intellectual requirements of a number of erudite men and women, including three judges, he was forced also, as he ruefully relates, to consider the wishes of "many old-fashioned people who did not want strong meat." His carefully prepared sermons of this period were, in consequence, models of elegance, inoffensive to the orthodox, and almost completely lacking in explosive political or social views.

Just after being offered the living of All Saints', Inge had become engaged to Mary Catharine Spooner, whom he had met the year before at the house of his uncle, F. G. Inge, whose wife was a sister of Miss Spooner's father. "Kitty," as Inge called her, had in her family background an ecclesiastical and scholarly tradition that was at least a match for his own. Her father was Archdeacon of Maidstone, her grandfather was Bishop Harvey Goodwin of Carlisle, and an uncle was the Warden of New College whose wayward tongue created the original "Spoonerism." In May of 1905, the young couple were married in Canterbury Cathedral by Archbishop Davidson, a relative of the bride. Their new home was at 34 Rutland Gate, in one of those quiet little West End squares which even yet retain their air of elegant respectability in the midst of the hectic life of twentieth-century London. His marriage was destined to be a long and happy one.

The General Seminary in New York invited Inge in 1906 to deliver the Paddock Lectures. During this visit he had lunch with President Theodore Roosevelt and traveled to some extent over the northeastern portion of the country. He cannot be said ever to have been really well acquainted with the United States or thoroughly versed in its thought and traditions. He nevertheless found frequent cause for alarm in the implications of certain ideas and social processes developed in America and expressed his alarm in no uncertain terms. The Paddock Lectures, published in 1907 under the title *Personal Idealism and Mysticism,* mark his real emergence as an internationally recognized critic of contemporary life and thought.

Less than three years after he had become Vicar of All Saints', Inge was elected to the Lady Margaret Professorship at Cambridge, the oldest Chair in the university, and one dignified by having been held by several famous men. Upon his election, he was also invited to become a professorial Fellow of his third College—Jesus College at Cambridge. He found the society pleasant and entered with enthusiasm into what he was later to regard as his most productive period of scholarly work. A pleasant residence called Brook House in Trumpington Street enabled him for the first time in his life to have a garden, and it was with some relief that he returned from the more hectic pace of London life to the ordered quiet of an academic routine.

The teaching of divinity students, he found, required more attention to elementary work than had been the case with his honors men at Oxford whom he had instructed in the classics. The position had compensations, however, which more than made up for this disappointment. The teaching duties were light and vacations long. Almost unlimited time and materials were available for private study, and the freedom which he enjoyed as a professor was much greater than he had experienced at All Saints'. This period of his life was, therefore, productive of some of his best lectures, sermons, and books. His thinking, however, still remained in its classical and scholarly mold. He was not yet to develop that keen interest in contemporary criticism

and twentieth-century morals which was to bring him
world-wide fame.

A quiet and pleasant home life added to the joys of the
Cambridge period. Already the parents of one child,
Craufurd, born during their London residence, the Inges
added three more, Edward, Catharine, and Paula, during
their four years at the University.

Into this idyllic existence Mr. Asquith, then Prime
Minister, threw a bombshell. In April of 1911 he wrote
to Inge, stating that he had nominated him to the King
for the appointment as Dean of St. Paul's. By tradition,
this position carries more literary prestige than any other
in the Church of England. It had been held by such eminent men as Colet, Donne, Tillotson, and—in more recent
years—Milman, Mansel, and Church. The Prime Minister
hoped that, by appointing a scholar of Inge's caliber, he
would be able to touch off a revival of the literary tradition,
which had for some time been in abeyance. Inge knew
that he was not an ecclesiastic in the usual sense of the
word. He also was not pleased with what he heard of the
conditions existing within the Chapter at the time. Against
this, however, he recognized an obligation to the Prime
Minister and to his friends, who had, without his con-
nivance or knowledge, worked diligently to obtain the appointment for him in the hope of establishing a liberal
churchman in one of the most important positions in England.

"A man ought to have some very good reason for refusing an appointment offered in such a way," Inge wrote
later, "and I had no good reason except that I was very
happy where I was, and that I was terribly bored by long

musical services. I therefore accepted after a few days' consideration."[22]

The most unpleasant aspects of the new position made themselves evident almost immediately. Under normal conditions, Inge could have expected to move without delay into the Deanery, an impressive mansion filled with portraits of past deans, and within a short walk of the Cathedral. By a curious arrangement, however, Dean Gregory, the retiring Dean, had been assured that he could continue to occupy the house as long as he lived, and the new Dean found himself confronted with the exacting moral demand of wishing long life for his predecessor while at the same time putting up with the inconvenience occasioned by his survival. The inconvenience was by no means inconsiderable. His wife and family remained in Cambridge, and Inge himself took rooms in a hotel in Bloomsbury, some distance from the Cathedral. He remained there until December of that year, when Dean Gregory died.

An ominous note was also sounded when he conferred with the Archdeacon of London about some of his plans and was informed that so long as two canons, whom the Archdeacon named, were there, the Dean would not be allowed to do anything. The power of the canons was brought into play a few weeks later in an incident which startled Inge considerably. He quotes the story as he wrote it in his diary for Sunday, June 18, 1911:

A number of colonial troops were present at the morning service, and they asked that the organ should play a verse of the national anthem while they marched out after the sermon. The Archdeacon of London, who was in residence, gave his consent. On hearing this, the senior Minor Canon rushed into the vestry, where our guest, the Dean of Gloucester, was robing, and in a voice trembling with excitement announced that the Minor Canons would walk out of church if this was done. In order to avoid the awful scandal of an insult to the King in St. Paul's, the Archdeacon revoked his consent, with my approval.[23]

The canons had no responsibility for the services, and their conduct in this case puzzled Inge. He admitted—rather reluctantly, perhaps—that they were not Communists, and concluded that their act was due to "some cryptic objection to that hymn, or perhaps any hymn, being played at that point of the service."[24]

Inge's difficulties were occasioned largely by the fact that, although the Dean is expected to supervise the activity of the Cathedral in routine matters, he is deficient in independent power. Inge, admitting that administration of this sort was not his forte, accepted what he felt a more self-assertive man would have regarded as a humiliating position and permitted the smoothly-running machine organized by his predecessor to function without much interference. Concerning his association with the Chapter, he commented later that he thought their relations were good, "by the not very high standard of Cathedral Chapters, which have a bad name for quarrelling."[25] When complimented by Archbishop Davidson on the way in which he had kept such "a difficult team" together, he felt that the honor was undeserved. He and his associates, however much they might disagree on many matters of faith and policy were, nevertheless, usually in agreement on the question of the general nature of the services in the Cathedral. St. Paul's had come to symbolize the religious life of the British Empire and Commonwealth in somewhat the same way that Westminster Abbey symbolizes that of England. Inge's conviction that "Prayer Book" or "Central" churchmanship should set the tone for its practices was shared by most of his colleagues. It is true now as it was then that few Anglicans are likely to find anything in the services of the great church to offend their sensibilities.

Inge apparently was not without some feeling of nostalgia for the lost joys of university life. He had an opportunity of accepting the principalship of Hertford College, Oxford, but was restrained from doing so partly by his recognition of the fact that it would have caused smiles for him to throw over a second London position to retreat to a more sheltered academic environment. Furthermore, he was beginning to enjoy being Dean. At the end of 1912 he wrote in his diary:

So ends my first complete year as Dean. My relations with my colleagues are tolerably pleasant, and my home life ideally happy. I own that I enjoy being a person of consideration, little as I desired it. But my literary work has got on badly. We are making very interesting friends in London.[26]

In December of 1915 he became the father of a fifth child, a son named Richard.

London presented Inge in his new position with unprecedented occasions for broadening the scope of his interests, and he was not slow in responding to his opportunities. He was elected president of several societies and helped to found the Religious Thought Society, which was to have an active life of about twelve years before succumbing to a post-war lassitude. He was also active in the work of the Clergy Home Mission Union.

One of his most significant and productive affiliations with an organization was with the Modern Churchmen's Union. This organization had been founded by persons within the Church whose opinions were regarded as sufficiently unorthodox to subject them to the dangers of heresy hunts. It was felt that a union of these liberals would provide for "mutual protection against episcopal persecution."[27] The Union published, under the direction of Dr. H. D. A. Major of Ripon Hall, Oxford, an excellent journal, *The Modern Churchman,* to which Inge was one of a number of eminent contributors. The Dean served as president of this influential organization, succeeding Hastings Rashdall, Dean of Carlisle, in this position. Rashdall, one of the leading figures in the movement, had been known to register some bitterness over the ease with which Inge, whom he considered more heterodox than himself, had soared with serene immunity to heights in the Church normally denied the unorthodox. When told of Inge's appointment to St. Paul's, Rashdall had commented, "Why not? Inge is a Buddhist!" A part of Inge's capacity for survival is explained by his conviction that a liberal clergyman "has no right to cause unnecessary distress to old-fashioned believers." Though the grounds for his own conviction may be quite different from those on which Christian doctrines have traditionally been accepted, the modern churchman should, according to Inge, stress the positive aspects of his own faith without unnecessarily attacking more traditional formulations. Though not always successful in following his own advice, Inge nevertheless managed to remain successfully within the historic framework of the Church with views which, it must be admitted, would in a less cautious man have occasioned continual battles over his alleged heresies.

The Modern Churchmen's Union was probably instrumental in securing for liberal thinkers within the Church a greater degree of tolerance. By the time of his retirement from the Deanship, Inge was able to regard the battle as won, in that the Church was ready to give as great a degree of freedom to modern thinkers as he felt they could legitimately claim. At any rate, Inge never wished to be identified as an extreme "Modernist," for he had an ineradicable respect for the traditional Thomistic philosophy of the Catholic Church. He recognized a sharp distinction between Roman Catholic liberalism, with its separation of truths of faith from truths of fact, and the Protestant liberalism for which he and the other members of the Union spoke.

The cosmopolitan society in which Inge found himself in London also imposed upon him the necessity of taking a more active interest in problems of the day outside the realms of philosophy and theology, which had previously dominated his professional interests almost to the exclusion of everything else. He became interested in the work of the Tavistock Clinic, later called the Institute of Medical Psychology, an organization concerned with the treatment of psychological disorders. He was also associated with the work of the London Library, the Council of Malvern College, and the National Portrait Gallery, of which he was a trustee.

Among the matters of public interest in which the Dean became involved was the study of eugenics. A friend of Sir Francis Galton, the founder of the science, Inge was a member of the council of the Eugenics Society from the time of its organization. Through the years he remained convinced that the improvement of the human race necessitates changes, not merely in the environment, but in the inherited qualities of the persons subjected to it. He realized early in the history of the movement that he and his associates would have to face the opposition of the Roman Catholic Church, "which will pass no coins that do not bear the stamp of its own mint," and of the bulk of the politicians, "who only reflect that the unborn have no votes."[28] If our society is to be made so humanitarian and so noncompetitive that inferior types survive in large numbers, he felt, we must adopt systematic methods for breeding them out to replace the processes of natural selection with which we have interfered. He saw no difficulty in reconciling his advocacy of eugenic principles with Christianity, in which, indeed, he thought such principles to be implicit. Christianity, he maintained, involves the saving or betterment of man, rather than his environment. He even held that Christ was enunciating eugenic precepts when he said, "Do men gather grapes of thorns, or figs of thistles? A corrupt tree cannot bring forth good fruit, neither can a good tree bring forth evil fruit. Every tree which bringeth not forth good fruit is hewn down and cast into the fire."[29]

Closely related to Inge's interest in eugenics was his general enthusiasm for vital statistics. This led him to a study of the population question resulting in the discovery that, except in certain Oriental and Slavic countries, there had been a significant decline in the birth rate since about 1878. This decline, he believed, was the only thing which could have saved the world from intolerable overpopulation. He further maintained that, in view of the fact that modern sanitation and medical practices have reduced those causes of early death which formerly kept the population within reasonable bounds, birth control should be seriously considered as a possible alternative to natural selection, particularly in heavily populated countries like England. Quite accurately, he regarded himself as a courageous pioneer with regard to this subject, and years later, on his retirement as Dean, he was to survey his accomplishments with some satisfaction.

I believe I was the first clergyman to face obloquy by urging that the question ought to be discussed as freely as any other social and economic problem; now, several well-known ecclesiastics openly support the restriction of families. That the taboo was enforced mainly by intimidation, is shown by the fact—very regrettable on eugenic grounds—that the lowest birth-rates are those of the clergy, doctors, and teachers, the three professions from whom denunciations of the practice were most frequently heard. I find, by consulting *Who's Who,* that, of the forty diocesan bishops, one has five children, two others four each, the remaining thirty-seven only twenty-eight among them.[30]

He recognized, however, the dangers to the population involved in birth control, particularly in view of its greater prevalence among the upper classes who, according to Inge's eugenic views, should be the sources of the strongest and most valuable elements in society.

As a result of his growing and vigorously expressed interest in contemporary sociology and morals, Inge was invited to speak to a number of scientific groups on subjects not directly connected with his earlier philosophical and theological studies. A group of these lectures, together with the Romanes Lecture at Oxford and the Rede Lecture at Cambridge, constituted the material for two volumes which had a tremendous sale, partly due, no doubt, to the title under which they were published—*Outspoken Essays*. Inge, regarding the essays as not particularly provocative, admitted that a more appropriate title might have been chosen. Undoubtedly, however, they are notably frank and lively for a classical scholar, clergyman, and Dean of St. Paul's. At any rate, they contributed significantly to his growing fame as a man of letters.

In the Romanes Lecture on "The Idea of Progress," published both separately (1920) and in the second volume of *Outspoken Essays,* Inge maintained that the idea of a steady flow of human progress, so popular in the nineteenth century, is not warranted by any evidence from science or history. Accumulated experience and material advancement do not constitute any real improvement in the nature of human beings themselves. The "superstition of progress" has been responsible for a falsifying of history, a perversion of the ends of philosophy, a misinterpretation of religious values, and a lowering of political science to a position where its efforts are largely directed at attempts to determine the most practical methods of flowing with the tide. From what he regarded as the secure standpoint of Platonism, which this essay in part describes, Inge struck out at American democracy and its worship of the ballot box; at the "progressives," with their belief that whatever is "coming" is therefore right; at the labor movement, which lays undue stress upon material things; and at the conservatives, who associate liberty altogether with property. In an even earlier work (*The Church and the Age,* published in 1912) Inge had attacked Socialism and the labor movement. Revolting against the dominance of the "spirits of the age," he turned to "the Spirit of the ages" as the only hope for the inhabitants of a world where progress is so illusory. This refuge he found most fully developed in Platonic Christianity.

The publicity naturally accompanying the movements of a Dean of St. Paul's was now augmented by that attendant upon this particular Dean's willingness to speak and write on subjects of contemporary interest.

Shortly after taking office, he had been asked to deliver four lectures to the Women's Diocesan Association on the subject of "The Cooperation of the Church with the Spirit of the Age." The request was, as Inge himself tells us, like waving a red flag in front of a bull.

I was moved to tell them that there are many spirits of the age, most of them evil; that we were not agreed what the Church means; and that it is not certain that religious bodies ought to co-operate with secular movements at all. Also, if you marry the Spirit of your own generation you will be a widow in the next. Unfortunately reporters were present, who took down all my gibes, and this was the beginning of the legend that I am a desperate pessimist.[31]

His direct challenge to the then-current spirit of secular optimism inspired the *Daily Mail* to dub him "The Gloomy Dean," and the sobriquet stuck. The press on Fleet Street learned that reporters had only to climb Ludgate Hill to find stories which would attract general attention. Inge's amazement at his journalistic fame was genuine. He expressed clearly his dislike of some forms of the publicity to which he was being subjected, and on some occasions felt it necessary to refuse to speak in public unless reporters were excluded. That he actually was persecuted by the less responsible press was recognized even by men of eminence

who disagreed with his views, among them such prominent figures as George Bernard Shaw. They leaped into the
fray on behalf of the "shy scholar" against the newspapers,
and at length, their efforts, Inge's own further accomplishments, and the passage of time won for him fairer and
more accurate treatment in the newspapers.

His improved relations with the press were profitable for
him. He became a regular contributor to a number of
newspapers with wide circulation, including the *Evening
Standard,* for which he continued to write after his retirement as Dean. He was well paid, and felt that if he had
bargained through an agent rather than accepting the first
amount offered and if he had kept up the pace for a few
more years, he could have become a very rich man. At any
rate, with his children to educate, the money received for
his writing was welcome, and his relations with the press
became much more cordial, although he still occasionally
complained of his mistreatment at the hands of "the gutter-
snipes of Fleet Street." He welcomed the opportunity of
writing in a lighter style and of expressing himself freely
on matters of literature, politics, religion, and a number of
other subjects. His wit and forceful style won for him a
large audience, and published collections of some of his
newspaper articles had a good sale.

Some of his attacks on political phenomena which
seemed to him to violate the aristocratic spirit of Platonism
and to exaggerate the importance of transitory things
aroused the anger of the Socialists, some of whom began to
attack him as an arch-conservative and an enemy of the
working man. Inge did not think this fair. He simply felt
that the dictatorship of the laboring class would not be

preferable to any other tyranny in history, despite the admitted desirability of providing by any legitimate means
for a broader base of material prosperity for the whole of
the nation. He conceded that the industrial system had
made a few persons unreasonably rich, but feared that the
reforms of a powerful Socialist state might be both immod-
erate and impermanent. "A ruling class always rules itself
out," he commented, and he expressed his distaste for those
of his clerical colleagues whom he considered overhasty in
allying themselves too definitely with the labor movement.

The masses at Rome were not elevated by an unlimited provi-
sion of *panem et circenses*. And therefore I do not like to see the
clergy, who were monarchists under a strong monarchy, and
oligarchs under the oligarchy, tumbling over each other in their
eagerness to become court chaplains to King Demos. The black-
coated advocates of spoliation are not a nice lot. "I take what I
want," said Frederick the Great; "I can always find pedants to
prove my rights."[32]

The harshness of the criticisms hurled at him by a minority of the labor press, most of the Roman Catholic press,
and one Anglican Church paper, did not perturb Inge un-
duly. He doubted the power of newspapers to damage a
man of his reputation to any great degree. His attitude toward criticism was summed up in the succinct remark,
"This is the manure which makes my reputation grow."[33]

He frankly admitted, however, that not all of the criticisms leveled against him were entirely without justification. His failure to realize the seriousness of the plight of
the unemployed permitted him, during the year of the general strike, to engage in bitter criticism of the strikers in a
historical volume, *England,* which he wrote for the "Modern World" series. Acknowledging his error, he rewrote

part of the book in 1933 to incorporate an expression of what he had come to accept as more judicious political and social views. Holding that revolution is not necessary to bring about social justice, he advocated that the genuinely serious unemployment problem be solved by reducing the home population, preferably by systematic colonization rather than by a still greater lowering of the birth rate. Once this is done, he held—admitting, however, that it would not be soon—technological advances will permit shorter working hours, universal prosperity, and the necessity for constructive hobbies to fill the resultant leisure time. This temperate and hopeful prediction hardly amounted to a social program, but it did demonstrate a recognition on Inge's part that serious economic problems did in fact exist.

A somewhat unconventional position with regard to the First World War contributed to his unpopularity in some quarters. He had not wanted to see England embroiled with Germany and, convinced that the Kaiser had not sought war in the West, was inclined to place the blame on Wilhelm's military advisers. However, he was deeply shocked by reports of German atrocities and loyally supported the British cause. Characteristically, he refused to adopt an optimistic view of the probable outcome. An entry in his diary for December 14, 1917, appears prophetic in the light of subsequent events.

A Meeting of the 'League for promoting International Friendship through the Churches.' I took the opportunity to tell them some unpopular truths. 'We cherish three impossible hopes: (1) that we can destroy German militarism. We cannot; they will only live for revenge. (2) A restoration of the balance of power. This means a mad competition in armaments and the suicide of

Europe. (3) That we can force Germany to adopt our democratic system. They do not want government by mass-bribery,
and will prefer a military dictatorship.' I do not want to be un-
duly discouraging. There is a real horror of war among the
peoples; but in spite of the proverb it takes only one to make a
quarrel.[34]

Public response was prompt. Inge's entry for December
17 reads:

The newspapers are attacking me more furiously than ever, for
my speech on the 14th, and I have a swarm of abusive letters.
One good lady says: 'I am praying for your death; I have been
very successful in two other cases.' The whole nation seems to
be mad with rage and hatred. Nevertheless, on reading my
speech again, I think it was rather unwise and provocative.[35]

There are also evidences in Inge's writings of his alarm
over the Russian Revolution. For all his dislike of the
course followed by Germany in the twentieth century, that
country never inspired in him the fear and distrust that he
felt for the Soviet Union.

It must not be supposed that Inge, during the early years
of his tenure at St. Paul's, was theologically and philosophically inactive. Having at last completed the study of Plotinus, on which he had been at work since his Oxford days,
he used it for the Gifford Lectures which he delivered at St.
Andrews in 1917–18. These lectures, his most scholarly
work, were published in two volumes entitled *The Philosophy of Plotinus*. As a book, it turned out somewhat differently from what he had originally intended because of
the conditions placed on the use of the material in a lecture
series, but Inge was satisfied with the resultant greater
emphasis upon the thought of Plotinus as a living philosophy rather than merely as a matter of historic interest.

He records that his visits to St. Andrews were pleasant ones and that his heart was quite won by the old town—a reaction shared by many other eminent men who have had some association with the Scottish university. As most of the students were in the armed services during those closing days of the First World War, his audience consisted largely of professors and their ladies, but he was still engaged in delivering the second series of lectures when the Armistice was signed. On the following Sunday he preached in the Kirk, where there was a satisfying "general fraternization."[36]

In 1923, Inge suffered one of his greatest sorrows when his little daughter Margaret Paula, then eleven years old, died after an illness of eighteen months. To a little book of sermons entitled *Personal Religion and the Life of Devotion,* the Dean, always reticent about his private life, appended a chapter in which, for once, the curtain was lifted to reveal something of the depth of the sorrow occasioned by the tragedy. The frontispiece of the little book shows us a wide-eyed, curly-headed little girl, posing a bit timidly to be photographed in a starched organdy dress. A Latin poem, *"In Memoriam Filiolae Dilectissimae,"* tells eloquently of Inge's devotion to the child, and in the appended chapter he describes her character and the radiance which surrounded her last days with a tenderness which his literary public did not often see from his pen.

It is not congenial to me [he wrote] to tear aside the veil which secludes the sanctities of a happy home. There are some things about our little girl which I could not bring myself to say in English, or in prose, and which are therefore kept for the metrical dedication which I have written. But it has been my strange privilege, as I believe, to be the father of one of God's saints, a character as pure and beautiful as many which are recorded in the Church's roll of honour; and I offer these pages which are to follow as a thank-offering for that precious gift, not without hope that my readers may be able, from this slight and meagre record, to realise something of the beauty and fragrance which accompanied that short but not imperfect life of eleven years.[37]

In the little biographical essay, we get glimpses into the quality of the Inges' family life. We hear one of Paula's brothers exclaiming, "O Paula, I wish you would get better," and the little girl's reply: "No, Richard, you must not say that. God has spared me for a whole year to be with you all, and it has been the happiest year of my life."[38] "I am the happiest little girl in all the world," she said, even after she was no longer able to use her paintbox and pencil, and Inge believed her happiness to be due to her consciousness of God's protection and the return to her of the love which she gave so freely to those around her.

We see Inge as a father, reading Milton's sonnet on his blindness to Paula several days before her death and, upon reading the line, "They also serve who only stand and wait," saying to her, "Paula, I should like you to remember that last line. You will never know how much you have done for all of us in this house, and for many others, simply by being what God has helped you to be."[39] We are shown the picture of a "Fairy Princess," who "lived in a sweet imagination, loving all things beautiful, and doing things as a Princess should."[40] This same little Princess could, during her last weeks, tell her family, in asking to be permitted to say her prayers silently, "If you do not mind, I should like best to be quite alone with God."[41]

The book containing Paula's story was the most popular Inge had ever written. "I rejoice," he wrote later, "to know that it has helped to comfort thousands of parents who have had to bear the same grief. Many of the letters which I received were inexpressibly touching, and illustrated the words of the medieval visionary, Julian of Norwich, 'To me was shown no higher stature than childhood.' "[42] In his last days, Inge still kept fresh and bright in his memory the time in which his life had been touched all too briefly by his little daughter's shining personality.

In 1925 the Dean and Mrs. Inge traveled to America, where, in addition to other public appearances, Inge was to deliver eight lectures at Yale University on "The Preaching of the Kingdom of God." Upon his arrival in New York on the old Mauretania, he was besieged by reporters who wanted to know what he thought of prohibition.

"I am quite willing to stick it for three weeks," the Dean replied, "but, since you ask me, I think cold water, with which the Psalmist says wild asses quench their thirst, is a poor beverage to offer to a human being."

"Well, Dr. Inge," he was asked, "what do you think of the morals of the modern flapper as compared with those of her grandmother?"

"The early indiscretions of the flapper's grandmother I neither witnessed nor shared," he said.[43]

He was given a great deal of newspaper publicity in America.

This visit is the most extraordinary experience of our lives [he wrote]. I am boomed like a first-class celebrity. I am surrounded by reporters and photographers, and I believe I have been filmed for the 'movies' more than once. The Americans say that perhaps Bernard Shaw or Rudyard Kipling would have as great a reception, but nobody else.[44]

He was pleased with the hospitality shown him by the Americans and with his growing popularity in England. Nevertheless, his pleasure in his status was not unalloyed. At the end of the year 1925 he wrote:

This has been a happy year. I am treated with great consideration, but I sometimes fear that I am beginning to run dry. I preach too many old sermons touched up, and accept too many invitations. My devotional life is not what it should be; I do not meditate enough on the great things.[45]

During the latter part of his career at St. Paul's, Inge demonstrated considerable interest in contemporary problems connected with Christian ethics, an area in which he believed the conflicts between Christianity and its opponents to be most acute. Two trends had, he realized, been the source of most of the controversy. The first was the change in the allegiance of the younger generation, following the demise of the Victorian era, from the somewhat Puritanical moral code subscribed to by the Church during the lifetime of the old Queen, to a hedonistic or utilitarian ethic which regards happiness as the greatest good. The second was the development of a scientific approach to ethics "which bids us aim at the improvement of the race, and also recognizes a moral duty to show humanity to animals, and not to spoil the beautiful things in the world."[46]

In his *Christian Ethics and Modern Problems,* published in 1930, Inge applied himself to the question as to what the attitude of a Christian should be concerning these developments. Recognizing that traditional Christianity had failed to provide specific answers for many of the personal and social problems of twentieth-century life, Inge, with some reservations, came out on the side of the new morality, particularly in so far as it stems from scientific humanism. He warned, however, against attempts to base the new ethical thought on secularism. The absolute Goodness of God is the necessary ground of all that can really be judged to be good in the world. Inge's acceptance of a considerable amount of contemporary ethical thought indicates no capitulation on his part to the despised idea of inevitable progress, but merely his growing recognition that new conditions frequently demand altered applications of old principles. Quite daring in some respects, his views in other instances show a resolute adherence to traditionally accepted modes of thought.

Inge had intended the book on Christian ethics to be his last major work. "I felt that I had said my say and given my message," he tells us, "and that I did not wish to become a bore."[47] However, in addition to numerous minor works, he was still destined to produce a volume which—although it failed to satisfy him, because of his feeling that he had lost his old "frosty brilliance" of style—contributed immeasurably to his already considerable reputation as a critic of contemporary scientific thought. Invited to deliver the Warburton Lectures in Lincoln's Inn Chapel, he used the resultant series, delivered in 1931 and 1932, as the basis for *God and the Astronomers,* perhaps his best-known book. Possibly he stretched a point in making these lectures the vehicle for an expression of his views on science. Bishop Warburton's trust deed provided that the speaker should select subjects connected with Old Testament prophecy or the errors of the Roman Church. Inge chose to speak on the Second Law of Thermodynamics, a topic which he felt to be sufficiently related to prophecy, though perhaps not

of the Old Testament variety. The Roman Church received
only incidental attention. In the course of this work, Inge
developed what he regarded as his most mature theological
convictions. He therefore considered it worth while, despite
his agreement with his French admirer and critic, the
Abbé Nédoncelle, that there was *"rien de bien nouveau"*
in the book. The public, which accepted the work with
enthusiasm, must have agreed with the Abbé's further
characterization of the work as *"un bel effort de synthese."*

From a series of talks given to undergraduates of Cambridge in February of 1933, Inge produced a further volume, *Things New and Old,* containing his message for the
younger generation. The beginning of his first talk shows
the skill which he had developed over the years at St. Paul's
in establishing contact with widely diverse audiences:

I have accepted the great honour and the great responsibility of
addressing the younger members of this University in a series of
talks, extending over eight days. You will have the opportunity,
if you wish to avail yourselves of it, of hearing me on the evening of every day this week, and on next Sunday. Some of you
may well ask, was it a wise choice to invite an old man, who became a Scholar of King's as long ago as 1879, to give advice to
young men who might be his grandsons? Am I not necessarily a
fossil, a dug-out, a mid-Victorian, almost an antediluvian, since
I lived nearly three-quarters of my life before the great deluge
swept over the world in 1914, obliterating old landmarks, and
leaving nothing as it was before? Is it likely that I shall be able to
understand you and sympathise with you? Well, that will be for
you to decide when you hear me. There is a great deal that I
wish to say to you; and perhaps we are not really so very far
apart; for though there have been great changes since I was
young, human nature, I think, remains much the same. The hidden man of the heart, who is our real self, has much the same
battle to fight whether he is born in the nineteenth century or

the twentieth; and possibly a man sees some things rather more
clearly at seventy than he did fifty years earlier. If life has taught
him nothing, he must be very stupid.[48]

The response of the students was gratifying. Inge pro-
ceeded to try to convince them of his position that the
foundation of Christian Mysticism and Platonism is a firm
one to stand on while making those adjustments to contemporary problems which cannot be solved adequately by
blind reliance on tradition. The book incorporating the
talks, the second to be published since he had resolved to
write no more, was widely read.

One of the advantages of the office which Inge held for
so long was the opportunity for association with the great
and near great. Added to the prestige of his office and his
literary fame were many honors which in themselves
might have been sufficient to insure him a social position
suited to his temperament. Not the least of these was his
designation in 1930 as Knight Commander of the Victorian Order. A frequent house guest of Lord Haldane and
Lord and Lady Burghclere, he also numbered among his
acquaintances and friends many of the eminent literary,
clerical, and political figures of Britain. He liked George
Bernard Shaw, despite their many areas of disagreement.
"He is a good man, and a great man," he wrote of Shaw
in 1926, "and he is kind enough to wish to be our friend."[49]
On a Mediterranean cruise together the two men had a
photograph made which Inge treasured for the rest of his
life. It shows him resolutely facing the camera with a properly ecclesiastical expression, "looking too good to be true,"
as he put it. With him is Shaw, even more merrily Mephis-
tophelean in appearance than usual. Shaw greatly enjoyed
the picture and named it "The Temptation."

During the early nineteen-thirties, Inge seems to have become increasingly dissatisfied with the course of his career. Fearful that his faculties might be waning, he worried about his tendency to be repetitious, inevitable in a man who spoke as often in public as he did, but noticeable also in his writings. He asked himself whether he was "too fond of money," but concluded that his reluctance to part with it was due rather to his recognition of the duty of a Platonist to practice some measure of asceticism. Despite this favorable conclusion, he felt a little guilty about the money he was receiving from writings which he feared he had not really earned. The enmities he had incurred through his outspokenness appear to have weighed a trifle more heavily on him than formerly, and he felt the necessity of consoling himself with thoughts of the real friendships he had formed.

Shortly after his seventy-fourth birthday, in the autumn of 1934, Inge decided to send in his resignation as Dean of St. Paul's. He regretted that leaving London would involve the loss of intimate association with many of his friends, his connection with the Mansion House and the City Companies, and his meetings with his two dining-clubs, "Nobody's Friends" and "The Brotherhood." However, he felt that his mission had been accomplished and that it was his duty to step aside. His resignation was accepted. The entry in his diary for October 1, 1934, is a brief one: "I went back into trousers."[50]

He and his wife had decided to purchase Brightwell Manor as a residence for the years of his retirement. Solidly planted in the rolling Berkshire country near Wallingford, the old house, of mixed Tudor and Georgian architecture, was a suitable habitation for one of Inge's temperament.

From it, a man who owed little of his philosophy to the century could look with critical detachment at movements which seemed in many ways alien to his spirit. However, his home was a haven from which he frequently sallied forth, and his retirement was far from complete. Even at Brightwell he could not escape the effects of the Second World War and suffered the loss of his youngest son, Richard, who, as an airman, died in a heroic attempt to save a companion trapped in the wreckage of a burning aircraft. Some four years after the end of the war, he suffered his crowning sorrow in the death of his wife.

Neither grief nor turmoil served to dull his mordant wit or the facility with which he expressed himself. To the last, he remained a nonconformist. "Any dead dog can float with the stream," he commented, and he continued to furnish the public with proof that he was far from dead.

The celebration of Inge's ninetieth birthday was noted nationally and brought him felicitations from old friends, acquaintances, and complete strangers. From King George VI came a telegram assuring him that "the Queen and I send you our Best Wishes and Hearty Congratulations on your 90th Birthday." The Queen Mother Mary, herself not far from Inge's age, wired, "I send you my Warm Congratulations and Best Wishes on this interesting anniversary." Nine-tenths of a century, much of it lived in the public eye, had left him during his lifetime almost a legendary figure to his youthful contemporaries of the atomic age, but older persons who remembered him from earlier days did so not only with respect but with some affection. C. C. J. Webb, himself living in retirement in the country after a life of academic eminence, recalled with amusement the occasion on which the Dean, after the interment of the Unknown Soldier of the First World War, muttered, "I'll bet they buried a Boche!" Other stories about him were legion. It was recalled how, on one occasion, he had accepted wine, cigars, and other luxuries offered him by his hostess, while some of his exalted clerical colleagues primly refused. After several instances of his acceptance and their rejection, he turned to the hostess and remarked in mock confidential tones, loud enough, nevertheless, to be generally heard, "However, they have other vices." Jokes and limericks, many of which he probably had never heard, were attributed to his authorship. He was, in short, no longer recognized merely as the author of some well-known books, but as a celebrity. Time did not dull his wit, and his criticisms of the "spirits of the age" continued to be sharp. In a letter to the writer in the fall of the hectic year 1951, he demonstrated the lively interest that, as a nonagenarian, he still took in public affairs.

We are in the throes of a General Election [he wrote], having closed that silly 'Festival of Britain,' as if we had anything to be festive about. Last year I was sitting next to Lord Halifax at dinner, and asked him about foreign affairs. He said, 'The Russians may have to climb down in Korea, but if they do it will be only to make more trouble for us elsewhere, *very likely in Persia.*'
You will soon have to add another star to your flag, to represent poor little Britain.

His own reminiscences of the ninety years were for the most part pleasant ones. Among those he liked best to recall were the seven Mediterranean cruises which he had taken to places congenial to his spirit in company which stimulated his mind. "The Mediterranean is such a friendly sea," he remarked; "not at all like the Atlantic," and in those words gave a key to that personality which for so many years had engaged in an intellectual quest for another friendly sea to which faith and thought might lead him and where he might find a refuge from the storms of the changing time.

He regretted that he could travel no more. In America, he had never gotten farther south than Virginia or west than Niagara, and he would have liked to see more of the country. "However," he remarked with a sudden grin, "my next journey will probably be with Charon."

A lifetime of thought had led him to the conclusion that there are three things that we do not know a great deal about. These are, first, the nature of the individual personality and its survival; second, the problem of time and eternity; and finally, the problem of evil.

He could still draw fire from his critics. His occasional intemperate remarks about Martin Luther did little to endear him to Protestants, and he had never been very gentle with the Roman Catholic Church. However, he did not regard himself as anti-Catholic in the strictest sense of the word. He had been greatly influenced by the Roman Catholic theologian Baron von Hügel and had frequently expressed some admiration for the tradition of Thomas Aquinas, although he admitted as late as his ninety-second year that he knew Thomas only by more modern works about him. He expressed great respect for several modern Roman Catholic writers with whose work he was directly familiar, particularly Fulton Sheen.

For the most part, though, his intellectual roots were too classical and mystical for him ever to feel at home in Catholic institutionalism or Protestant Biblicism. Augustine, he said, was "too much a bishop, too little a heretic," and he felt much more akin to men like William Law, whose works, he said, had influenced him strongly.

His attitude toward institutional Christianity was, in fact, critical enough to cause him to question whether he had followed the right calling. "If I could live my life again," he said, "I don't think I should be a clergyman. . . . Perhaps it will be said of me that as I grew older I became a better Christian and a worse churchman."[51]

He still poured his own tea and that of his guests with a steady hand, and now quite deaf, listened courteously to their shouted conversation with his hand cupped around his ear to make an improvised hearing aid. His own rather high-pitched voice was of undiminished vigor and clarity, and he still talked rapidly and precisely. Asked on one occasion in years past why he talked so rapidly, he had replied, "If I talked more slowly, what I say wouldn't sound nearly so good."

Inge was no doubt aware that the elegance of his written English would effectively counter any libel that his words might imply with regard to his use of the language. He could also go to some pains to combat his reputation as a curmudgeon by a display of exquisite manners and open-handed hospitality. However, he made no pretense of feeling universal good will.

"I do not love the human race," he said flatly. "I have loved just a few of them. The rest are a pretty mixed lot."[52]

When Inge died of an attack of bronchitis on February 26, 1954, *The Christian Century* summed up the feelings of a public which saw in his uncompromising figure the personification of a vanished era. "In his passing the grandeurs as well as the limitations of a period which ranks in British history beside the golden age of the first Elizabeth return to march in ghostly review before our eyes."[53]

Victorian though he may have been in temperament, however, it is not as a representative of any age that Inge thought of himself, but as a citizen of a realm of timeless values. From what he believed to be an eternal and unchanging vantage point, he viewed—if not always with compassion, at least with keen interest—the plight of a civilization enmeshed in a period of history characterized by dramatic and far-reaching changes in the structure of its thought.

2 DISCIPLE OF PLOTINUS

In INGE'S JUDGMENT, Plotinus was the last of the great Greek philosophers. The Platonic tradition in which he taught was, according to the Dean, central in Hellenic thought, despite the tendency of some modern critics to regard Plato himself as un-Greek. Convinced that true Platonism is timeless, Inge holds that the schools which go by that name have obscured the real message which Plato has for those who personally would follow his way. "The true Platonist," he writes, "is he who sees the invisible, and who knows that the visible is its true shadow."[1] It is this ability to apprehend concepts more clearly than sensory phenomena which is responsible for the doctrine of ideas on which all Platonic systems are based. Without such clarity of spiritual perception the Platonic doctrines tend to become corrupted and the doctrine of ideas minimized or misinterpreted. The professors of Plato's school in Athens, in spite of their professed orthodoxy, departed more than they realized from the thought of their master. Finally they fell into skepticism and eclecticism, and the central teachings of Plato entered into a period of decline until Plotinus rescued them.

Plotinus, however, was not merely a commentator on
Plato. His highly original and creative mind absorbed
many streams of ancient thought and transmuted them
into elements of his own intellectual system. Inge maintains that his thought is almost wholly Greek. Alleged influences from Oriental philosophy, particularly Buddhism,
are, he holds, only indirect.

The principal source for our knowledge of the life of the
great Neoplatonist is Porphyry, from whom Inge derived
the biographical material included in his Gifford Lectures.
Plotinus' racial origins are obscure, primarily because of
his distaste for talking about anything pertaining to his
mundane existence—a distaste based, apparently, on the
shame which, according to Porphyry, he seemed to feel at
being "in the body." He was born somewhere in Egypt in
204 or 205 A.D., and his name was a Roman one. He attended an elementary school in the town of his birth and
completed his formal education at Alexandria. He went
from philosopher to philosopher in the Egyptian capital
until he was twenty-eight years old, seeking guidance in
his quest for truth. His search was in vain until, on the
advice of a friend, he went to hear Ammonius Saccas,
called "The Porter," a former Christian who had reverted
to the Greek religion. Ammonius did not commit his
teachings to writing, but his instruction was of such quality
that Plotinus stayed with him until he was thirty-nine
years old. Despite Inge's insistence on the essentially Greek
character of Plotinus' thought, Plotinus himself seems to
have been interested in finding out directly something of the
character of Oriental philosophy, for he accompanied the
army of the Emperor Gordian on an expedition against

Sapor, King of Persia, in the hope of having an opportunity "to consult the Magi, and perhaps even the Brahmans, in their own homes."[2] When Gordian was assassinated in Mesopotamia, Plotinus got as far back as Antioch, but instead of returning to Alexandria, went to Rome in 244 A.D. He lived there the rest of his life, conducting a school which attained great popularity. He enjoyed the favor of the Emperor Gallienus and his wife, and on one occasion was given permission to found a city called Platonopolis based on the principles enunciated in the *Republic*. The permission, perhaps fortunately for Plotinus' reputation, was rescinded before the project could be started. Until he was fifty years of age, he communicated his philosophy orally and committed nothing to writing. Then he began the production of the *Enneads,* the source of our direct knowledge of his philosophy. Inge recognizes that the *Enneads* are poorly written and difficult to read, but maintains that they are supremely worth the effort. "If Plotinus had been studied with half the care that has been bestowed on Plato and Aristotle," he writes, "the continuity of philosophical and religious thought in the early centuries of the Christian era would be far better understood, and the history of Greek philosophy would not be habitually deprived of its last chapter."[3]

Plotinus was a saintly man whose principal concern was not with intellectual achievement, but "to bring back souls to 'their heavenly Father.'"[4] A man of fine countenance and engaging simplicity, his natural modesty was almost excessive. He would never permit his portrait to be painted. "Is it not enough to have to bear the image ($\epsilon \check{\iota} \delta \omega \lambda o \nu$—the mere simulacrum of reality) in which nature has wrapped me, without consenting to perpetuate the image of an image, as if it were worth contemplating?"[5] he asked. A portrait was, however, painted from memory by an artist who attended his lectures.

Despite the generally Christian tenor of Plotinus' life and personality and Inge's conviction that his philosophy contains the essential elements of Christian Platonism, the Egyptian never became a convert to the faith of Christ. Unlike many mystics, he claimed no spectacular visions or private revelations, although he did believe that he had on several occasions experienced the beatific vision.

When he realized, while at a country house in Campania, that he was about to die, his only close friend in the vicinity, the physician Eustochius, was sent for from Puteoli. Eustochius did not arrive in time to give him medical aid, but did hear his last words, which are seemingly thoroughly characteristic of the man: "I was waiting for you, before that which is divine in me departs to unite itself with the Divine in the universe."[6]

Inge has referred to himself frankly as a "disciple" of Plotinus. His allegiance to the great Neoplatonist found expression in his Gifford Lectures, delivered at the University of St. Andrews in 1917–18. Later published under the title *The Philosophy of Plotinus,* these lectures, in addition to being a scholarly treatment of Plotinism, are also a thorough and systematic treatment of the basic principles of his own thought.

In Plotinus' mysticism Inge sees a genuine pursuit of "ultimate, objective truth."[7] Unlike some of the questionable forms of mysticism which have appeared in the history of Christianity, as well as in other religions, that of Plotinus was not devoted to the attainment of "levitation, incandescence, transverberation, visions and auditions,"[8] but, as Inge—quoting Coventry Patmore—says, to "the science of ultimates, the science of self-evident reality."[9] Such an approach cannot be understood by psychological examination of the mystical experience, for whereas psychology is interested in the content of the mystic's consciousness, the mystic himself is concerned with the truth of what he purports to discover.

He cares very little whether he is conscious or unconscious, in the body or out of the body. But he is supremely interested in knowing God, and, if possible, in seeing Him face to face. His inner life is not an intensive cultivation of the emotions. It develops by means of what the later Greek philosophy calls 'the dialectic,' which Plotinus defines as 'the method and discipline which brings with it the power of pronouncing with final truth upon the nature and relation of things, also the knowledge of the Good and of its opposite, of the eternal and of the temporal.' This knowledge gained, the dialectic, now freed from all deceit and falsehood, 'pastures the Soul in the meadows of truth'; it has a clear vision of the eternal Ideas, and points the way to the supreme Unity that lies behind them. Then at last, and not before, it rests, leaving behind the operation of the discursive reason and contemplating the One who is also the Good.[10]

Inge deplores the tendency of modern thought to make philosophy of religion a matter of epistemology, psychology, and ethics, while little or no attention is paid to the question of the nature of ultimate reality. Mysticism is not simply a method of attaining information, but a total spiritual philosophy which, through the combined activity of thought, will, and feeling, reveals the true nature of the universe. Inge's epistemology, like that of Plotinus, rests firmly upon his metaphysics and cannot be considered apart from it.

In common with many other idealists, Inge holds that reality is at its core a unity. The one-ness of the whole is, however, somewhat dissipated by the fact that we apprehend it as two worlds. The higher of these is the intelligible world, whose principle is νοῦς, or the content of the divine mind. This is the "real" world, which has as its numerical symbol the One-Many, indicating that in it the antithesis of the One and the Many has no real existence in the higher unity. The lower world is the soul world. It is the world which we experience through the senses in space and time. To Inge it represents "a partial disintegration of reality."[11] In this sphere, to which the numerical symbol of "the One and the Many" is applied, the sharp distinctions in subject-object relationships occur. Here, God appears, not as the unifying principle underlying all reality, but as a superior entity coexistent with a number of inferior entities. In the lower world evil seems to be a positive force. Though it is, according to Inge, somewhat less than real, it must in the soul world be treated as being actually existent and powerful. In this lower sphere, we may also talk meaningfully of time, for Inge holds to Royce's idea that "time . . . is the form of the will, and will or purposive action is the characteristic quality of the soul-life."[12]

The difference in degree of the reality of the two worlds seems to constitute the principal reason for man's attempts to gain access to the higher world, it being accepted that the *ens realissimum* must of necessity be also the *summum bonum*. The attempt to establish a bridge of knowledge from the lower world to the higher has a long tradition in classical philosophy, from Plato through Plotinus and the Cambridge Platonists to Inge. For thinkers of Neoplatonic persuasion, the attainment of spiritual enlightenment consists in adapting our natures in so far as possible to the eternal things of the spirit rather than to the flux of the temporal order. That Plotinus was successful in this attempt seems to Inge to be evidenced not only by his formal philosophy, but by the spirit which shines through his writings. He was "able to breathe freely in the timeless and changeless world which is the background of the stage on which each generation struts for its brief hour and then is gone. He lives among the eternal Ideas; he never refers to the chaos which surrounded his peaceful lecture room."[13] Plotinus' apparent indifference to mundane affairs was not, Inge maintains, due to callousness, but to the fact that he was convinced that evil is not a part of the "real" world and has no substance of its own. The real world is the world of values and is eternal. Inge was fond of a statement of Plotinus that "nothing that has real existence can ever perish."[14] Moreover, the questing intellect cannot forever be kept from finding its true home, for "no earth-born cloud can long prevent the beams which stream from the eternal fount of light from illuminating the dark places of this lower world."[15]

Inge points to two basic triads in Plotinus' thought: the trinity of divine principles involving the Absolute, spirit, and soul; and the division of the nature of man into spirit, soul, and body. Recognizing that this particular feature of the system stems from the somewhat superstitious reverence in which the number three was held in the ancient world, Inge defends his master against any charge of undue concern with numerology by pointing out that the triad was not as important to him as to Proclus or Hegel. Plotinus' philosophy, he holds, does not contain "hard boundary-lines drawn across the field of experience," but rather "contour-lines, which, as in the designs of modern surveyors, are to be understood to indicate not precipices but gradual slopes."[16] Although we may use the metaphor of Plotinus and speak of the world "here" and the world "yonder," we must realize that these designations are but figures of speech, and that we are not actually dealing with two worlds having independent existence. In order to understand the Platonic cosmology, we must, according to Inge, accept some form of the notion that man is psychologically tripartite, not merely with reference to the faculties of intelligence, will, and feeling, but also from the standpoint of the distinction among spirit, soul, and body. Inge holds that this classically recognized division is as fundamental to Christianity as to Greek philosophy. The term "body" refers to the world as apprehended by the senses; "soul" refers to the idea of temporal and spatial order apprehended by the discursive reason; and "spirit" indicates the soul which has attained the spiritual perception which alone can guarantee true knowledge.

Since, as we have seen, neither Inge nor Plotinus treats time and space—the manifestations of the soul life—as ultimately real, the same unreality must be attributable to matter, or that which exists in time and space. Thus, Inge writes:

The world as apprehended by the senses is . . . devoid of reality. It may be doubted whether there is such a thing as perception without conception. "Matter," for the Platonist, is not ponderable stuff, but the all-but nothing which remains when we have stripped phenomena of all that the mind brings to their interpretation. The elementary blunder of supposing that Plato's ὕλη is "material" is responsible for much misleading talk about "dualism" in the Platonists. It will be easier to understand the Neoplatonic view of matter if we realise that it is a relative term. Matter is matter only as the passive recipient of form above it. The same thing may be form in relation to what is below it, and matter in relation to what is above it.[17]

With reference to the question of whether the world of appearance is merely the intelligible world as viewed in distorted fashion, or an actual though inadequate copy of reality, Inge inclines to the latter, more Platonic view, although at the same time he insists, without acknowledging any contradiction, that we must not actually think in terms of two coexistent and more-or-less independent worlds. One may well ask in this connection what Inge means when he describes the lower created world as "actual" but not "real." At times, and indeed in general, Inge uses "real" as applying only to the world of spirit. But there must be some sense in which we can say of the world "here" that it *is*, though it may not even be the real world seen imperfectly. Plotinus attributes to matter only a dependent sort of existence and argues that its very incompleteness points to something beyond it. Matter could have no "determinate existence" without form. But this form cannot, as the Stoics claimed, be reduced to "states of matter."

Life, he [Plotinus] says, cannot be generated by an aggregation of lifeless particles, nor can intelligence be produced by things without understanding. If it be suggested that when the molecules are arranged in a certain *order,* life results, then the prin-

ciple which produces the order, and not the molecules which are
so arranged, should be called the Soul or vital principle. Body is
produced, through the agency of the seminal *Logoi,* by Soul,
which gives form to indeterminate 'Matter.' Every body is compounded of Matter and Form. But the Soul is by definition an
uncompounded substance; it cannot then be Body. Nor can it
be a simple manner-of-being of Matter; for Matter, being pure
indetermination, cannot give itself Form.[18]

Inge accepts as valid this attempt by Plotinus to establish
not only the inferior status of matter, but also its dependence upon a higher principle. It might, of course, be objected that if matter needs form for its determination, form,
by the same token, needs matter for its actualization. Each,
in its own role, may be as real as the other. But Plotinus,
Platonist that he was, could not admit the equal reality of
"superior" and "inferior" principles. Inge tells us that his
master shows "by other arguments of the same kind"[19] that
"the very conception" of the soul precludes its explanation
in terms of body, whereas body can be explained by soul,
since it "plainly has a 'form' which does not belong to the
material part of it."[20] The conceptualistic character of this
line of thought is evident. Plotinus and Inge ask that we
accept certain definitions based on ideas which may be
held concerning possible categories of existence and that
we then take the nature of the conception as sufficient
guarantee of its truth in the world of reality. The basic assumption is made that a "lower" principle can only be
generated by a "higher." This, it may be noted, is not identical with the more frequently advanced argument that a
lower principle cannot generate a higher, which has occasionally been used with some effect in denying that mind
can be a derivative of body. As for the use of the more

questionable assumption to justify the assignment of a lesser degree of reality—whatever that may mean—to the physical world, such a performance is unconvincing. Inge, in fact, never seems to have been quite at ease about it, despite the fact that much of his argument depends upon it.

Matter, then, for Inge and Plotinus, is not ponderable and extended stuff. It is a bare abstraction considered apart from form. However, Inge does not feel that Plotinus would have gone along with some of the modern physicists in their denial that anything but energy exists. Energy must act on something, even if the "something" is not much. It is "no thing" in itself, says Plotinus, but it is not "nothing," a curious distinction which he elaborates in a passage remarkable, in Inge's opinion, for its half-humor, but, it may be maintained, no less for its obscurity.

Matter is incorporeal, because Body only exists after it; Body is a composite of which matter is an element. . . . Being neither Soul nor Spirit nor life nor form nor reason nor limit (for it is indefiniteness) (ἀπειρία), nor a power (δύναμις); for what does it produce? but falling outside all these things, it cannot rightly be said to have Being, but should rather be called Not-being (μὴ ὄν). . . . It is an image and phantom of extension (εἴδωλον καὶ φάντασμα ὄγκον), an aspiration to exist (ὑποστάσεως ἔφεσις). It is constant only in change (ἑστηκὸς οὐκ ἐν στάσει); it is invisible in itself, escaping him who wishes to see it. When one is not looking at it, it is there; when one gazes at it, it is not seen. It is made up of contradictions; it is great and little, less and more, defect and excess. It is a phantom which can neither stay nor flee. Flee it cannot, for it has received no strength from Spirit, but is the negation of all being. In consequence it deceives in all that it professes to be. If it is represented as great, it straightway appears as little; if as the more, it appears as the less. Its being, when one tries to conceive it, appears as not-being; it is a fugitive bauble (παίγνιον), and so are the things that appear

to be in it, mere shadows in a shadow. As in a mirror the sem-
blance is in one place, the substance in another, so Matter seems
to be full when it is empty, and contains nothing while seeming
to contain all things. The copies and shadows of real things
which pass in and out of it, come into it as into a formless
shadow. They are seen in it because it has no form of its own;
they seem to act upon it, but they produce nothing; for they are
feeble and weak and have no power of resistance. But neither
has Matter any such power; so they go through it like water
without clearing a passage.[21]

The "matter" thus treated is, of course, not palpable
stuff, but is, rather, any passive principle in the presence of
an active one. The term is, thus, "purely relative,"[22] for a
thing may be matter in one relation and form in another.
Only the highest and lowest stages can be merely form or
merely matter.

Matter, however, does not appear to Plotinus or to Inge
simply as a passive principle or a negation of real being. It
also plays the role of villain in the cosmic drama. At times
Plotinus speaks of it as maleficent, and not only in a
negative sense. The tribulations of an enmattered soul are
"due not to the privation of something which it ought to
have, but to the presence of something which ought not to
be there."[23] This view so obviously contradicts the view of
matter as nothingness or simple passivity that Inge himself,
though he appears to accept both views, is constrained to
point out the difficulty and to attempt to explain it away.
He does this by reference to the interrelation between two
"scales" on which judgments may be made—those of existence and of value. Existence can be judged only on a positive scale ranging upwards from zero. Value admits of
negative judgments. But Inge will not sanction a view in

which the dualism implied by a discrimination on this basis is real. Value judgments must be forced to correspond to a monistic interpretation of reality, with the result that the positive character of matter becomes merely appearance, and evil merely "defect of goodness"[24] when viewed under the aspect of eternity. Inge admits that Plotinus was not at his ease in this solution, for he was too cognizant of the facts of morality which seem to militate against it. There are, therefore, passages in which Plotinus refers to matter as "the first evil"[25] and curious attempts to show that matter, though "without qualities" is evil by "nature" on that very account.[26] Inge finally attempts to rationalize his way out of his master's difficulties by the somewhat doubtful expedient of declaring, "When he attributes a positive evil nature to Matter, Plotinus is thinking of the materialist's Matter, not of his own doctrine."[27] It is apparent that Plotinus could not easily fit all the data with which reality confronted him into his system even by his sometimes Procrustean techniques.

Matter cannot, in the last analysis, have for Neoplatonists such as Plotinus any suggestion of an independent or real existence. Inge is thoroughly convinced of the truth of the Platonic doctrine that "like alone sees its like."[28] It follows, then, that the perceiving soul is aware of matter only because matter is actually only an appearance. This product of soul exists only because it is endowed with a "spurious substantiality" by an "illegitimate kind of thought."[29] When the soul is "awake," matter does not exist. Such a view seems to dispose of it quite neatly. However, having seemingly accomplished something in the way of clearing up the subject by frankly denying its reality, Inge, apparently aghast at having killed it off, restores it to partial life by the following statement:

Matter has no reality (οὐσία); but the activity of the irrational Soul which produces these phantasms is none the less a fact. In denying reality to Matter, we do not affirm that it is absolutely non-existent.[30]

Inge admits, in effect, that Plotinus' treatment of matter involves ambiguity. Usually Plotinus means by the word the indefinite abstraction "on which the Soul in the exercise of its lowest and least spiritual activities impresses a vague and fugitive form."[31] However, he also speaks on occasion of "divine Matter" and justifies this use of the term by his second conception of matter as—in Inge's language—"that which, in any stage, occupies the same position in relation to that which is next above it, that Matter, in the world of appearance, occupies in relation to Form."[32] Some spirit must, then, be also matter, and it is only at the bottom of the scale that we would expect to find the "nebulous substratum" with which we started the discussion. Even this substratum, Inge holds, somehow becomes refined and sublimated, for it

is redeemed in giving itself as the recipient of Form. In so doing, it is an image of the great self-surrender whereby the World-Soul receives illumination from Spirit, and of the ineffable self-surrender by which Spirit itself awaits the visitation of the Absolute Godhead.[33]

The obscurity of this statement prepares us for Inge's acceptance of Proclus' description of matter as a "true lie."[34]

It must be emphasized, however, that even Inge does not find Plotinus' treatment of matter entirely satisfactory. He recognizes its inadequacy particularly with reference to the implications it contains for moral philosophy. The recognition of the incompleteness of matter and the Plotinic view that evil stems wholly from this incompleteness does not satisfy the moral consciousness, for which the struggle against evil is real.

The radical optimism of his philosophy makes him reluctant to give evil any footing within the world of reality, which is eternal; in the flux of Matter he found a kind of symbol of reality in a state of complete disintegration. It is the symbol of the indeterminate and dark, and these qualities are evil. Whatever is material (or rather, transient and changeable), is not yet what it ought to be. It embodies the subordinate pessimism which results from a radical optimism, since each concrete fact or phenomenon is condemned by reference to a standard of perfection.[35]

In light of the contention that the physical world has only a very ephemeral reality—if, indeed, it may be said to be real at all—it is evident that space and time must have an equally gossamer-like quality. Their appearance to us is attributable to our point of view from a particular "here" and "now"—a limitation not shared by the Absolute, who does not, therefore, experience reality under the categories of space and time. Ultimate reality, then, is infinite and eternal, and these two qualities are not merely extensions of the "phenomenal" forms under which we have our experience. These present forms are unreal in a certain sense, but as forms they must point to some reality of which they are the forms. How to define the realities behind them provides a problem for Inge and Plotinus no less than for any other idealists, but we are told that of the two, space is of lower value than time. It is "the lowest rung of the ladder," for it gives us merely scenery and stage, whereas, "Time gives us the play itself."[36]

As for time, Inge admits that we may have an instinctive notion of it, but, being temperamentally incapable of accepting such a notion at its face value, he must attempt to analyze and explain it. Time, for Inge as for Plato, is "the moving image of Eternity, which it resembles as much as it can."[37] It is the sphere of soul as eternity is the sphere of spirit. Views which treat time as ultimately real involve an absurdity, according to Inge, for they postulate an unreal past, an unreal future, and a present which is an unextended point. Things are mere abstractions unless their whole spans of existence are somehow real. Activity is real in the nontemporal Absolute, but it does not involve succession, for,

in Eternity the whole is in each part; all is present together in its realised meaning and achieved perfection. Will is not destroyed, nor activity paralysed; but will and satisfaction, activity and rest, are taken up into a higher unity.[38]

The monistic austerity of this assertion is softened somewhat by Plotinus' admission that "Time is natural ($\phi \acute{v}\sigma\epsilon\iota$); it had to be,"[39] and by Inge's comment that Plotinus "wishes us to understand that there are some things in philosophy which we have to accept as given facts of experience."[40] Time is, for the life of the soul, a necessary thought form.

Any explanation of Time in terms of discursive thought must necessarily be inadequate; but the contradictions which modern thinkers have found to inhere in the notion of Time are not of a kind to condemn it as 'contrary to nature.'[41]

This admission cannot be completely harmonized with a number of attacks on the reality of time found throughout Inge's works, but it serves to illustrate the uneasiness which is implied in his frequent attempts to get rid of the reality of a thought form which experience persists in guaranteeing as real. Time itself must be considered as, in a sense, eternal, for it has no beginning and no end. "It is 'the span of the life proper to the Soul; its course is composed of equal, uniform, imperceptibly progressive movements, with a continuous activity.' "[42] The endlessness of time cannot be considered, however, as identical with the eternity of the world of spirit. The soul, to be sure, finds itself impelled to regard the "not yet" and the "no longer" as belonging to different categories. The tendency which we have to recognize a real difference between space and time with reference to the coexistence of all their points is evidenced, Inge acknowledges, by the fact that, whereas many people desire to be immortal, few would care to be ubiquitous. However, Inge does not regard time, even though it be infinite in duration, as providing an adequate theatre for the realization of values. He holds that the soul creates time along with the phenomenal world and that in the spiritual life it transcends time. Nevertheless, this transcendence is not attained at the expense of the very real "before" and "after" relationship existing among events. It involves, apparently, not the sacrifice of the reality of the present, but the attainment of the reality of the past and future. For a Platonist of the Dean's persuasion, "all real psychical ends belong in the spiritual world. Ends are striven for in Time, but there can be no ends in Time, which swallows her own children."[43] Human hopes cannot be satisfied within the time series. The soul is regarded as functioning on a different perceptual level from that of the "body," for, in Platonic language, "The Soul does not perceive objects of sensation, but their 'forms,' which belong to the intelligible world."[44]

Inge's view of the nature of man is in great measure determined by his attitude toward the Absolute. In other connections there will be occasion to discuss more fully some of the important implications of his idea of human personality as related to ethics and religion. The question of man's essential nature, however, is one which he considers in the light of Plotinus' philosophy.

A highly significant question in this connection is that of the eternal existence of individual souls. Inge, although his own view of immortality seems somewhat indefinite, appears to regard Plotinus' position as being distinctly favorable to some notion of personal survival. The universe and all the ideas in it are eternal. There are ideas of individuals; therefore, individuality is an indestructible fact. Plotinus favors a cyclical theory of the world-order, according to which an infinite number of finite purposes are eternally worked out in a history which repeats itself over and over again. Inge holds this view to be superior to the perpetual-progress theories of a later age.

The world in which all this history occurs, though not, as we have seen, in the fullest sense real, is nevertheless a necessary avenue of approach for the soul in its attempt to know divine principles.[45] The world of sense is not to be despised, for it is closely akin to the world of spirit, the only true reality. Everything in the eternal world is also here, though in imperfect form. Our realization of the imperfections is evidence that our true abode is elsewhere.

Plotinus attempts in his writings to reconcile two views about the nature of the soul. One of these regards the soul as a sort of universal principle; the other stresses the individuality and plurality of distinct souls. Plotinus, as a good Platonist, tries to preserve the universal principle without sacrificing all the individuality. Inge says that the soul stands, not at the summit, but at the center of Plotinus' philosophy. It is "midway between the phenomenal world, of which it is the principle, and the world of Spirit, which is its principle."[46]

It is not, however, simply an intermediary between the real and the phenomenal world. All the universe and all its principles are represented in the soul. It has a life proper to its nature and infinite possibilities for expansion without losing its identity. Nevertheless, it shares the nature and being of the Absolute. When, through its expansion, it becomes spirit, Plotinus tells us,

it will see God and itself and the All; it will not at first see itself as the All, but being unable to find a stopping-place, to fix its own limits and determine where it ceases to be itself, it will give up the attempt to distinguish itself from the universal Being, and will arrive at the All without change of place, abiding there, where the All has its home.[47]

It is the "offspring" of spirit, and though essentially of the nature of spirit, is lower in the hierarchy of divine natures. It is timeless and spaceless, and thus not subject to physical barriers against interpenetrability. It differs from spirit in a number of ways, one of them being that it has desires and thus works to create what it has experienced in the completely fulfilled spiritual world. It is to spirit as word to thought, activity to power, manifestation to essence.[48]

Plotinus was accustomed to refer to soul and spirit in collective, plural, and singular fashion. Thus, we are confronted with "Soul," "individual Souls," and "the Universal Soul." This latter is admittedly rather hard to distinguish from "Spirit." It is the source of all the being which the world possesses, and it contains the world. It is in contemplation of the Universal Soul that the individual soul understands itself. It creates and sustains the world from necessity, because a complete universe must contain all possible grades of being, and discordant elements are thus necessary to universal harmony.[49] The world is, therefore, good as a whole. The Universal Soul directs the world and is conscious, but its consciousness is not *in* the world, and it is not incarnate in the world. The Neoplatonic idea of an oversoul which has its own consciousness without being involved in the consciousness of individual entities existing within its body is carried by Inge to such a point that he seriously considers the notion that consciousness may be an attribute of the heavenly bodies. "Each of our bodies," he writes, "is a world, populated by millions of minute living beings. We are not conscious in them, nor are they conscious of the unitary life of the organism to which they belong. Why should not our planet have a life of its own, thinking thoughts of which we know nothing?"[50] This is not to say that such an oversoul need be good. If, for example, there were a racial soul, it admittedly might be evil.

Furthermore, the Universal Soul cannot be regarded as the real whole of which individual souls are merely parts. Universal Soul and particular souls proceed from spirit. They are united "up to a certain point" and may be said to "form one Soul in so far as they do not belong to any particular being." However, they "presently diverge, as the light divides itself among the various habitations of men, while still remaining one and indivisible."[51]

Inge assures us that Plotinus was "anxious to preserve human individuality."[52] Each soul must be considered as an "original cause,"[53] and as self-directed. It is difficult, however, to reconcile this insistence with Plotinus' flat statement that "all souls are one" and his attempt to show that sympathy implies that the one who feels it has a substantial as well as a metaphorical unity with its object.[54] The distinctness of each individual soul rests in its *raison d'être,* which is the goal for which it strives. It is, then, "the distinctness of this personal goal which constitutes the distinctness of each individual life."[55] In interpreting a passage of some difficulty written by Plotinus, Inge holds that

there are three planes on which a man may live, and . . . his rank in the scale of existence depends on the choice which he makes. He may live a purely external life, obeying his natural instincts and not reflecting. Or he may live in accordance with his discursive reason, the life of an intelligent but unspiritual man. Or lastly, he may live on what is really a superhuman plane —'that of the gods and godlike men,' the life of Spirit. The Soul, as a microcosm, has within it the potentiality of all three lives; but it chooses which of its faculties it shall develop, and which shall remain latent. If we have to choose one kind of activity as characteristically *human,* and say that our personality as individuals resides in that sphere of activity, we must select the second grade, that of the discursive intellect; because the merely sensuous life is infra-human, and since in the life of the Spirit we are really raised above the conditions and limitations of earthly existence, no man, while in the body, can live permanently on this level.[56]

The soul is a wanderer and an exile. It is continually compelled to make choices between that which is above

and that which is below it. It is striving to realize its true
self and attain its true home in the world of spirit and, to
that extent, it seeks a less personal life. Inge sees a difficulty
here and admits that the very sympathy and love which
impel persons toward unity might be destroyed if the unity
became a fact. According to Plotinus, true individuality is
attained only in the spiritual world, where each individual
soul, though real, attains perfection as "the centre of an
infinite circle," from which vantage point it "in complete
self-forgetfulness looks up with yearning eyes to the Absolute One, in whom there are no more persons. And while
thus looking, it creates unceasingly in the world of Soul."[57]
The obscurity which characterizes Plotinus' discussions of
the soul is hardly diminished by this explanation. Nor does
Inge's reference to the life of the universe as an eternal
systole and diastole help us greatly. All grades of being
are in this metaphor represented as the product of a perpetual stream of creative activity, through which "every possible manifestation of Divine energy, every hue of the Divine radiance, every variety in degree as well as in kind, is
realised somewhere and somehow."[58] The creative flow is
not, however, the only manifestation of the cycle, for beside
it is a return current which takes created things back toward their source. Created beings have as their purpose the
attainment of a closer resemblance to the "Divine image"
through the yearning which they feel for the home from
which they are away. "This aspiration," says Inge, "which
slumbers even in unconscious beings, is the mainspring of
the moral, intellectual, and aesthetic life of mankind."[59]
The soul may, according to Plotinus, live one or more than
one life on earth, but its task is a divinely commissioned

one, and its mandate is to co-operate with the divine plan. Why the soul must be incarnated is not clear. Incarnation may be merely a necessary aspect of the creative activity of God, or it may be a deliberate defection—a fall—of the soul itself, bringing about its imprisonment in the body. The former view seems to be the one favored by Plotinus. At any rate, it is possible for an individual to live so as to experience the life of the spirit while still in the body. The descent and ascent are thus activities which have relation to the here and now. The relationship between soul and matter is analogous to that obtaining between spirit and soul, with the descent of the higher principle to the lower and the ascent of the lower to the higher constituting a necessary part of the universal harmony. With reference to the question whether the "descent" of the soul is complete, or whether, on the contrary, there rests at the core of the individual self a "Divine nucleus" which cannot consent to sin, Plotinus takes the latter view, holding that the soul is "here" only in appearance—an opinion in which many of his Neoplatonic successors decline to defer to his judgment.[60] In Inge's own opinion, the soul has heaven within it even while it is in the body.

Its inmost life and being are safe, because the Soul is the child of God; but it is not allowed to remain always on the mount of vision; there are devils to be cast out in the plain below. The return-journey is rough and arduous, because the task given to great souls is great and heroic. Temporary failure is of no importance; God has all time to work in, and the Soul has all eternity in which to enjoy that rest which is another word for unbroken activity in accordance with the law of its being.[61]

Inge poses the problem—without going into a full discussion of it—of handicapped persons whose souls appear not

to have descended "entire." He is particularly concerned
with persons who suffer from such physical defects as a mal-
formed brain. Plotinus' notion enables Inge to regard the
plight of these unfortunates as different only in degree from
that of the rest of humanity. "In all of us there are some
hindrances to a perfect life, hindrances which cannot be
overcome," he says. "It is a legitimate hope that in another
life the Soul may be able to act more freely."[62]

The real world, for Inge as for Plotinus, is "the spiritual
world as known by Spirit, or Spirit as knowing the spiritual
world."[63] This realm is "fully real," as opposed to the partially real soul world. The term spirit is Inge's translation
of the Greek νοῦς, and in his opinion, a much more accurate translation than the more frequent terms such as *intellect, reason,* and *mind* by which modern expositors of
Neoplatonism have indirectly attributed to Plotinus intel-
lectualistic or idealistic tendencies which do not fairly reflect his thought. Two related terms used by Plotinus
(νόησις and τὸ νοητόν, or τὰ νοητά) are, in English,
called respectively spiritual perception and the spiritual
world. These three constitute "the trinity in unity in which
reality consists."[64] The soul is real only in so far as it can
"rise into the world of Spirit, and be active there, without
ceasing to be itself."[65]

Spiritual perception is defined as the apprehension of
that which is incorporeal, "a seeing of the invisible."[66] Although it is an activity of spirit, it is not one by which
spirit creates the spiritual world, for the ideas perceived by
spirit really exist. But the difference between some modern
idealistic positions and the Neoplatonic one becomes
somewhat negligible when Inge attempts an answer to the

question as to whether the ideas are external to the perceiving spirit. Neither he nor Plotinus could admit that they
are, for then the spirit could possess only images of the
ideas and not the ideas themselves. For an answer, he goes
back beyond Plotinus to Plato himself.

Plato, when he says that νοῦς sees the νοητά, means that it possesses them in itself. The νοητόν is νοῦς, but νοῦς in a state of unity
and calm, while the νοῦς which perceives this νοῦς abiding in itself is an energy proceeding from it. In contemplating it, it becomes like it and 'is its νοῦς because it perceives (νοεῖ) it.' It is in
one aspect νοῦς, in another νοητόν.[67]

Not satisfied with a statement of "bare identity," however,
Inge follows Plotinus into the intricacies of a position in
which, as the Egyptian says, "The perceiving Spirit must
be one and two, simple and not simple." The common principle shared by spiritual perception and being is the One,
which is their cause. Inge climaxes this singularly difficult
discussion with the curious assertion that "the relation between them is one of essential identity actualized under the
form of essential reciprocity."[68] Plotinus actually reduced
the three categories to a unity, and it seems that the distinction which he made among the three terms of his reality represent a distinction of function rather than substance.
" Noῦς and νόησις are one; and νόησις is the activity of
νοῦς. The νοητά, however, are the product not of νοῦς but
of the One. The whole spiritual nature (νοητὴ φύσις) proceeds, like the rays from the sun, direct from the One, and
not through the medium of νοῦς."[69] Every idea, in the Platonic sense, is a thought of spirit, but, as spirit itself, is also
an eternal aspect of reality. Ultimate reality consists in the
kingdom of ideas, as known by spirit. In the words of
Plotinus,

What then is the activity of Spirit, in virtue of which we may say that it is the things which it knows? Plainly, since Spirit has real existence, it knows and posits reality. Spirit therefore *is* all that really exists. . . . The objects of spiritual knowledge cannot be in the world of sense, for sensible objects are only derivative. The νοητά existed before the world; they are the archetypes of sensible things, and they constitute the true being or reality of Spirit. . . . Spirit is the first lawgiver, or rather it is itself the law of being. This is the meaning of the saying 'To know is the same as to be'; and *the knowledge of* immaterial things is identical with the things known. . . . Thus Spirit and the real world are one.[70]

The question of whether being is antecedent to spirit or the other way around is rendered meaningless by the assertion of the real identity of the two terms. Being and spirit are one and the same thing, and in the final analysis, all the ideas which constitute the real world involve spirit as perceiver, the act of perceiving, and the property of being perceived. Inge holds that the fluidity of Plotinus' terminology in dealing with these concepts is rather to be admired than deplored. He is operating in a realm of discourse above the logical faculty and is thus at liberty to ignore "sharp distinctions and hard boundary-lines."[71]

Plotinus' doctrine of ideas appears clearer to Inge than that of Plato. Recognizing that Plato never really succeeded in determining the ultimate status of the ideas, or forms, which are the ultimate categories of reality in his philosophy, the Dean points to several possible interpretations which have been made of them with which Plato himself seems to have toyed at various stages in his career. From a hypothesis, as in the *Phaedo,* the doctrine attains the status of a revealed certainty in the *Republic.* The categories in the *Theatetus* tend more to be regarded as forms of thought than are the ideas of the earlier works. As Plato grew older, Inge holds, the logician and dialectician increasingly crowded out the mystic, and the ideas became more and more dependent on the thinker's mind, although Inge does not think that Plato ever regarded them as merely subjective. As a matter of fact, whenever it appeared that a chain of reasoning was leading him toward the notion that ideas are in the soul, he would react against it with some violence. Inge points out that Plato's idealism is not subjective even in the sense of regarding the ideas as thoughts in the mind of God. They are not processes, either of divine or human thought, but are rather that which is known. He cites with favor A. E. Taylor's argument against a mentalistic interpretation of Plato in which Taylor rigorously distinguishes between objective fact and that which is thought about it and contends that the former is not contingent on the latter. Inge admits to a slight difference in emphasis which distinguishes his own position from that of Taylor in that the Dean believes that "God cannot 'think' without *ipso facto* actualizing His thought."[72] At any rate, Platonism is not, for Inge, to be regarded as consonant with spiritual pluralism. "A spiritual world," he remarks, "is not the same thing as a world of spirits."[73] Soul, in Plotinus' philosophy, is to be attributed in varying degrees to all things, although the Egyptian did not share with Plato the opinion that there are ideas of artifacts.

Inge summarizes Plotinus' conception of the realm of ideas in this somewhat difficult passage:

The doctrine of Plotinus is that so far as every thought in Spirit is also an eternal Form of being, all the thoughts of Spirit

are Ideas. Spirit embraces all the Ideas, as the whole its parts.
Each Idea is Spirit, and Spirit is the totality of the Ideas. The
Kingdom of the Ideas is the true reality, the true beauty. They
are unity in diversity, and diversity in unity. Their number cannot be infinite, though it is immeasurably great, for beauty and
order are inseparable from limitation, and the number of possible Forms is not, strictly speaking, infinite. There are as many
Ideas Yonder as there are Forms Here. The only objects Here
which are not represented Yonder are such as are 'contrary to
nature.' There is no Idea of deformity, or of any *vie manquée*.[74]

Inge gives a brief account of the gradual displacement of
the ideas in Plato's thought by the categories, the list of
which was progressively developed until by the time of the
Timaeus it was quite similar to the classification adopted
by Aristotle. Plotinus disliked the Aristotelian system, and
his own is considerably less elaborate, consisting of three
pairs of opposing categories which, as is to be expected,
"are reconciled in the spiritual world."[75] They are "Spirit
and Being, or Thought and Thing (νοῦς and ὄν); Difference and Identity (ἑτερότης and ταὐτότης); Stability and
Movement, or Permanence and Change (στάσις and
κίνησις)."[76] Plotinus does not follow this classification consistently, sometimes omitting the first pair, and sometimes
omitting νοῦς and positing being, movement, and stability
as the three categories recognized separately by spirit, with
identity and difference added because an analysis of the
primary three shows "that they are both identical and different."[77] Inge himself, not particularly interested in the
subject of the categories, rightly acknowledges that in thus
following Plato's *Sophist* Plotinus has done nothing to
clarify "a very obscure argument."[78] In a highly technical
critical passage, Inge himself accomplishes very little by
way of clarification. Altogether, the question of categories

seems to have very little importance in an understanding of the essential features of Plotinus' philosophy or that of Inge.

One doctrine based on a pair of Plotinus' categories, however, is very closely related to Inge's conception. Inge describes the Egyptian's treatment of "the Same and the Other" in these words:

The great doctrine which Plotinus expresses as the reconciliation of 'the same' and the 'other,' is that all the barriers which break up experience into fragmentary and opposing elements must be thrown down, not in order to reduce life to a featureless mass of undifferentiated experience, but in order that each element in experience may be realised in its true relations, which are potentially without limit. Otherness and sameness help to define and emphasise each other. The whole, as Plotinus tells us repeatedly, is in each part. Individual Spirits are not parts of the one Spirit. They exist 'in' each other; each is the whole under a particular form. The universal is implicit in the particular. The νοητά are 'many in one and one in many and all together.' They are not separated in the slightest degree from each other; the whole Spirit lives in each centre of life. There must be differentiation; otherwise no communion of Spirits, no interaction on the spiritual plane, would be possible. It would not be enough that distinctions exist on the plane of Soul; for then Spirit would need Soul in order to come to life. 'Spirit itself is not simple,' any more than the Soul.[79]

The passage quoted above is expressive of a conviction about the soul which finds expression in Inge's reflections on personality and immortality. The conception of differentiation, combined with the exceedingly difficult notion of interpenetrability, apparently gave Inge a considerable amount of trouble in formulating a conception of personal identity and survival which would preserve the purity of his Neoplatonism and at the same time satisfy the demands of Christian doctrine. Some of the problems which he encountered in the attempt to reconcile the two traditions on this subject will be further explored in the chapter dealing with Inge as a Christian theologian.

Movement and stability ($\kappa \acute{\iota} \nu \eta \sigma \iota s$ and $\sigma \tau \acute{\alpha} \sigma \iota s$) are considered by the Dean as involving simply another form of the antinomy presented by difference and identity. "That which changes and yet remains the same, that which moves and yet abides unshaken, is at once 'the same' and 'another' in its relation to itself." The question of activity as related to "Spirit," however, soon involves us in the difficult concept of nontemporal activity, for the idea of movement as expressed in the pair of categories refers to the nature of the "real" world, whereas activity in time is, in Plotinus' view, mere appearance. In the "real" world, movement and stability are somehow reconciled in the sort of timeless activity appropriate to spirit. But movement does not disappear in the reconciliation. It simply ceases to be dependent upon time and loses its involvement in the antithesis between itself and stability. Inge says in this connection:

The purposes of Spirit are realised, by its creative power, as processes involving temporal succession. In these processes, subject as they are to time and place, Movement is of course opposed to Stability, though the two are necessary counterparts of each other. But this movement, which might truly be called imperfect activity ($\dot{\alpha} \tau \epsilon \lambda \grave{\eta} s \ \dot{\epsilon} \nu \acute{\epsilon} \rho \gamma \epsilon \iota \alpha$), is also imperfect movement, if we compare it with the movement of Spirit, which does not need Time ($o\dot{\upsilon} \ \delta \epsilon \hat{\iota} \tau \alpha \iota \ \chi \rho \acute{o} \nu o \upsilon$).[80]

Inge insists that this doctrine, which, of course, completely denies the ultimate reality of temporal change, is entirely compatible with, and indeed essential to, Christianity as well as Platonism. The spiritual world is regarded as per-

manent, unchanging, and perfect. It does not evolve and is
not in the stream of time. It is to his conception of that
world that Inge, following in the steps of Plotinus, con-
stantly invites our attention. He admits the difficulty presented by the task of reconciling change and permanence
without having them "fall apart again." However, he is
insistent that no final meanings can be found in time, but
rather that "the whole meaning of movement and change
is to be sought in the direction taken by the movement, and
in the values which the movement, taken as a whole, suc-
ceeds in realising."[81] These values, he declares, reside in the
eternal world.

It is with this introduction of the idea of eternal values
that Inge, apparently with considerable relief, abandons
the discussion of the categories of Plotinus. Convinced
that the "dialectical puzzles" provided by the antinomies
of his master really have no place in the realm of the eternal verities, he maintains that the real direction of Plotinus'
whole philosophy tends rather toward an ontological treatment of a kingdom of values embracing all spiritual things.
The ultimate values, three in number, appear to constitute
the whole of reality.

The highest forms in which Reality can be known by Spirits,
who are themselves the roof and crown of things, are *Goodness,
Truth,* and *Beauty,* manifesting themselves in the myriad products of creative activity. Things truly *are,* in proportion as they
'participate' in Goodness, Truth, and Beauty. These attributes of
Reality, which, so far as can be known, constitute its entire essence, are spiritual; that is to say, they belong to a sphere of
supra-temporal and supra-spatial existence, which obeys laws of
its own, and of which the world of common experience is a pale
copy.[82]

Inge maintains, in fact, that Plotinus should have abandoned the Platonic and Aristotelian categories altogether and recognized the values he names as the attributes of spirit. Plotinus does consider a value theory recognizing the categories of "the Beautiful, the Good, the Virtues, Science (true knowledge), and Spirit"[83] but argues against regarding it as accurate. He refuses to accept without qualification Plato's identification of the Good as ultimate reality, arguing that when one speaks of the Good in that sense, he must mean the Absolute, "which we only call the Good because we have nothing else to call it."[84] Inge rejects the argument as "hardly worthy of Plotinus," pointing out in the process that in referring to Goodness as an attribute of $νοῦς$ or $νοητά$, he is speaking of "Goodness in its proper sense,"[85] rather than as another name for the Absolute. The same argument was used by Plotinus in disposing of the Beautiful and is refuted by Inge in the same way. As for Knowledge, or $ἐπιστήμη$, which, of the attributes discussed by Plotinus, most closely corresponds to Inge's "Truth," Plotinus had rejected it on technical grounds which Inge considers contrary to the Egyptian's own philosophy.

Not finding sufficient support in the doctrine of his own master for the recognition of the trinity of values as constitutive of reality, Inge turns to Proclus, "the ablest thinker of the school next to Plotinus himself."[86] The Dean had already formed his own view before becoming acquainted with the work of Proclus and was pleased to find there a full expression of it.

Having postulated his theory of value, Inge rejects altogether the quantitative categories, considering them ap-

plicable only to temporal and spatial relations and as being
of no assistance in arriving at an understanding of the spiritual world. It is only through a direct apprehension of
value rather than through the discursive reason that we
attain knowledge of spiritual matters. But it must be
understood that in apprehending values we are not discovering a subjective something superimposed upon experienced reality, but the very nature of reality itself.

The attributes of Reality are values. But values are nothing unless they are values of Reality. Truth, for example, is, subjec-
tively, a complete understanding of the laws and conditions of
actual existence. It is the true interpretation of the world of sense,
as knowable by Soul when illuminated by Spirit. Objectively, it
is an ordered harmony or system of cosmic life, interpreted in
terms of vital law, and nowhere contradicted by experience. If,
as is notoriously the case, perfect law and order are not to be
found in the world of ordinary experience; if perfect Beauty and
Goodness are not to be discerned by the Soul except when it
turns to Spirit, we have to suppose that these imperfections are
partly due to our faulty apprehension, and partly to the essential
conditions of a process which is doubly split up by Space and
Time, and which is so disintegrated precisely in order that spiritual values may be realised through conflict with evil.[87]

Inge acknowledges that in substituting value judgments for
judgments of existence as descriptive of the real world, we
introduce a graduated conception of reality in place of the
simpler view which would invoke the law of the excluded middle in asserting of anything either that it does or
that it does not exist. However, in Inge's view, this problem
cannot be altered by the arbitrary elimination of value
considerations from judgments of fact in an attempt to
make reality amenable to quantitative description. Value
judgments are smuggled in when "an abstract method of

inquiry" concerns itself with concrete reality.[88] The Platonist, unwilling to smuggle, meets the problem more honestly. "His ontology . . . compels him to identify Reality
with achieved perfection; and this involves the difficulty of
postulating degrees of existence corresponding with degrees of value."[89] Nor can the graduation be regarded as
merely a matter of appearance, as in the philosophy of
F. H. Bradley, for to do so, Inge maintains, is to recognize
an unbridgeable gulf between a world of ideas which has
value but no existence and a world of matter which has existence but no value. The solution to the problem must be
found in the conclusion "that the world is most adequately
conceived under the form of spiritual values, rather than
under the form of commensurable quantities."[90] The will
and the intellect, acting together, have as their goal the attainment of Goodness, Truth, and Beauty, which are ultimates in our experience.

Turning to Plotinus' attempt to explain the nature of the
spiritual world, Inge concerns himself with the relationship between "Universal Spirit" and "particular Spirits,"
which, it appears, is much the same as that between universal and particular souls.

The Great Spirit exists in itself, and the particular Spirits exist
equally in themselves; they are implied in the Universal Spirit,
and it in them. Each particular Spirit exists both in itself and in
the Great Spirit, and the Great Spirit exists in each of them as
well as in itself. The Great Spirit is the totality of Spirits in
actuality (ἐνεργείᾳ), and each of them potentially (δυνάμει). They
are particular Spirits (ἐνεργείᾳ), and the Great Spirit (δυνάμει).
As to the source of particular Spirits, he [Plotinus] says that
when the Great Spirit energises within itself, the result of its

activity is the other Spirits, but when outside itself, Soul. Thus, the Great Spirit is exactly analogous to the Universal Soul on the next rung of the ladder.[91]

It is this "Great Spirit" which is the Neoplatonic God. It is not itself the Godhead in its completeness, but it is the fullest manifestation of the Godhead to us. Its nature finds expression in Christianity, Inge says, in the doctrine of the Logos-Christ, and the relation of the Great Spirit to other spirits is illustrated by the metaphor of the vine and the branches. An individual self, it seems, can find its true meaning only in an ultimate reality which is supra-personal. Inge states, with the assurance of one quoting an axiom, that rather than passing by abstraction from the particular to the general, we apprehend the general immediately. "We see resemblances before we see the objects which resemble each other,"[92] he remarks—a strong statement even for one who accepts the reality of universals. We are more than "our psycho-physical ego," which is asserted to be object rather than subject for us. The individual spirit is, on a higher plane, the same as the individual soul, characterized by "something unique, which gives it individuality," but somehow capable of "mutual inclusion" in its relation to all other spirits.

It is with reference to the life of the spirit that the concept of eternity ($\alpha\iota\acute{\omega}\nu$) enters the Neoplatonic philosophy. In the words of Plotinus,

Spirit possesses all things at all times simultaneously. It possesses all things unchanged in identity. It *is;* it knows no past or future; all things in the spiritual world co-exist in an eternal

Now. Each of them is Spirit and Being; taken together, they are universal Spirit, universal Being.[93]

The terms "was" and "will be" have no meaning, Inge holds, in the eternal life of the real. There is no loss and no change. Eternity is not extraneous and accidental to ultimate reality. It is identical with it. It is, Plotinus says, "God manifesting his own nature . . . life which is infinite because it is universal and loses nothing of itself, having no past and no future."[94] Thus, to live eternally is something quite different to Inge from endless existence in time. In the soul life, the awareness of time is interpenetrated with that of eternity, and we tend to separate them in our thinking, but genuine spiritual experience does not find them divided. Time resembles eternity "as much as it can"[95] and everything in time is also "in an eminent sense" in eternity.[96]

In considering the nature of the Absolute, Inge's loyalty to Plotinus involves him in an attempt to reconcile two attitudes which are not always easy to entertain simultaneously. As a Christian, he is committed to a personal theism, to be discussed in a later chapter. Along with this, he accepts with equal positiveness the Neoplatonic idea of the ineffable Godhead as "the Absolute." It is in response to the demands of this latter conception that Inge reinterprets the theories of Plotinus to present the Absolute as the completely unified trinity of Goodness, Truth, and Beauty. In the light of this identification, the emphasis which he lays upon the three attributes of the soul life—will, intellect, and feeling—becomes quite clear. "The goal of the Intellect is the One. The goal of the Will is the Good. The goal of the Affections—of Love and Admiration—is the Beautiful."[97] These three concepts do not really represent separate attributes of Deity. Though apparently distinguishable from one another from our point of view, they are ultimately a single undifferentiated reality.

Dialectic is the path to Truth or "the One," for it shows us that the intelligible world (which Plotinus called the spiritual world) *must be,* by demonstrating "that the idea of plurality implies that of unity, that of imperfection a perfect."[98] But Plotinus and Inge concur in the belief that "the One" is not a term with merely numerical significance.

In this, the numerical sense, unity and plurality are correlatives, so that we cannot have the former without the latter. In this sense, the Absolute One would be an impossible abstraction. But for Plotinus the One is the source from which the differentiation of unity and plurality proceeds; it is the transcendence of separability rather than the negation of plurality.[99]

In the metaphysical sense, then, the One, as Plotinus said, "is not one of the units which make up the number Two,"[100] but rather the supreme Unity which is the source of all plurality. The guarantee of its truth is the fact that all progress toward reality seems to be from lower to higher unities; we must, therefore, postulate at the top an Absolute, a unity "above all differentiation."[101]

In describing the One as "beyond existence," whatever that may mean, Inge and Plotinus admit at the outset that we cannot actually know the nature of the Absolute and can give no accurate description of its characteristics. Nevertheless, both then proceed to describe it in some detail. Plotinus tells us at some length of an Absolute Who does not will and yet is all will, Who does not think, and yet knows everything, and Who, without being conscious, is supremely awake. However mystifying such a description may seem to many theists, Inge seems to have felt that it says too much rather than too little and agrees with the criticism not infrequently leveled against Plotinus that, after telling us that the Absolute cannot be described, he gives us so much information about it that one is almost forced to "postulate some still more mysterious principle behind the Monad."[102]

In *God and the Astronomers,* Inge himself, in furnishing a description of the Deity, makes a distinction between the Godhead and the God of religion, Who, he maintains, are epistemologically, though not metaphysically, differentiable. Such a step, he says, is necessary if we are to avoid the *via negativa* of some of the Indian and European mystics, who make only negative statements about God, a process "which has been unsympathetically compared to peeling an onion,"[103] inevitably ending in nothing. The imperfect pictures which we can make of the Absolute furnish us with the God of religion, and, indeed, have some positive value in showing us the true nature of God. The convenient distinction between the two concepts enables Inge, despite his criticism of Plotinus, to elaborate a doctrine of Deity.

That "the One" is indeed "beyond existence" is a part of the creed of Neoplatonism, and the conclusion is the product of three links in a chain of reasoning described by Inge as follows:

(1) The nature of the Godhead is certainly unknown to us; we are unable to form any idea of the absolute and unconditioned. (2) It is a principle of this philosophy that we are not cut off from the highest form of life—the eternal and universal life of

Spirit. (3) We have, in the mystical state, an experience of intuition which is formless and indescribable, and which is therefore above the spiritual world of Forms or Ideas.[104]

Inge acknowledges that this line of thought, if carried to an extreme, might lead to a sort of nihilism in which everything would be swallowed up in an undifferentiated and formless Absolute. However, he makes no attempt to evade the implication of the *via negativa* that beyond the world of sense and even beyond the knowable world of the ideas, there must be an infinite and ineffable Being about Whom negative statements are more easily made than affirmative ones.

When Plotinus posited the Absolute as being all will, but not as willing, he was expressing his conviction that, whereas all will must be contained in the Absolute, since the One is its own cause, we cannot speak of will in this connection if by will we mean the desire for something not present. All things are eternally comprehended in the Absolute, and thus all will and all necessity.[105] For Plotinus, it is similarly true that the Absolute does not think. Nevertheless, He is not asleep. He has a form of "self-discernment," in which the subject-object relationship is transcended. The sort of thinking which He does not do is that which involves any sort of duality. So anxious was Plotinus to avoid any sort of dualism that he denied of the One even that He has ordinary self-consciousness, on the ground that "that which is absolutely self-sufficing does not even need itself."[106] The Absolute is "superconscious." He "abides in a state of wakefulness beyond Being."[107]

Inge, as before mentioned, admits that Plotinus perhaps says too much about the Absolute if the concept sought

after is strictly that to which the necessities of logic lead
us. However, he does not recognize in the admission any
serious weakening of Plotinus' position. He comments:

> Here we are concerned with a number of statements about the
> One, which are intended to make us understand *what* he is,
> though we know that strictly he is not. Plotinus was well aware
> that *omnis determinatio est negatio;* but one cannot worship the
> privative. He would probably not have been seriously troubled
> by the above criticism, for he has no desire at all to separate his
> three Divine Principles sharply from each other. He might per-
> haps have accepted our suggestion that the God of practical reli-
> gion is the universal Soul, the God of devout and thankful con-
> templation, the Great Spirit, the God of our most inspired
> moments the Absolute. 'And these three are one.' This is not so
> for the dialectic, if we treat the dialectic as a logical structure
> leading to a climax; but we have seen that for the Platonist,
> dialectic is the method of acquiring knowledge of the eternal
> verities; and scholastic logic, which does not recognise the fluid-
> ity and interpenetration of concepts in the spiritual world, gains
> lucidity and cogency at the price of truth.[108]

In criticism of Plotinus' description of the One as "fundamentally infinite," Inge urges that the word infinite cannot be applied literally to God because it is a term which
implies the real existence of space. God cannot be described
in spatial terms any more than eternity can be described as
endless temporal existence. Nevertheless, Inge says, we
may adopt the metaphor of Augustine and the Scholastics
"that God has his centre everywhere, and his circumference nowhere."[109] The Absolute, in one sense, stands in a
causal relationship to the world. As the One, it is first
cause; as the Good, it is the final cause of everything. However, since the One is no more eternal than the spiritual
and phenomenal worlds which are aspects of it, the concept of causality as applied to the whole of reality merely

indicates its internal hierarchical nature, "leading up to an all-embracing Absolute in which everything is contained, and which in the world of becoming is the primary source and final consummation of every process."[110] In a later chapter some attention will be given to the status of the created world in Inge's philosophy from the point of view of his criticism of certain views prevalent among those philosophers who have drawn the bulk of their methods and conclusions from modern science. As a disciple of Plotinus, however, he tends to identify the created with the Creator in so far as possible. Our own minds can come to know something of inorganic nature, apparently only because of this fundamental indentity. These minds are, in reality, part and parcel of God Himself, and, on the other side, the seemingly mechanical operation of lifeless matter is merely a revelation of the nature of the divine mind. It is, in fact, only the immanence of God in natural processes that makes any knowledge of nature possible on our part. Inge quite rightly regards his own opinion as a sweeping denial of naturalism as it is usually presented, but it may be maintained that he has not provided an effective refutation of a dualism recognizing both mind and matter. It is not inconceivable that minds may have the capacity for apprehending physical objects with no implication whatsoever of an identification of the knower with the thing known. It is true, however, that such a unity is presupposed in Neoplatonic doctrine. Inge insists that his belief in the fundamental identity of perceiver and perceived does not involve him in mentalism, though his view is undeniably idealistic. Mind does not create things by thinking about them; the perception *is* the thing perceived. An attempt which he makes to elucidate this idea may be held only to suggest its obscurity: "Reality, as this medieval philosopher (Maimonides) perceived, is neither thought nor thing, but the indissoluble unity of thought and thing, which reciprocally imply each other. The relation between them is one of essential identity actualized under the form of essential reciprocity."[111] It seems that the reciprocity occurs in the soul world, where the unity of thought and thing is not completely discernible. Thus, says Inge, the created world represents "a partial disintegration of reality." The question never seems to be answered satisfactorily as to the relationship of the created world to the Absolute and what may be the reason for a disintegration within the divine nature.

The world studied by the scientists is a mental construction based on the inadequate data of the senses.

The world, according to the school of Plato, is created by the Universal Soul, after the likeness of the Spiritual World, which it ever contemplates. "Nature," "the lowest of the spiritual existences," is its intermediary. Nature is the rational, and therefore unvarying, expression of a perfect intelligence. It follows that, though the material objects which science studies are themselves without real being, the construction built up by human thought and observation upon it belongs to the intelligible or real world. What is real in science is the realm of law which "Soul" both makes and finds there. I have insisted, in opposition to the mentalism of some modern physicists, that science begins with what it *finds,* not with what it makes.[112]

It is not surprising to find Inge admitting that we cannot answer the question *how* the Absolute produces distorted copies of its own real categories. As to *why* it does so, Inge agrees with Plotinus that, without the lower world, the intelligible world would not be "in act." This is not taken to mean that God needs the world, but that since creativity is a part of His nature, the world had to be created. Plotinus and Inge do not, however, give us any genuinely cogent reason for the creation of an inferior copy of reality. They tell us of a God, in Himself perfect and complete, compelled by His own nature to create a deceptive world in order to make active the values of a higher one! If such activity results in a more desirable state than is the case without it, then it can hardly be said that the Absolute does not need it. On the contrary, it is a necessary part of perfection.

Beauty and Goodness are considered as of equal importance with Truth in a description of the Absolute, but Inge has devoted a good deal less attention to them. That the importance of each value is not in direct ratio to the amount of space devoted to it is apparent from the fact that Inge presents Beauty as, in a certain sense, the highest of the values if, from the mystic's point of view, it is regarded as the consummation of the way of love. Considered thus, it is the last of the absolute values to be attained by the mystic, for it is in this value that the love which the mystic seeks is most fully expressed. In this connection, he writes, in *Personal Idealism and Mysticism:*

Platonism and Christianity are at one in representing the final consummation as a passing of knowledge into love. The "intellect in love" loses itself in the supreme transit which is its goal and the end of its labours.

Logically, the system is incomplete without this ideal completion of the spiritual ascent, though it has but little relation to any facts of experience. Love the unifier is ours; but to be "made perfect in love" belongs not to our present state.[113]

Farther on in the same work, after describing the ascent of
the soul through the stages of will and intellect, he declares: "And when at last love suffuses all the mind—
love of God and His laws, and love for our neighbour as
made in His image, and the chief mirror of His goodness,
then indeed the yoke becomes easy and the burden
light."[114]

Neither in his description of God, then, nor in his discussion of the life of devotion, does Inge show any willingness
to subordinate aesthetic and emotional considerations to
intellectual or moral ones. He goes to some pains to reconcile with his own position some passages of Plotinus' works
which seem to indicate a tendency to place the Beautiful
in a somewhat lower category than the True and the Good.
Both the latter seem to be identifiable in Plotinus' thought
with "the One," which Inge recognizes as the goal of the
intellect and thus as particularly bound up with the True.
The Beautiful cannot, according to Inge, be so identified,
for the One is formless, and that which is formless cannot
be the Beautiful. It can, however, be *Beauty*, or the source
of that which is beautiful, and so Plotinus refers to the Absolute by three names—the One, the Good, and Beauty.
However, Inge shows that at times Plotinus uses "the Beautiful" in the same sense. The term "First-Beautiful" is always for him interchangeable with "Beauty."[115] Inge himself draws no sharp distinction between "the Good, the
True, and the Beautiful" and "Goodness, Truth, and
Beauty."

Inge appears to have experienced no difficulty in postulating Truth and Beauty as attributes of a God Who exists in
neither space nor time, for these two fields of value lend

themselves with some readiness to abstraction. A consideration of God as Goodness, or the goal of moral effort, on the
other hand, faces us with the problem of finding in Inge's
philosophy a real ground for ethics. In admitting the close
relationship between time and will, Inge sounds the key-
note of the difficulty which many idealists have experienced in establishing an adequate moral philosophy coherent with a metaphysics which denies the reality of the
phenomenal world. For if morality belongs to the world of
time and individuality and Goodness belongs to the world
of eternity and unity, what relationship can exist between
them? Can the individual will *create* moral values, or can
it merely *apprehend* them in much the same way that
Beauty and Truth are said to be apprehended by the feelings and the intellect?

In his treatment of Plotinus, Inge is able to avoid the
problem to some extent by pointing out that in Greek philosophy the notion of "the Good" does not have essentially
moral connotations. It rather involves three ideas which,
according to Inge, cannot be separated:

(1) The Good is the supreme object of all desire and aspiration.
(2) The Good is the condition of knowledge; it is that which
    makes the world intelligible.
(3) The Good is the creative and sustaining cause of the
    world.[116]

The Good is, thus, the final end for which a reasonable
man must strive, for it is the principle grounded in his
rational nature which gives life its meaning and which
"makes things what they are."[117]

Plotinus' view, though based on Plato's, exalts "the
Good" to an even loftier height. It is the Absolute, and is

"beyond being" for even the highest intelligence. Inge maintains that only loyalty to Plato's terminology prevented Plotinus from referring to it rather as "Goodness" —the source of the Good—much as he spoke of "Beauty," rather than "the Beautiful." He did, in fact, disclaim the strict accuracy of the term, explaining that the One is "the Good" only in relation to us.

Morality, for Inge as well as for Plotinus, must somehow be transcended in the Absolute in such a way that, strictly speaking, it would be incorrect to refer to God as morally good. Moral goodness is only a step in the ascent to perfection, but that perfection when attained no longer has moral connotations, for it is beyond the realm of the antithesis between good and evil.

Whereas, in his earlier writings, Inge frequently declared that the Absolute is independent of all temporal processes, he seems to imply in his later works that some activities occurring in time are required for the actualization of the eternal values. This is particularly true with reference to morality. Truth is dependent upon logical rather than temporal processes. Beauty can be appreciated in a "specious present." Goodness, however, as the goal of the will, appears to be dependent upon activity in time, for it is inextricably bound up with moral activity.

Time is the arena in which any purpose is achieved or frustrated; that is its main character as we know it. Time then belongs to the psychic stage in the hierarchy of existence. It is as real as the conflict between good and evil. In our higher activities, and even in the exercise of the moral Will itself, we vanquish Time.[118]

This statement is, in part, ambiguous and obscure. The affirmation that time is "as real as the conflict between good

and evil" makes the reality of each dependent on that of
the other, but does not provide anything remotely resembling an unequivocal answer to the question of whether
morality is real or illusory and evil positive or privative.
Inge's frequently-expressed doubts as to the reality of the
temporal process indicates his apparent willingness to rele-
gate the whole of ethics to a subordinate level of reality.
However, the last sentence of the paragraph just quoted
suggests that, after all, moral actions are in some way related to eternity.

Inge in one place states that "man does not make values
any more than he makes reality."[119] It is, therefore, rather
surprising to find him saying on the following page that
"I have said that morality is concerned not so much with
the apprehension of values, as with their production and
increase."[120] The problem is cleared up to some extent by
his explanation that the values thus created are instrumental rather than absolute. What effect these instrumental
values have on the ultimate value of Goodness is never
made quite clear. Apparently we must be content with the
conclusion that the moral values of the soul world must be
produced in order that the Goodness of the Godhead may
be "actualised." "The human Will introduces final causes
into the processes of nature,"[121] but apparently does not increase the sum total of value in the universe. The effect of
its strivings on the soul level in the overcoming of evil is a
question which must be reserved for the discussion of the
relation of religion to human life—a matter which will
be considered in a chapter dealing with Inge as a theologian.

Inge himself, though firmly convinced that the way of

truth lies in mystical experience, does not base his position
so much on personal experience as on a rational examination of the selected testimony of celebrated mystics. It is
no surprise, therefore, to find him quoting at length from
the works of Plotinus when he wishes to give us some ink-
ling of the nature of the "vision of the One." In Plotinus'
description, as in Inge's exposition, we find a reluctance to
ascribe positive attributes to the ultimate object of the mystical vision which in effect places it above intellectual, aesthetic and moral categories.

We must not be surprised [Plotinus says] that that which excites
the keenest of longings is without any form, even spiritual form,
since the Soul itself, when inflamed with love for it, puts off all
the form which it had, even that which belongs to the spiritual
world. For it is not possible to see it, or to be in harmony with it,
while one is occupied with anything else. The Soul must remove
from itself good and evil and everything else, that it may receive
the One alone, as the One is alone. When the Soul is so blessed,
and is come to it, or rather when it manifests its presence, when
the Soul turns away from visible things and makes itself as beautiful as possible and becomes like the One; (the manner of preparation and adornment is known to those who practice it;) and
seeing the One suddenly appearing in itself, for there is nothing
between, nor are they any longer two, but one; for you cannot
distinguish between them, while the vision lasts; it is that union
of which the union of earthly lovers, who wish to blend their
being with each other, is a copy.[122]

We are told that in this condition the soul is unconcerned
with itself but that this state represents the pinnacle of its
blessedness. It despises all its former concerns, considering
them worthless in comparison with the attainment by the
soul of the happiness of becoming again "what it was formerly, when it was blessed."[123] It values not even "spiritual
intuition," which is inferior in that it implies move-

ment. There is no longer room in the vision for contemplation of anything else. "Even so," Plotinus says, "a traveller,
entering into a palace, admires at first the various beauties
which adorn it; but when the Master appears, he alone is
the object of attention."[124] The exclusive contemplation of
the One produces supreme satisfaction, but also entails a
loss of sharp distinction between subject and object, analogous, for Plotinus, to intoxication. It may be sought by
"looking forth out of" other concerns to which one applies
oneself, if in so doing one does not concern oneself with
the "externals." The One "does not lie in one place and not
in another, but it is present everywhere to him who can
touch it and not to him who cannot."[125]

God, as Plato says, is not very far from every one of us; he is present with all, though they know him not. Men flee away from
him, or rather from themselves. They cannot grasp him from
whom they have fled, nor when they have lost themselves can
they find another, any more than a child who is mad and out of
his mind can know his father. But he who has learnt to know
himself will know also whence he is.[126]

The natural movement of the soul is not in a straight
line, but in a circle around a center—or possibly, Plotinus
suggests, it seeks "some point at which all centres as it were
coincide."[127] It is presumably our failure to recognize the
centrality of "the One" which keeps us from a clear vision
of our own true nature.

The One does not strive to encircle us, but we strive to encircle it.
We always move round the One, but we do not always fix our
gaze upon it: we are like a choir of singers who stand round the
conductor, but do not always sing in time because their attention
is diverted to some external object; when they look at the conductor they sing well and are really with him. So we always

move round the One; if we did not, we should be dissolved and no longer exist; but we do not always look towards the One. When we do, we attain the end of our existence, and our repose, and we no longer sing out of tune, but form in very truth a divine chorus round the One.[128]

From the utter dependence of our being upon "the One" and from the idea that attention—even exclusive attention —to it is a necessary condition of blessedness, Plotinus concludes that "our life in this world is but a falling away, an exile, and a loss of the Soul's wings."[129]

We must then hasten to depart hence [Plotinus goes on], to detach ourselves as much as we can from the body to which we are unhappily bound, to endeavour to embrace God with all our being, and to leave no part of ourselves which is not in contact with him. Then we can see Him and ourselves, as far as is permitted: we see ourselves glorified, full of spiritual light, or rather we see ourselves as pure, subtle, ethereal light; we become divine, or rather we know ourselves to be divine. Then indeed is the flame of life kindled, that flame which, when we sink back to earth, sinks with us.[130]

Ultimately the quality of the ecstatic experience seems to be as indescribable for Plotinus as for Inge. Involving, as it allegedly does, a transcendence of all the properties of the subject-object relationship, it cannot properly be said even to be an experience of "seeing" or of "knowing" but rather of "merging." It is for this reason that the mystical vision must be regarded as ineffable, communicated only in inadequate symbols, and concealed in mysteries. Words are inadequate to convey the real nature of the experience. Plotinus says:

These are but figures, by which the wise prophets indicate how we may see this God. But the wise priest, understanding the symbol, may enter the sanctuary and make the vision real. If he has not yet got so far, he at least conceives that what is within the sanctuary is something invisible to mortal eyes, that it is the Source and Principle of all; he knows that it is by the first Principle that we see the first Principle, and unites himself with it and perceives like by like, leaving behind nothing that is Divine, so far as the Soul can reach. And before the vision, the Soul desires that which remains for it to see. But for him who has ascended above all things, that which remains to see is that which is before all things. For the nature of the Soul will never pass to absolute not-being: when it falls, it will come to evil, and so to not-being, but not to absolute not-being. But if it moves in the opposite direction, it will arrive not at something else, but at itself, and so, being in nothing else, it is only in itself alone; but that which is in itself alone and not in the world of Being is in the Absolute. It ceases to be Being; it is above Being, while in communion with the One. If then a man sees himself become one with the One, he has in himself a likeness of the One, and if he passes out of himself, as an image to its archetype, he has reached the end of his journey. And when he comes down from his vision, he can again awaken the virtue that is in him, and seeing himself fitly adorned in every part he can again mount upward through virtue to Spirit, and through wisdom to the One itself. Such is the life of gods and of godlike and blessed men; a liberation from all earthly bonds, a life that takes no pleasure in earthly things, a flight of the alone to the Alone.[131]

The Good, for Plotinus [Inge says], is *unity as the goal of desire*. This desire, he says, is universal. The Good is the fulfilment of the natural desire (ὄρεξις) for self-completion and self-transcendence, which every finite centre of consciousness feels. Our life indeed *is* that desire; all life is a *nisus* towards its proper goal. This unity which is the Good of all finite life is also the source of all individual being. All being begins and ends in the Good. Spirit flows over into Soul, unconsciously. Soul returns to Spirit, consciously; and Spirit is rooted in the One. 'From the great deep to the great deep he goes.'[132]

All in all, Inge decides the term "the Perfect" is a better term than "the Good" to designate the Absolute. The term "Good" is properly applied to finite experience to indicate

the stage of development beyond that which we ourselves
have reached. This ascent of the soul has as its final goal
what Inge calls "the vision of the One," in which the spirit,
"carried out of itself by aspiring love . . . the unplumbed
depths of its being stirred . . . *becomes* for a moment that
which it can never *know,* the absolute ground of all being."
This process, which cannot properly be referred to as "understanding," is dependent upon the identification of the
knower with the known. "We can know the unknowable,"
the Dean says paradoxically, "because in our deepest
ground we are the unknowable,"[133] and he quotes Eckhart's
"The eye with which I see God is the same with which
God sees me. My eye and God's eye are one eye, and one
sight, and one knowledge, and one love."[134]

Essentially, Inge, like Plotinus, is concerned not so much
with a personal God as with the Absolute, Who as such is
unknowable to man. In so far as He can be apprehended as
object, He is seen as the absolute values of Truth, Goodness,
and Beauty. As Truth, He makes Himself known to us
primarily as the immanent, but at the same time transcendent, Creator of the universe. As Beauty, He is the source of
all that is beautiful. As Goodness, He is the reality toward
which all the moral activity in the universe is directed. As
for the God of religious devotion,

we must admit that the whole character of the mysticism of
Plotinus is affected by the fact that the ideal object of the quest is
a state and not a person. At no point in the ascent is God conceived as a Person over against our own personality. The God
whom Plotinus mainly worships—the Spirit—is transcendent as
well as immanent in the world of Soul, but purely immanent in
his own world, Yonder. In that world He is no longer an object but an atmosphere.[135]

Inge acknowledges that the conception of the Deity held by Plotinus is not entirely in accord with the more highly personal one which has been meaningful to many Christians in their devotion to the heavenly Christ. It is, with its implication that God must be loved disinterestedly without expecting love in return, more akin to Spinoza's conception, and admittedly the saints who have found personal affections an essential feature of the ascent to God will find the summit attained by Plotinus bleak and cold. Inge goes so far as to concede that the Neoplatonic view of God may have a special attraction for many lonely persons who are unsuccessful in their interpersonal relationships. "In all ages," he says, "there are some who fancy themselves attracted by God, or by Nature, when they are really only repelled by man."[136] The loneliness of the true mystic, however, he regards as something quite different, and he holds that even the Christian saint must pass beyond personal devotion and that his love for the exalted Christ must be of another kind from that felt for the historical Jesus. Ultimately, he maintains, the difference between Christianity and Platonism on this score is not as great as might be supposed.

Plotinus' view of ethics, of specifically religious matters, and of aesthetics, are wholly dependent on his metaphysics and his conception of proper human development as an ascent of the soul toward reality. Despite his admitted disinclination to engage in a thoroughgoing examination of specific data in these fields, Inge maintains that he provides a guide for investigation of such data which is in no significant way incompatible with authentic Christian philosophy.

The Egyptian's ethical system is conceded to be deficient in some respects, although Inge seems to concur in his judgment that morality is not a category which can be applied to the highest order of reality. Plotinus' own aristocratic disdain for those who concern themselves with problems of distribution of wealth caused him to differentiate sharply between virtuous men on the one hand, who can attain a vision of reality, and are therefore apparently entitled to such of the world's goods as they need—and "vulgar and earthly persons" on the other, who sometimes "dream of virtue and participate in it to some small extent," but who sometimes "form only a vile crowd, and are only machines, destined to minister to the first needs of virtuous men."[137] Inge points out that a man like Plotinus would not be a heavy burden on the community which supported him and would be worth his keep. He does recognize that Plotinus may have erred if he assumed that lowly occupations are necessarily a barrier to the higher life. He also regards Plotinus' ethics as defective when compared with Christianity in the degree to which it encourages moral isolation. "The dependence of Souls *on each other* for the achievement of their perfection is a truth which Christianity taught and Neoplatonism neglected,"[138] he says. It is only because of Plotinus' own character, which made him "lovable and beloved," that Inge finds it possible to excuse even these defects in his master's ethical teachings.

As in the case of ethics, Inge attempts to minimize in so far as possible the differences between Plotinus' religious doctrines and Christian theology, while admitting that there are differences which cannot be ignored. The trinity of the One, Spirit, and the World Soul are not precisely

analogous to the Christian Trinity, and Plotinus leaves
room in his philosophy for devotion to the gods of popular
theology and belief in daemons. It is to these beings that
petitionary prayers are properly addressed, whereas in the
higher reaches of religion only contemplation and meditation are appropriate. Just so, the question of personal immortality can be of real interest only to those who have not
yet realized the oneness of the individual soul with the
"Great Soul."

The Soul that never dies is not something that belongs to us, but
something to which we belong. We shall belong to it after we
are dead, as we belonged to it before we were born. Its history is
our history, and its super-historical existence is our immortality.[139]

While recognizing the points at which Christianity di-
verges from Plotinus, Inge maintains that the differences
between the two systems have been overemphasized by
most critics. He charges Augustine, in his progressive alienation from Greek culture, with failing to do full justice
to the debt he owed to Plotinus and the Platonists. Inge attempts to set the record straight on this score by placing
Augustine squarely within the Platonic camp. "The religious philosophy to which Augustine was converted and
in which he found satisfaction," he says, "was the Platonism of Plotinus with the doctrine of the Incarnation
added to it."

In Plotinus' discussion of aesthetic matters in the *Enneads,* we have the formulation of a position with respect
to art which Inge rightly regards as an advance upon Plato.
The function of the artist is not to copy nature, but to attempt to reveal through whatever medium he may be em-

ploying something of the nature of the Beautiful. Inge says:

The true artist fixes his eyes on the archetypal Logoi, and tries to draw inspiration from the spiritual power which created the forms of bodily beauty. Art is not only genuinely creative; it is among the highest and most permanent forms of creation. Some spiritual values are revealed only in art. The artist has more freedom than is possible to mechanical skill or to outward action. Art, therefore, is a mode of contemplation, which creates because it must.[140]

But as is the case with every other human activity, the work of the artist belongs to a lower plane of being than that which is the ultimate goal of the spiritual quest. Ultimately, religion, ethics, art, and, indeed, all the concerns of human society must be left behind us. The Platonist's quest reaches beyond them.

He must expect to outgrow many early enthusiasms before the end of his course. For this life is a *'schola animarum,'* as Origen said; and we are learners to the end. The future is hidden from us; but through the darkness the light of heaven burns steadily before us; and we know that 'yonder,' amid the eternal ideas of Truth, Goodness, and Beauty, is our birth-place and our final home.[141]

3 CHRISTIAN THEOLOGIAN

Rᴀꜱʜᴅᴀʟʟ's ᴄᴏᴍᴍᴇɴᴛ upon Inge's appointment to St. Paul's that "Inge is a Buddhist" casts some doubt on the Dean's reputation for Christian orthodoxy. Inge himself felt that Shaw was more accurate when he called him a Quaker. The opinion of some of the more eminent of the English clergy is that Inge derived too little of his theology from the historic doctrines of the Christian Church. Nevertheless, he himself was an ordained priest within the Anglican Communion. He spoke from a position of authority in the Church. He related his opinions to Christian doctrine. It is therefore impossible to effect an over-all evaluation of his thought without some attention to his attitude toward fundamental questions of Christian theology.

The development of his position on these matters is somewhat oblique. Having repudiated Church and Bible as sources of final authority in matters of religion, Inge had to appeal to another perennial approach to belief which he recognized as having a place within the framework of historic Christianity. This he found in the "Great Tradition" of the Continental and English mystics, whose reports of the states of awareness resulting from their devotions seemed to Inge to fit best into a Platonic system of thought. Accordingly, he drew no line between the intellectual system of reality derived from his study of Plotinus and his reflections on the Christian faith, which he regarded as a continuation and fulfillment of the "Great Tradition." Pointing out that Augustine learned from his study of Plotinus and the other Platonists the true meaning of the judgment "God is Spirit," he further cites the passage in the *Confessions* in which Augustine admits that the Platonic philosophers expressed most of what he wanted except the Incarnation. These admissions constitute for Inge clearer evidence of the close relation between Neoplatonic thought and Christian mysticism. To a considerable extent, then, the Dean's treatment of Christian theology becomes an examination of the mode of religious awareness and its data as related to the central Christian doctrine that God as person became incarnate that men might be lifted up to Him.

Inge's view of the nature of religious awareness stems from his rejection of dogmatic authority and of rationalism as sources of final answers to fundamental questions in theology. Institutional or Scriptural authority cannot be final, for they must themselves rest on some other ground.

Although Inge makes the claim that the majority of his doctrines are as essential to Christianity as to Platonism, it can be seen almost invariably that when it is necessary to alter one to fit the other, it is generally Christianity which suffers the violence. This observation must not be taken to imply any dishonesty on Inge's part, for among the several philosophical systems to which the fundamental tenets of the Christian faith may be adapted, he was genuinely constrained by his own nature to choose Platonism. Having done so, he showed unusual vigor and ingenuity in reconciling the data with the system. He firmly believed that the central tradition of the Christian faith is found in the line of thought which he adopted as his own. He chose his scriptural references carefully and frequently made them imply concepts which might have startled the men who wrote them. However, he found in many passages of the New Testament, especially in the writings of St. Paul and St. John, statements which seem to provide real support for his views. He therefore experienced little difficulty in effecting a harmony between Neoplatonism and Christianity sufficient to satisfy his orderly mind.

In Inge's view, the assumption that man can attain true wisdom by rational procedures alone is a misconception concerning the role of logic in a philosophy of religion. An essential feature of the religious life is the mystical experience involved in his conception of the term *faith*. Despite his confidence in reason as applied within its proper sphere, Inge holds rationalism in small esteem as a method for discovering eternal truth. In a sermon delivered at St. Paul's in 1892, he said:

Should we be glad, in our best moments, to see the Divinity of Christ proved like a proposition in Euclid? Should we wish to forfeit entirely the blessing on those who have not seen, and yet have believed? the last beatitude of the gospel, as it has been fitly called. For in what way can poor mortals show *love* to an omnipotent Being? In one way only—when He condescends to ask us to trust Him. . . . The idea of religion as a series of propositions to be examined by the rules of evidence has no place in the spiritual history of the real saint.[1]

A somewhat more philosophical presentation of this position is found in a sermon delivered at Saint Mark's, Marylebone Road, London, in 1903: "When religious faith is challenged to justify itself, it is almost obliged to argue and give reasons. But in reality it knows that it cannot be acquitted or condemned by the categories of the understanding: its inspiration and its energy are drawn from a deeper and a more mysterious source."[2]

The word faith may be used in such a fashion as to have no particular reference to religion. When so used, it usually signifies "the holding for true of something which is not already verified by experience or demonstrated by logical conclusion, or confidence in the wisdom and integrity of a person."[3] The two attitudes described here may be designated as *belief* and *trust*. As employed in religious language, the term faith has a somewhat more circumscribed meaning. It refers to a conviction in regard to the universe and our relation to it. The conviction is not based merely upon intellectual belief. "It involves an eager and loyal choice, a resolution to abide by the hypothesis that the nature of things is good, and on the side of goodness. That is to say, Faith, in the religious sense, is not simply belief; it is inseparable from the sister virtues of hope and love."[4] Through the life of faith we may enter into a real communion with God. Faith is the human side of religion, corresponding to grace on the divine side. The two are indissoluble in any religious act and only appear as separate because in our imperfect experience we have not yet been able to fuse them. Faith cannot exist without grace; any attempt to eliminate the latter results in rationalism or magical supernaturalism. Inge's idea of faith is summarized briefly and well in the following statement:

Faith is, on the practical side, just the resolution to stand or fall by the noblest hypothesis; and, on the intellectual side, it is a progressive initiation, by experiment which ends in experience, into the unity of the good, the true, and the beautiful, founded on the inner assurance that these three attributes of the divine nature have one source and conduct to one goal.[5]

According to Inge, the intelligible world can be known only through a form of mysticism which cannot be accepted unless we admit at the outset that the soul may perceive truths otherwise than by means of the sense organs. This position may be more clearly understood if we think of man as a microcosm who reflects within himself the nature of the macrocosm, and if we recognize the Platonic division of man's nature into the three realms of body, soul, and spirit. The spirit is not a separate entity or faculty, but the soul when it "enters into its full rights as a denizen of the spiritual world."[6] The recognition of such a distinction does not, of course, in itself establish the nature of the religious consciousness. In making the distinction, Inge is simply affirming his conviction that the ability of man to apprehend religious truths is due to a part of his essential nature which has as its principal function the attainment of spiritual goals. His evidence for this contention is in part empirical and statistical. We must believe in the objective validity of religious experience, he holds, because of the important role that it has always played in human life.

Doubt concerning the fundamentally religious nature of the universe always indicates a spirit of skepticism; but

Inge regards complete skepticism as unbearable, even if intellectually tenable. Forced by his own nature to take some form of positive position, the doubter usually falls into that form of pseudo-agnosticism which arbitrarily divides the world of experience into "dreams" and "realities." Although ideas of God are usually included under the "dream" category by the agnostic, he nevertheless often classifies aesthetic appreciation and the higher emotions as "realities." The reason usually advanced for this inconsistency is that the agnostic "feels" aesthetic and emotional values and must, therefore, recognize their reality. If this is the case, Inge quite properly demands, by what right does the doubter deny the same treatment to religious awareness? If his only argument is that he does not "feel" it, the sensualist has a perfect right on the same ground to deny that the higher emotions can yield any knowledge. If the agnostic points to the many disagreements occurring among religious people, he can be answered by pointing out that all religions agree on at least one thing—that the limits to knowledge set by the agnostic are wrong. To the question whether mysticism is a source of real information, Inge recognizes only two alternative answers: "Either religious belief is a natural and normal product of the healthy human mind,—and as we have no possible appeal from the highest human consciousness, that is much the same as saying that it is true,—or it is a mental disease, a form of insanity."[7]

Inge further argues that the agnostic should not rule out a vast mass of evidence merely because he has not himself had any experience of the kind. A person who demands physical proof for all facts rules out a great many things which neither common sense nor reflective thought can well banish from the picture of reality. An absurd world view is the inevitable result of such a procedure. When one considers the part played by religion in history, one cannot say that the whole thing is a delusion without becoming more skeptical than the agnostic wishes to be. The Dean seems quite justified in turning to the history of religion itself to substantiate the claim to objectivity made by all religions. Whatever one may think of his specific claims concerning the nature of the religious consciousness, the religious person can at least agree with him that not all legitimate knowledge is a product of science or rationalism.

In the collection of sermons called *Faith and Knowledge,* one of his earlier works, Inge maintains that the spiritual consciousness is a kind of instinct, lying in the subconscious region of the mind, and comparable in its protective and preservative functions to the instincts of the lower animals. Its particular task, however, is to keep the lower impulses in subjection and direct a man in the path that he would deliberately choose if he were further advanced intellectually and morally. Religion is still in the instinctive state because the "higher life" has been open to the human race for only a few thousand years. The religious instinct is apparently what is referred to in *Christian Mysticism* as a "dim consciousness of the *beyond*"—a capacity for extending the limits of our consciousness.

Mysticism arises when we try to bring this higher consciousness into relation with the other contents of our minds. Religious Mysticism may be defined as the attempt to realise the presence of the living God in the soul and in nature, or, more generally, as

the attempt to realise, in thought and feeling, the immanence of
the temporal in the eternal, and of the eternal in the temporal.
Our consciousness of the beyond is, I say, the raw material of all
religion.[8]

The religious impulse is identifiable with the instinct
which forces us to order our experience according to a
scale of values. Inge maintains that when ideas of objects
pass through our minds, they necessarily fall into different
categories of value or disvalue, some being called good and
others bad, some beautiful and others ugly, some true and
others false.[9] The religious significance of this valuational
process is readily understood when we recognize that, for
Inge, God Himself is Goodness, Truth, and Beauty. When
we assign values to our experience, we are to that extent
coming into some sort of harmony with the mind of God,
Who is the embodiment of the eternal values in all their
fullness.

So fundamental an energy as the religious instinct is not
peculiar to will, feeling, or intelligence. Each of the three
faculties has its own religious state, and the one which is
strongest in a particular personality dominates, or tries to
dominate, the whole mind. Inge, as a disciple of Plotinus,
does not hold the faculties to be separate departments of
the mind, but treats them merely as different functions of
the total personality. However, he does present a description of three religious types, based on his faculty psychology.

Religion of will is conducive to an attitude in which the
whole of life is bound up in morality. It is found in the
New Testament in the Epistle of Saint James, and to some
extent, perhaps, in I Peter. To the moralist, God is the

Great Taskmaster, in Whose eye human beings must strive ever to live according to law. Inge says, in criticism of religion of the will in general, "This type of religion is strong in its insistence of human responsibility, and in the unassailable supremacy which it assigns to the moral over the aesthetic and speculative faculties; but it is weak in sympathy and imagination, and, above all, in its practical negation of Divine immanence."[10]

Religion of feeling is essentially emotional and aesthetic. According to Inge, it is the religion of the heart, which regards love as the fulfilling of the law and blessedness as "loving communion with God, and salvation in ultimate union with Him."[11] He cites St. Paul, St. John, and the devotional mystics as exponents of emotional religion in the sense described. Inge points out that religion of feeling presents only one aspect of the truth. "Pure feeling" is for him no guarantee of the truth or falsity of an idea and cannot, therefore, be regarded as the primary ground of faith. He continues:

Feeling is the mirror which reflects ideas and ideals. It has been defined as the 'passive echo in consciousness of the unconscious psychical process.' It creates nothing; it seems to project ideas and ideals, because it reflects unconscious motions of thought and will. Feeling in itself is neither good nor bad, true nor untrue. It is simply a fact of the soul-life. Its truth depends on the truth of the idea which determines it; its goodness on the goodness of the motive which is bound up with it.[12]

Emotion must not, therefore, be stimulated artificially to secure "immediacy of religious feeling," as is done in many primitive religions and in others supposedly more highly developed. Following a description of the frenzied revels of

an early Dionysiac cult, Inge points to the abiding detri-
mental effect of such practices upon the worshiper.

This is one of the most important empirical discoveries about the
religious emotion which man has made. The result of employing
it is to arrest the development of Faith at a very early stage. This
kind of religion may be intense; it may become the predominant
interest in life; but it can hardly produce any of the proper
fruits of Faith: it is an abortive Faith, a monstrosity and a perversion. The undifferentiated Faith-state was not given to us to
use or enjoy in this way. It must be developed, rendered explicit,
unravelled, as it were, through will, thought and appropriate action.[13]

This is not to say that feeling can be eliminated from religion. It is implicit in the religious consciousness, both in
the form of love—which cannot be reduced to the level of
mere feeling—and in the aesthetic ground for faith. Both
emotional and aesthetic feeling constitute the most direct
approach to "Beauty," and thus one of the three avenues
to Inge's triune God.

The third type of religion is that of the intelligence. Here
metaphysics and science furnish the material for a theory
of reality which is then set up as the law of God, with
which man is said to be obliged to live in harmony. Inge
cites as examples of religion of the intellect the words of
the 90th Psalm, the Epistle to the Hebrews, the works of
Marcus Aurelius and the other Stoics, Calvinism (which
he calls "Christianized Stoicism"), and all the philosophies
of religion which derive their inspiration from Spinoza.

Although he consistently recognizes the intelligence as a
legitimate road to a knowledge of reality, Inge is opposed
to rationalism as a final method of establishing truth, holding that it leads to a variety of philosophical aberrations,

among them pragmatism—of which more will be said in a later chapter. Rationalism has, however, made valuable contributions to philosophy, and Inge attaches some importance to its famous three "proofs" for the existence of God. Recognizing the many fallacious versions of the ontological argument which have developed in the course of Christian history, Inge nevertheless regards it as a good argument when it merely states the conviction that the only possible source of our knowledge of God is God Himself. In this form, rather than in Anselm's, it recognizes the place of faculties other than the intellect, and thus probably seemed to the Dean to be less tainted with rationalism. At any rate, he concedes that neither in this nor in any other form can the argument provide a conclusive proof for the existence of God. The cosmological argument carries a certain amount of conviction when it states that experience points to the existence of an immanent "World-ground," Who is the eternal source of transitory phenomena. If it merely points to the existence of a Prime Mover rather than an immanent Spirit, it is not, by Inge's definition, pointing to God at all. With reference to the teleological argument, he affirms that Darwinism and modern science in general have not provided any refutation of the idea that through the apparently mechanical processes of nature there runs some purpose which is the manifestation of a divine mind, whose unity may be postulated because of the harmony which the various parts of the world seem to exhibit in their relations to one another.

It may be noted that Inge's interpretation of all these "proofs" is thoroughly in accordance with the Neoplatonic doctrine of Plotinus, and further, that his willingness to recognize them as having some merit is conditional upon their being stated in such a form as to involve more than the "pure reason" which the rationalists consider sufficient. The following evaluation of the teleological argument expresses equally well his opinion of the other two:

> We have to face the objection that this conviction may have a purely subjective origin. But we have already conceded the righteous and reasonable demand of Faith that when our whole personality—will, thought, and feeling—tells us that we are in the presence of objective truth and reality, we shall believe it.[14]

The same transcendence of rationalism is implied in Inge's denial that the so-called "proofs" render their contradictions logically untenable, for

> atheism is not unthinkable or illogical; it is only 'absurd,' in Lotze's sense of the word. It is rejected by Faith as a hypothesis which would reduce the world to a chaos, a malignant trick, or a sorry joke. Being ourselves what God has made us, we have a right to call this hypothesis absurd, and to let it go. But this is not the rationalistic idea of proof.[15]

The dangers of intellectualism lie in the fact that as rationalism it has a tendency to become naturalistic pantheism, and as speculative idealism it tends toward idealistic pantheism. In either case, the result is merely a theory of cosmology which has little to do with religion. Rationalism is further tainted by its tendency to lead to pragmatism, instrumentalism, humanism, or other forms of "action" philosophies which lay excessive emphasis upon the will at the expense of attention to objective truth. This tendency exists largely because the type of "pure intellectualism" condemned by Inge leaves no room for faith.

It confounds Faith with knowledge. It is easy to recognize this type. Its God is 'the One.' He is triumphantly monistic, for that is almost all that is required of Him. His worshippers easily fall into a lofty disdain of the unphilosophic vulgar. This was a weakness of Greek philosophy, and it has reappeared wherever Faith and knowledge have been identified. In the field of practice, we see from the history of the Italian Renaissance how easily intellectual morality becomes Machiavellian, and how, in the region of feeling, intellectualism substitutes artistic sensibility for charity and affection. It is never long before this type proves its unsoundness by passing out of religion altogether. Thus the fatal results of one-sidedness are once more brought home to us.[16]

Inge's chief objection to rationalism, then, is that it ignores two of the three primary grounds of faith. The rationalists are, to be sure, correct in asserting that reason cannot be excluded from religion, and, indeed, if men advance to a less primitive state, we may expect that it will play a greater part in religion than it does today. Its principal function is to test the attainments of faith and determine whether they are authentic. Rationalistic philosophies cannot, however, be sufficient, for they attempt the impossible task of *proving* faith by logical processes and fail to arrive at true γνῶσις. They try to find a place for God in their world pictures, but "God, 'whose center is everywhere and His circumference nowhere,' cannot be fitted into a diagram. He is rather the canvas on which the picture is painted, or the frame in which it is set."[17] They prematurely attempt to make a synthesis of reality, which can never be adequate from Inge's viewpoint until there is no differentiation between thinker and thought. In other words, never in our experience as human beings can a completely adequate explanation of the universe be made. The only satisfactory approach to reality from the human viewpoint must include the will and the feelings as well as the intellect.

The religious instinct finds its true expression, not in any one of the three, but in the "higher reason," which is the totality of all of them working in perfect harmony. The higher reason is not a separate psychic organ or a special faculty, but rather the complete functioning of the entire personality. Its capacity for giving us access to God rests on the intimate relationship of the value-sensitivity in man's nature to God Himself, Who is the embodiment of the eternal values. Rudolf Metz in comparing Inge's position with Harnack's says, "the latter defines Mysticism as Rationalism applied to a sphere that lies beyond Reason; while Inge defines it as Reason applied to a sphere that lies beyond Rationalism."[18]

According to Inge, mysticism as a type of religion rests on four "articles of faith": that *the soul . . . can see and perceive,* by channels other than the organs of sense; that, "since we can only know what is akin to ourselves, *man, in order to know God, must be a partaker of the Divine nature";* that *"without holiness no man may see the Lord";* and that *"the true hierophant of the mysteries of God, is love."*[19] The foregoing discussion has been related to the first two. How the others fit in with Inge's theory of knowledge may be explained by a brief exposition of the manner in which the higher reason operates in aiding us to establish contact with the intelligible world.

The "Trinity within us"[20] of will, feeling, and intelligence is actually a complete unity, but in our imperfect experience the three elements seem discordant. The conflicts which result from our lack of understanding often affect the images which we form of God. The person who has not to any great extent developed his capacity for apprehending religious truths often looks for delusory outward proofs of religion, such as miracles and signs. Attempts of this sort are inevitably doomed to failure, for an outward sign can never be a positive guarantee of the thing it is supposed to signify. If it offers itself to the understanding of the observer, it cannot prove the truth of something which he cannot understand, for, as Inge says, "In proportion as a truth is external, it is either not revealed or not spiritual. For in the spiritual world there is no outside and inside. Spiritual things, as Plotinus says, are separated from each other not by local division, but only by discordance of nature."[21] To avoid this error, one must so live that the faculties of will, feeling, and intelligence may become unified to such an extent that the religious consciousness can operate with as little hindrance from the physical world as can be attained.

The religious consciousness is concerned with the attempt to eliminate sin from the mind, and Inge regards pride as the root of sin. Self-consciousness, self will, and self-seeking are the forms under which sin manifests itself. Inge lays at the door of pride all the human evils which afflict the world—the wars between capital and labor, the defacement of the natural beauty of the world, and even the nervous overstrain resulting from competition in business which seems to be sterilizing good families and allowing inferior persons to people the earth. The way to eliminate the evils of human nature is, he holds, identical with the road of Christian mysticism—the progressive denial of the false concept of individual selves through an attempt to identify oneself with ultimate reality. This leads to a consideration of the *scala perfectionis* of the mystics, the ladder which is supposed to lead from earth to heaven through an increasingly effective negation of self.

The steps of the upward path are referred to as the purgative life, the illuminative life, and the unitive life, which is really the goal of the pilgrim's effort rather than a part of the ascent.[22] The first stage of the journey is effected by *contrition, confession,* and *hearty amendment.* In practice, the civic virtues must be included in this step. They occupy the lowest position, not because they are less important than the others, but because everyone must acquire them, whether or not the other steps of the ascent are taken. We learn from the civic virtues the principles of order and limitation, which are attributes of God. Self-discipline is a necessary part of the purgative life. Asceticism, in the popularly understood meaning of the word, is not implied in this discipline, but a measure of "austere simplicity" may prove helpful if the mystic is careful to direct his attention outward rather than toward himself. Extreme asceticism of the type practiced by many medieval monks is a perversion of the mystic's creed. "Mysticism enjoins a dying life, not a living death."[23]

In the illuminative life the mystic concentrates all his faculties—will, feeling, and intellect—upon God. The good works of the first stage, although still practiced, are under the control of the intellect rather than the struggling will and are now habitual and without strain.[24] In the last stage, "man beholds God face to face, and is joined to Him."[25] So long as religion exists, the union can never be complete, for the union itself would be the annihilation of religion. The unitive, or contemplative, life is an infinite process, although the union is, in a sense, accomplished in this stage. ". . . as its end is part of the eternal counsel of God, there is a sense in which it is already a fact, and not merely a thing desired."[26] The recognition of a sharp distinction between Creator and created, so dominant in much Christian thought, is conspicuously absent in Inge's theology, despite his recognition that religion demands that the soul as subject must retain some vestige of its relationship to God as object or face annihilation as an entity. It will be noted that, although all three of the faculties of the higher reason are employed at each stage of the ascent, there is a close correspondence between them and the three steps of the *scala perfectionis*. In Inge's view, the religious man employs will, intelligence, and feeling in ascending through three stages related to these faculties to a God Who is Goodness, Truth, and Beauty.

The intelligible world is the realm toward which the individual ascends in the spiritual quest. According to Inge, the final goal may be "the One beyond Intelligence,"[27] even though we may never hope to become identical with the Absolute. The mystic must first attempt, however, to reach a state in which thinker and thought become identified with each other and in which the mind, having included within itself all possible experience, passes into a condition of undifferentiated being, a condition in itself a fuller reaffirmation of the original religious state—"an undifferentiated feeling of the Beyond, a feeling in which all possible developments of the moral, intellectual, and emotional life are implicit."[28] Having attained this happy state, the soul is ready for the consummation of the ascent,

which Inge calls "a passing of knowledge into love." He
admits that the idea of being "made perfect in love" is
quite inconceivable in our present state, although we can
now know "love the unifier."[29] He is rather doubtful with
reference to those revelations provided by the mystical
ecstasy characterized by a "swooning into the Absolute."
Nowhere in his writings does he definitely brand the process as a psychological aberration, but it is plain that he
does not consider it an essential part of the mystical process.
In our present state, our knowledge must be of the God of
religion and not of the Godhead. In the same fashion, he
refrains from passing final judgment on the visions which
have often accompanied the mystical experience of the
saints. To a reserved and orderly mind like the Dean's such
phenomena are somewhat distasteful, and he appears to
have felt that many of them are of a pathological nature,
but he does not deny that some of them may be associated
with genuine mystical experience.

In a number of his writings, he expresses a similar distrust of miracle as providing evidence for religious truth.
Recognizing that a good many people find it comfortable to
believe in a thoroughgoing dualism of fact and value in
which the natural order may be altered by divine intervention and frequent miracle, Inge nevertheless regards such a
solution as an undesirable return to outmoded thought
forms. His objections are essentially pragmatic and aesthetic. Science, he says, would not be able to function
properly if suspensions of natural law were likely to occur.
Furthermore, he admits to a distaste for the idea that divine acts are intercalated among natural events. "Belief in

miracle as a fact of experience despiritualises religion,"[30] he says.

It is difficult to see how this last objection is justified unless Inge is willing to admit to an almost Manichean view of matter which would be quite inconsistent with the rest of his philosophy. His real objection to miracle appears to have a different basis. He treats the intellectual constructs of science as reflections of eternal truths. Any disturbance of the order and uniformity of nature would seem to imply that in the value structure of the eternal world there might be an element of caprice, which would, of course, be intolerable to Inge. Faith in the uniformity of nature, he holds, is not so much a product of materialism as of the conviction of science, whether recognized by scientists or not, that the ultimate value of truth admits no disorder in its realm. Miracle, as "the bastard child of faith and reason, which neither parent can afford to own,"[31] would seem to Inge to admit a lawless element into the realm of the spirit. In *Science Religion and Reality,* though the book is for the most part concerned with criticism of contemporary philosophy, Inge devotes some special consideration to the psychology of religious belief. He takes issue with Wordsworth's contention that we are in infancy surrounded by heaven. "The child's mind is a garden where flowers and weeds grow together," he says, and he writes of the "roots of unpleasant vices" which the "perverted ingenuity" of the psychoanalysts has found even in the apparent innocence of the nursery.[32] Children get many false ideas about religion in their early formative period. As a matter of fact, it is hard to tell what goes on in the child's mind. Much of his apparent religiosity may be artificial, and we know little of the fears and worries which beset him. Yet, Inge tells us, some children show an "exquisitely beautiful saintliness of character," and sometimes one who dies in childhood seems to have developed quickly all the genuine religious awareness that a lifetime rich in devotion and good works could have produced. In this observation, Inge gives us again a glimpse of the feelings produced by the life and early death of his little daughter Paula.

Inge holds that the storm and stress which is supposed to occur in religion during adolescence has been over-emphasized. In the field of sex, too, he accuses Continental writers of being guilty of too much exaggeration about adolescent difficulties, "unless we may flatter ourselves (and I am not sure that we may not do so) that a much larger proportion of young people in England preserve their innocence than in other great countries."[33]

Middle life brings maturity to our religion. One comes to understand that freedom is achieved by submission to God. Prayers include less petition. Creed becomes simplified and intensified. God is experienced more as an "atmosphere" than as an object. It is in this period of life that rich mystical experience normally becomes possible. Attempts to impute a psychopathological character to all forms of mystical awareness fill Inge with indignation, for it cannot be legitimately claimed that the abnormalities which may accompany some mystical experiences or the absence of such experiences in certain persons should shatter our faith in the mystical process. A moderate degree of mystical experience is normal. However, there are those who do not attain it, either because they are "religiously ungifted" or because they do not develop the capacity which they have for it. The testimony of the "specialist" in the spiritual life should be accorded the same respect as is given to authority in other fields. However, this claim leads to an admission of the necessity for critical examination of the experiences of those mystics who profess to have attained the highest rung of the ladder and to have become conscious of their one-ness with the Absolute. Inge assumes this "Vision of the One" to be a valid experience, although, impaled on the horns of a Platonic dilemma, he admits, with Plotinus, that "without some duality of thought and its object, there can be no existence."[34] Nevertheless, the mystics have claimed that in the final stages of ecstasy, the soul rises to a condition in which it is really merged with the First Principle. Inge does not profess ever to have experienced any such thing. He contents himself with the more modest claim that even in many aspects of our normally experienced "higher life" we rise above the forms of time and space and, to that extent, confirm the experience of those who reach the summit of religious experience.

The statement made by Metz concerning Inge's conception of God, that it "coincides with that of Christian theology,"[35] is, in view of the diversities among the opinions held by Christian theologians themselves, not very explicit. However, it is true that his view of God is one which is essentially theistic and in some sense trinitarian. The core of Christian thinking about God he describes as "the doctrine that the ultimate ground of the universe is a single supreme Being Who is perfect and complete in Him-

self."[36] Thus far, his position creates no undue strain between the Christian and the Plotinic elements of his
thought. He admits, however, that further reflections on
the nature of God as revealed in religion lead to some difficulty in reconciling one's conception of the God of religion with the concept of the Absolute. Sometimes, he
holds, we are almost compelled to think of them as different beings, although the distinction cannot, of course,
reflect the truth of the matter. The conception held in
popular religion stresses the other-ness of God and leads to
the conclusion that "God must be a Spirit among other
spirits, not the deepest life and final home of all spirits."
"Such a conception of the Deity, if counterbalanced, as it
should be, by that of a personal devil, is a useful piece of
symbolism for the conscience in its struggle with sin; but
if it is offered us as a metaphysical truth, we can only say
that such a God would not be God at all."[37] It seems obvious that the contention that "such a God would not be
God" can be justified only by accepting initially a sort of
ontological assumption that the idea of God necessarily involves the reality of the precise nature which Inge attributes to Him. Inge's refusal to admit the ultimate reality of a God who is "personal" in the modern sense of the
term is a logical outcome of the premises provided by his
theory of personality and his distaste for any view which
would tend to reduce God to the status of "a very con-
stitutional President in a society of free and independent
spirits."[38]

In contrast with a definite personal theism of this sort,
Inge accepts substantially the doctrine of Deity advanced
by Plotinus and discussed in the preceding chapter. Never-

theless, in the Dean's theological and devotional writings the Neoplatonists' God is described in the language of the Christian faith, and the insights of the Christian mystics are given full attention.

It is in his acceptance of the Logos Christology, the historicity of the Incarnation, and the doctrine of the Trinity that Inge places himself legitimately within the historic framework of Christianity. He affirms his belief that the Logos, the Word of God, "the creative and sustaining principle in the universe," Who "comprehends it, though as God He is not comprehended by it,"[39] was incarnate in Jesus of Nazareth in order that we might receive the revelation of God's love, as well as that of His power and beauty, already revealed in nature. That love, according to Inge, could only have been revealed in the Incarnation and Passion.

Christ is permanently related to the world in time. "So far as we can know, the reign of the Son as a distinct principle in the Godhead is co-extensive with time; it began 'in the beginning,' and will continue till 'cometh the end.' For us, the Son is the revelation of God in space and time."[40]

In an essay entitled "The Person of Christ" published in a work "by six Oxford Tutors" under the title *Contentio Veritatis,* he says:

What theology calls the Incarnation—*i.e.* not the conversion of the Godhead into flesh, but the taking of the manhood into God —is, so far as we are concerned, the supreme object of creation. Taking as our guide the unique historical Incarnation in the past, we may say that the complete revelation to man of God's purposes concerning man, and the complete subordination of the human will to the Divine Will, so that it may act unswervingly

in carrying out those purposes, are what constitutes union between the human and Divine natures, and that the realization of
this union in mankind, as it was once realised in Christ, is the
far-off Divine event towards which the whole creation moves.[41]

He maintains that the intellectual foundation for the
understanding of this doctrine was laid by such Greek
philosophers as Heraclitus and Socrates and that its formulation by the Church was simply the statement of a truth
guaranteed by the mystical experience of the Christian society. "The facts which supplied the framework of Christian dogma," he writes, "were not only the events which
occurred in Judaea in the reigns of Augustus and Tiberius;
they were also the experiences, repeated in each generation, of the human soul in its conflicts with sin, its suffer-
ings, its death unto sin, and its new life unto righteousness."[42]

Inge holds that the early church was right in its rejection of Adoptionism and Docetism and its preservation of
the Johannine Logos-theology. It is this last theory which
Inge sees as closest to Platonism of all the attempts to
formulate a doctrine of the Incarnation. However, he recognizes that the point at which the whole Christian position is in danger of breaking with the Platonic tradition
is the insistence in the former that "the Word was made
flesh." The tendency of Christian Platonists to substitute a
doctrine of general immanence for one of Incarnation in
Christ threatened the conception of Christ's personality
which Inge holds to be essential to the Christian faith.

The Christology of Arianism he dismisses as "hopeless,"
but he regards the opposite extreme of Sabellianism as
equally unsatisfactory. Recognizing that Monophysitism

and Monothelitism both have some germs of truth in them, he nevertheless maintains that the Church was probably right in condemning them. The Incarnation must not be regarded as an absorption of human nature into the Divine. If that were true for Christ, it would be true of humanity generally with respect to the ultimate state of the redeemed man. Inge recognizes here—more clearly than sometimes seems to be the case with him—that such is not the Christian position. "The ideal goal which we contemplate and hope for," he says, "is a state in which our nature and will shall be perfect instruments of the Divine nature and will, but in which they shall remain in a condition of free subordination to the Divine—not abolished or absorbed, so as to lose all possibility of *communion,* nor yet so separate as to admit only of an ethical harmony."[43]

Inge recognizes the difficulties involved in the question of the nature of Christ as both human and divine. He insists that the Godhead and manhood must be conceived as "not mutually exclusive, while at the same time neither is allowed to curtail the other."[44] Jesus grew and learned, but we must on no account say this of God, Who cannot, in Inge's view, be considered as in time at all.

Inge holds that the religious conciousness is primarily concerned with the search for symbols adequate to that which is symbolized. It does not confine itself to pure thought or conscious myth. Recognizing that, on occasion, manufactured myths have been accepted in good faith as historical truths, he nevertheless holds that there is some legitimacy to the conviction that spiritual revelations have as their concomitant certain occurrences in the natural order. Historical evidence in itself is insufficient to validate the theological claims associated with these occurrences, but they may nevertheless be regarded as true and significant for the believer.

For all Inge's natural reluctance to incorporate divine truth in any special way in a single historical event, he comes at last to the conclusion that belief that Christ was the Son of God in a special sense is an essential of Christianity for four reasons:

(a) If Christ did not claim to be the Son of God, in a sense which applied to Himself alone, the gospels are too untrustworthy to have any historical value. The real Jesus of Nazareth is lost to us irrevocably. (b) There is one essential attribute of divinity which Christianity can never consent to surrender in the case of Christ —namely, His sinlessness. If He was a sinner like ourselves, the union between God and man, which Christianity asserts to be a fact, is still an unrealised ideal. (c) The voluntary humiliation of the Lord of all is an integral part of Christianity. (d) The highest, most distinctive, and most potent parts of His teaching are bound up with the personal claim.[45]

His Christianity is therefore, perhaps, most noticeable in his occasional vigorous attacks on those who would deny the historicity of Christ or imply that He was a deluded Galilean peasant with a popular but vain eschatological message. Long after his disagreement with the Catholic Modernists had appreciably lessened, he was still saying that Schweitzer went "much too far," although it is not entirely evident why he considered Schweitzer more heretical than Loisy and Tyrrell.

As late as 1935, however, he was still enthusiastically engaged in a counter-assault against the "attack on Christianity itself" which he felt to be implicit in the contention of many theologians that all Jesus' utterances were made within the framework of a mistaken opinion that the world order would shortly be brought to a close and a new Messianic age ushered in. In a little Lenten book published in that year, the Dean included an essay written some years earlier, "The Kingdom of God," in which there is a wholehearted defense of a fairly traditional view of the nature of Christ's person and knowledge of His mission. The more lurid eschatological elements in early Christian thought, he holds, were not the result of Christ's teaching, which was invariably calm, unemotional, deeply spiritual, and universal in character. It is more reasonable to assume that these expectations of an early dramatic culmination of human history were grafted on to the Christian message as "innocent interpolations" of those who were originally attracted to Christianity in the pathetic hope that the day of the Messiah was at hand, but who may well have remained in the faith after it was evident that no such hope was implied or needed in the faith of Christ.

I do not wish entirely to exclude the possibility that our Lord, in becoming man, may have been willing to share, to some extent, the current popular illusions, both with regard to the Messianic hope, and demoniacal possession. But this must certainly not be stretched so far as to admit that He fancied himself filling the rôle of Daniel's Son of Man in the near future. Such a notion would not be compatible with sanity, far less with those attributes which all Christians believe Him to have possessed. What the disciples thought about Him is another matter. It may be laid down as a rule that a conversion always begins with a misunderstanding. We are attracted in the first instance not by the reality, but by some preconceived idea of our own, which drops off as we come to know the reality. Messianism in point of fact dropped off very early from Christianity, like a protecting shell which was no longer needed. It dropped off with hardly any convulsion. Not so very long after Christians ceased to pray "come, Lord Jesus," they began to pray *pro mora finis*—that the end might not come just yet.[46]

Trinitarianism has, Inge concedes, frequently been a stumbling block to modern minds, a fact due, in his opinion, to the current misconception of a "person" as a thinking subject rather than merely as an individual with legal rights and duties. He denies that the psychological as contrasted with the legal usage of the terms referring to personality had any meaning whatsoever for the Greeks and holds that it was in some measure—though not so greatly —alien to the Romans. A confusion in the meanings attached to the words denoting personality, as well as the Cartesian attitude toward the ego which obtains generally in modern thought, caused Christian opinion in the West to grow away from Modalism and toward Tritheism. Inge holds this development to be a corruption of Trinitarian doctrine as suggested by the Gospel of John. It may be inferred that an even more serious objection to modern ideas of personality from Inge's standpoint is their insistence on human individuality as an ultimate fact. As for the significance of earlier Greek conceptions of personality in their relation to modern Christianity, Inge regards them as pointing more in the direction of a view which would recognize more fully the real identity of the three persons of the Trinity. With that as a starting point, he launches into a discussion of the Logos-Christology, in which he traces its development from Heraclitus down to the present day. The acceptance of Christ, or the Logos, as a cosmic principle seems to him to be a recognition of the essential rationality of the universe. A man who bases his faith on that rationality cannot have it refuted "by the digging up of an old scrap of papyrus, or the ingenious lucubrations of some German professor."[47]

It sets us free [he continues] from that haunting fear—which is surely an unworthy and faithless fear—that the honest exercise of the highest intellectual faculties, whether in scholarship, criticism, or the study of nature's laws, may lead us to the discovery of something that had better not have been discovered.[48]

The doctrine is significant for personal religion in that it points to the real presence of God in the spirit of man. With his conviction that "only like can know like," Inge regards some kind of union between God and man as a necessary doctrine of the Christian faith. The idea of the Logos implies that knowledge of God is attained through the indwelling of God in the personality so that identity of subject and object is somehow realized. This doctrine of divine immanence, which Inge highly prizes, reached its peak with the medieval mystics such as the elder and younger Eckhart and Hugo of St. Victor. It is interesting to note the fullness of the development of this idea in the thinking of Meister Eckhart, who, in his defense against charges of heresy, writes:

it must be realized first of all that, without doubt, God himself being One, because he is not another, is undivided in Being through power, presence and essence, the Father unbegotten and the Son begotten; for the Father is not the Father unless begetting and unbegotten and the Son is not the Son unless begotten and himself One, as being God. Hence, wherever God is the Father and the unbegotten begetter, there is the begotten Son too. Therefore, since God is in me, surely God the Father begets the Son in me, and in me the begotten Son himself is one and undivided, since there is no other Son in the divine, except this One, and he is God.[49]

The mysticism of such men as this is, as Inge saw, inextricably linked with the Logos doctrine as well as with Platonic thought in general. Inge champions these views against all contemporary ideas of personality which deny the reality of divine immanence. In a passage which echoes the sentiments of Meister Eckhart, he says:

The life, death, and resurrection of the Word of God were not a solitary event, not an unique portent, but the supreme vindication of an universal law. It is exemplified and re-enacted in little, in every human soul among the elect; it is in the highest sense of the word *natural,* for to those who can understand Scotus Erigena's words: "Be assured that the Word is the nature of all things," nothing is "supernatural." The best that God can give us, the gift of His own presence, is all part of His original scheme, part of the inviolable laws under which we live.[50]

Belief in this sort of divine immanence produces a "natural religion," which does not rely on rational "proofs" for the existence of God. It is not pantheism, but it does produce for many thinkers a sympathy with panpsychism of the variety proposed by Fechner—a view with which Inge is by no means unsympathetic. He insists, however, that a philosophy of this kind does not render the traditional doctrine of the Incarnation meaningless by minimizing the importance of its historical features. Admittedly, "real" things are, for Inge, supra-historical, and only the "lesser" reality can be affirmed of events occurring now or in Judea and Galilee some two thousand years ago. However, those events are not merely allegorical. The Incarnation shows that "God reveals Himself most fully in the fullest and richest developments of being and actuality, in that form of life in which the processes of nature seem to culminate and converge, in the soul of the perfect man, in the soul of Christ."[51] Inge's view of the world of events seems to be somewhat self-contradictory. On the one hand, the world is, in the strictest Platonic sense, a copy, or a dissipated version, of reality. On the other hand, it produces the "richest and fullest developments" of reality. Inge draws the further conclusion concerning the Incarnation of Christ that it "teaches us that Goodness does not need the accessories of Power and Omniscience in order to be divine," even though in Christ they are only temporarily separated.[52] The historical Passion is symbolic of this Goodness as it may be incarnate in man. That which it symbolizes is found sporadically in the Church in the persons of the saints, and the history of the Church at its best is an assurance that the nature of Christ is better understood by the Church than by the writers of the Gospels. Inge believes that the revelation of Christ is yet incomplete, for the Church is still in its infancy. All generations and all nations since the Incarnation have tended to depict Christ in the guise of their own cultures. Inge holds, however, that the significance of Christianity is not so much in its view of Christ as the universal and ideal man as in its recognition that through Christ "the Word of God becomes incarnate in the hearts of the faithful."[53]

Using his conception of the nature of the persons of the Trinity as a springboard, Inge examines the question of human personality. It is with reference to this matter that the issue between the Personal Idealists and the Dean becomes most sharply defined. Those modern writers who place personality at the foundation of their metaphysics and ethics and do so in the name of Christianity are "at best translating Christian theology into an alien dialect."[54]

Inge chooses as his first opponent in the lists a rather extreme example of the movement he dislikes in the person
of Professor Andrew Seth Pringle-Pattison, whom he desig-
nates as a "representative" modern philosopher. He quotes
with distaste the Scottish writer's statement that "each self
is a unique existence, which is perfectly impervious to
other selves—impervious in a fashion of which the im-
penetrability of matter is a faint analogue."[55] Even if it be
understood that Pringle-Pattison is merely urging here that
one self may not merge with or become identified with
another, the view of personality which Inge endorses is still
widely at variance with his. The doctrine of "impervious
selves" is represented as being fundamentally opposed to
"the absolutely fluid conception of personality" found in
the New Testament. For evidence of this "absolutely fluid
conception," we are presented with the suspicions of the
Jewish masses that Jesus was Elijah, Jeremiah, or—more
significantly—John the Baptist, who had only recently
been beheaded. Although the uncritical notions of a very
few people may seem poor evidence for his contention that
the thought of New Testament days contained no conception of personality as it is understood today, Inge regards
the same attitude as evident in the more philosophical reflections of Paul and John concerning the vine and the
branches and the body and its members. This, he holds, is
not "fantastic and misleading metaphor," but a statement
of the Christian idea of personality, an idea which thoroughly repudiates the notion that selves are "impervious."
It may be submitted that Inge is not at his argumentative
best when, from such meagre linguistic and scriptural references as he has seen fit to cite, he assumes that most of

the persons in the Graeco-Roman and Jewish cultures had no conception of a view of personality which, far from being a philosophical abstraction, may be regarded as grounded on the experience of an impressive majority of the members of the human race concerning their own natures. It is true that some Personal Idealists have overstated the case in implying that real communication and interaction among selves cannot exist, but this has not been a frequent error. It is incorrect to derive from the fact that some highly speculative thinkers have regarded the self as fluid the unlikely conclusion that such a view has ever been generally accepted in any age. It seems more probable that the scarcity of references in ancient literature to the individuality of selves is due to the fact that ordinarily such individuality was taken for granted.

It is, moreover, open to serious question whether Inge interprets the position of his opponents with strict accuracy, for throughout his treatment of Personal Idealism he seems to attribute to its adherents the belief that each soul is a sort of spiritual buckshot, destined to spend the entire period of its existence in complete and unhallowed isolation from its fellows. Apparently overlooking the possibility that individual minds might have the capacity to establish contact with one another and work in complete harmony without any sort of actual metaphysical identification or merging, Inge appears to make spiritual fellowship dependent upon some such process. The result of such a procedure is to reduce individual personality to a semi-illusory status. "The individual assumed by the psychologist, and by the common political and ethical theories," he says, "is a half-way abstraction of the ordinary understanding, a bastard product of bad metaphysics and bad science."[56]

Since nothing in human experience indicates for him the existence of "self," Inge finds it fairly easy to build up a case for his metaphysical identification of subject with object. Once he says that we are merely parts of a whole. Nevertheless, he soon rejects even this analogy, for the whole of existence is not, according to his theory, dependent upon its parts; the parts are rather dependent upon the whole. The part-whole idea must, therefore, be rejected. In seeking a form of expression to replace it, Inge considers the metaphor of the vine and the branches. As even that is unsatisfactory, he falls back on a traditional Christian phrase, concluding that, in some way which cannot be adequately expressed, we are all "one in Jesus Christ," and thus members of the same body. Thus, falling into a trap against which he repeatedly warned religious philosophers, Inge demands, as almost the sole evidence for the unity he affirms, that language which may well be figurative be regarded as literal. Citing the relatively common experience of an apparent inner division of the personality, he quotes Paul's cry: "I live, yet not I, but Christ liveth in me."[57] In another place he argues that when Jesus said, "Believe Me that I am in My Father, and ye in Me," he was, if the Personal Idealists are right, "either using an extravagant oriental metaphor, or saying nothing."[58] Against Inge's contention, one may rightly object that it is not at all necessary to fit utterances such as these into his particular philosophical framework in order for them to be meaningful. The word *in* has spatial connotations that Inge is seldom ready to accept literally. Remove the implication of space, and these statements may be regarded as referring to something in the nature of complete harmony of will and purpose among individual spirits. At any rate, the idea of a non-spatial "in-ness" is subject to a variety of philosophical interpretations.

Although the human soul is not held to have an "independent existence," Inge maintains that it does have an "independent value."[59] This point is never quite explained in his writings, and it is extraordinarily confusing, contradicting, as it does, his insistence upon the ultimate identity of value with existence. At any rate, he goes on to say that the unity in which we are bound to the Logos is the unity of a system "in which parts and whole are equally real," or in which, as Proclus said, the parts and the whole are "woven together."[60]

Inge considers that we are forced to choose between a monistic conception and a thoroughgoing pluralism. If we attempt a compromise, as Leibniz did, we are nevertheless compelled to admit that all the things comprising reality ultimately rest in a system. This admission is all that Inge professes to need to point out that if the world is indeed composed of a number of "spirits" who constitute a moral kingdom by virtue of their relation to God, "this relation is a fact as much as their separateness, and a fact fatal to pluralism."[61] The relation, he thinks, is the most real thing about them. However, he overlooks the fact that if such an admission is fatal to pluralism, it is also fatal to the sort of monism he appears to have been upholding. In order for real relationships to exist at all, it is necessary for items to exist which are related. The unsubstantiated assertion regarding the greater reality of the relationship is

hardly sufficient to demonstrate that the individuality of
the members of the spiritual organization is not just as
important as any other facts about them. If Inge's contentions can be reduced to an argument for some form of order
in the universe, he is tilting at windmills, for few of his
opponents other than those at the extreme end of the
pragmatist movement would uphold the theory of a "wild
universe." The theory of an ordered cosmos does not demand souls which are "woven together" and which have
no independent existence. Nor does it necessitate the assumption that individuality is somehow "less real" than
unity. Certainly concepts of selves may overlap in our experience, but to attempt to show from this fact that there
is any metaphysical overlapping of the individual selves is
to identify concepts with the facts to which they refer.

The fact is that Inge never makes clear just how much
reality he is willing to attribute to individual personalities.
Yet no matter how anxious he may seem at times to preserve some degree of individuality in his view of human
selves, it seems, in the light of his entire philosophy, that
he is ultimately forced to sacrifice its most important aspects to the ideals of the Good, the True, and the Beautiful.
This becomes clearer when we consider his view of the
"transfigured self."

Real personal life, he holds, can be attained only by
reaching a consciousness of one-ness with God. Man has a
soul, or personality, which, although in a sense it is not his
at all, may nevertheless be "lost." It is "an ideal; not a given
fact."[62] Indeed, Inge claims, falling back again on a traditional Christian phrase, that it can become fact only for
those willing to "lose" it. He arrives at this conclusion by

substituting the word *personality* for the *soul* or *life* found in most translations of the New Testament. The "transfigured self" is attained by being willing "to forget ourselves entirely, to cease to revolve round our own selfish interests, to pass out freely into the great life of the world, constructing our universe on a Christocentric or cosmocentric basis, not a self-centered one."[63] If Inge is merely pleading here the value of an unselfish life as opposed to a completely self-centered one, few will disagree with him. Unselfishness is quite easily conceived of as an attribute of an individual personality. But if he is advancing this position as an argument to defend the idea that the personality may be actually lost by being merged with some greater entity constituting the "real" personality, it must be maintained that his evidence is inadequate.

Despite his strong disagreement with the Personal Idealists, Inge contends that his own philosophy does not deal any fatal blow to human personality. Growth to grace, to be sure, cannot be described as "an increasing consciousness of the barrier which separates the thinking subject from all other subjects;"[64] but, in another statement, we are told:

Those who are afraid of a philosophy which seems at first sight to depersonalize man should reflect that this is the philosophy which attaches the greatest importance to *unity* as a supreme attribute of God, and sets out the attainment of unity or personality by ourselves as the goal of all our striving. Not that our aim is to attain an individuality separate from or independent of the life of God. Such an aspiration would be philosophically absurd and religiously impious.[65]

But it may surely be asked how many of the defenders of Personal Idealism whom he attacks so vigorously ever suggested the position he here labels as "philosophically absurd."

Possibly because his *Personal Idealism and Mysticism* had not been regarded generally as of great philosophical consequence, or possibly because he came to feel that in it he had not really done justice to the fact of human personality, Inge in his later writings went to some pains to show that a certain type of real individuality is implied in his conception of man. In *God and the Astronomers,* he did this by making a distinction between the soul and the "abstract ego." If the two are identified, he states, the identification involves three assumptions with which he cannot agree. The first of these is the sharp distinction believed to be implicit in the subject-object relationship; the second is that "the subject, thus sundered from the object, remains identical through time"; and the third is the conception of the soul as in some way both oneself and one's property.[66] By denying the distinction between subject and object, the identity of the subject throughout time, and the idea that the soul is, or belongs to, one's "self," Inge endeavors to establish a view of the individuality of the soul quite different from that of the Personal Idealists. He says that in the world of spirit, there is "distinction without division," and "complete compenetration of all real existences, so that the whole is present in each part."[67] Nevertheless, he goes on to say:

Souls, being immaterial, cannot be divided quantitatively, nor can one soul be part of another soul. They are not parts of the Universal Soul, but are active powers of Spirits, who are fully real in the world Yonder. Both the Universal Soul and particular souls emanate from this higher world, and they preserve their rights in this higher world.[68]

This idea of completely interpenetrable souls emanated by "Spirits" which, though not "selves," yet have in reality some form of individuality sometimes appears to be nothing more than the notion that what is real in the individual is a "soul-centre" which, in practically all of Inge's writings, is identifiable with God—"Christus in omnibus totus."[69] He seems never really to have receded from the position expressed in his Paddock Lectures that man's individuality is but a shadow of God's. One's will never becomes truly effective until it attains, not merely harmony with the will of God, but identification with it. He writes:

Those who adopt a rigid theory of personality cannot think of the matter in this way. The utmost to which they can aspire is, it would seem, a complete ethical harmony between God's will and our own. But this is not the experience which the saints have described for us; and it would not satisfy them at all. There is no room in the universe for more than one will, existing in its own right. Our approach to the likeness of God is not an approximation to a *copy* of God. It is rather a transmutation of our personality into a state in which God can think and will and act freely *through* us, unimpeded by any wilfulness on our part.[70]

Thus, the only fully personal life which can ever be attained, according to Inge's philosophy, is apparently one "which we may claim in virtue of the very severity of our monism."[71]

One may question whether Inge is justified in assuming that adoption of the Personal Idealists' position necessitates renunciation of a belief in an ordered existence and the recognition of a lawless universe peopled by hard-shelled spirits. His opponents might very well admit all the evidence actually produced to support the Dean's position and still not be forced to accept the idea of the unreal

nature of personal identity. Despite the reverence with
which many philosophers have regarded the doctrine that
"only like can know like," it is open to serious question.
Even if it were admitted, however, it would still not necessitate a conclusion that likeness implies identity, or that
a man is in any real sense substantially identical with God
or with other persons. To reason from "likeness" to "in-
ness" involves a leap in logic which will give many
thoughtful persons pause. We cannot readily conclude that
the bonds of sympathy and common purpose which unite
a man with his fellow human beings imply his ontological
identity with his fellows, nor does the picture of human
personality given in the New Testament necessitate a denial of the full reality of individual selves.

On none of the subjects dealt with in a long and productive life of speaking and writing is Inge more vague than
he is with regard to the question of human immortality.
Most of his utterances on the subject give one the feeling
that, although he felt obliged as a Christian minister to
believe in some form of immortality, the question did not
assume a place of primary importance in his thought. He
points out two conceptions of immortality in Christian
theology, the first implying the idea of a state of blessedness into which we can enter here and now, and the second
the conception of a future life of reward and punishment
after death. In a sermon delivered at Westminster Abbey
in 1902 he stated that early Christianity appears to have
had no trouble in reconciling these two concepts. He insisted that we must, therefore, find room in our beliefs for
both. The accommodation of Inge's Christianity to his
Neoplatonism is nowhere more conspicuous than in his

discussions of this question. In most of these, the "state of blessedness" receives the dominant position, and the idea of survival after death tends to become extremely attenuated, if not nonexistent.

From the outset he recoils from the idea of probation, reward, and punishment as a crude concept which violates the balance of his value structure by laying too much emphasis upon morality. The traditional conception of hell is intolerable. In a sermon preached in 1906, he repudiated it without hesitation:

If hell were what it has been described to be, no one who deserved to go to heaven could bear to live there and know what was going on. Can we fancy ourselves singing, 'Just and true are thy ways, Thou King of Saints,' while contemplating even the less estimable of our acquaintances torn by red-hot pincers for all eternity? It is in the name of Christ that we dismiss these dreadful stories as a mere nightmare.[72]

Even the idea of mere survival in time without positive punishment is treated as an unpleasant one. The notion of eternal rest is intolerable. The alternative, a conception of immortality as an eternal struggle, is a fate which "condemns the Will itself to the doom of Sisyphus."[73] As a final blow to the popular conception of souls which exist for perpetuity in time and space, he states that "no habitation in space can be found for these deathless beings."[74] Whether the implication is merely that we are unable to locate such a place, or whether—as seems more likely— he would imply that space is incapable of holding all the souls which inhabit bodies at some time in the history of the cosmos, this argument seems curiously naive coming from a clergyman of Inge's stature, resembling, as it does, the words of the astronomer who declared that he had searched the heavens with his telescope without finding any signs of a God.

In lieu of an immortality in time, Inge endeavors to describe one which differs from mortal life principally in *quality*, but has indestructibility as one of its essential attributes. "What we *are*," he states, "remains; what we seem, get, lose, enjoy, suffer, passes."[75] It may seem to many Christians that in eliminating all these, he comes perilously close to losing the "we" as well.

The fact of the matter is that his real concern is not with individual immortality so much as with the concept of a world of values which does not involve space, time, or consciousness.

Faith in human immortality stands or falls with the belief in *absolute values*. The interest of consciousness, as Professor Pringle-Pattison has said in his admirable Gifford Lectures, lies in the ideal values of which it is the bearer, not in its mere existence as a more refined kind of fact. Idealism is most satisfactorily defined as the interpretation of the world according to a scale of value, or, in Plato's phrase, by the Idea of the Good. The highest values in this scale are absolute, eternal, and super-individual, and lower values are assigned their place in virtue of their correspondence to or participation in these absolute values.[76]

Any attempt to separate value from existence is, Inge maintains, doomed to failure. As the absolute values constitute real existence, they are eternal and cannot cease to be, he says, for he holds, in agreement with Plotinus, that "nothing that really *is* can ever perish," and with Höffding that "no value perishes out of the world."[77] Immortality, then, is the identification of ourselves with the eternal ideals of the Good, the True, and the Beautiful.

Anticipating two of the most important objections to this conception of eternal life, Inge makes a serious attempt to answer them. The first is that no guarantee of survival in time is included in such a doctrine. The second is that it offers only an impersonal immortality. He attacks the first objection by maintaining that time has no real existence outside the soul life of the individual. "If the soul were in time, no value could arise; for time is always hurling its own products into nothingness, and the present is an unextended point, dividing an unreal past from an unreal future. The soul is not in time; time is rather in the soul."[78] The "life-frame" of the Logos—the Universal Soul—is the whole of the cosmic process and is supra-temporal. No matter how important our lives in time may seem to us, any such importance is illusory. "If my particular life-meaning passes out of activity, it will be because the larger life, to which I belong, no longer needs that form of expression. My death, like my birth, will have a teleological justification, to which my supra-temporal self will consent."[79] The truly religious man does not, according to Inge, desire the shadowy form of existence which necromancers and materialistically-minded persons attempt to prove, but is quite content to die, confident that "what ought to be is eternally real and true."[80] The problem of whether or not after this life we are to be given a further period of probation, either in some other physical body or as a member of another spiritual realm, is dismissed because we can have no knowledge of the existence of any such state. "To these questions," Inge declares, "no answer is possible, because we are confronted with a blank wall of ignorance."[81] It is surely reasonable to ask at this point whether, if we can-

not have knowledge of the continuance in time of a spiritual life comparable with our present existence, it is possible for us to be aware of the non-temporal, non-spatial
existence suggested by the Dean.

In answer to the second objection, Inge reaffirms his
stand that personality is not a stable thing and that there
is no barrier between a subject and other subjects and between subjects and objects. He then points out that the
thinking subject is not identical throughout experience, but
is fluid and changing, even on the empirical level. In this
contention, however, he does not seem to discriminate between the contents of thought and experience, which obviously change from moment to moment, and the psychic
center which integrates these varied experiences and con-
fidently refers to itself as "I." The question of whether "my"
soul will live eternally seems to have no meaning for Inge,
holding, as he does, that a man must be willing to lose his
soul on the experiential level before he can attain eternal
life.[82] Thus he attempts to refute the second of the two
objections on the basis of his own conception of personality. In the second volume of his work on Plotinus, we find
the following statement:

'Mysticism,' says Keyserling, 'whether it likes it or not, ends in
an impersonal immortality.' But impersonality is a negative conception, like timelessness. What is negated in 'timelessness' is not
the reality of the present, but the unreality of the past and future.
Time is only forbidden to devour itself. So impersonality, for the
mystic, means simply the liberation of the idea of personality—
it is allowed to expand as far as it can. How far that is, we admit
that we do not know clearly; but the expansion is throughout an
enrichment, not an impoverishment. When Keyserling adds:

'The instinct of immortality really affirms that the individual is not ultimate,' we entirely agree with him. If this were not true, how could men die for an idea?[83]

Inge and Keyserling, from their separate viewpoints, assume conditions which do not appear necessary in a consideration of immortality. The assumption that a belief in immortality implies a denial that the individual is "ultimate" is unjustifiable, and with reference to Inge's question about dying for an idea, it is necessary only to point out that a man who believes the individual to be ultimate could quite easily die—*i.e.,* give up his present physical life—for an idea if he also believed that as an individual he would be immortal. The Dean's query is thus meaningless.

Inge admits that the question of personal immortality is not concerned with the extent to which the soul life may expand, but with whether or not the individual soul centers remain. The so-called centers are centers of consciousness, and thus, apparently, of will, which is in Inge's system a manifestation of the soul life. Consciousness as we know it must, therefore, be absent from the intelligible world. It really only comes into existence when the individual will begins to function and as a condition of its struggle. It is not a necessary attribute of life, for there is a life below consciousness and perhaps one above it. Keeping in mind the fact that we are using spatial and temporal metaphors in speaking of centers of consciousness and continuance of consciousness, Inge contends that the question of the nature of individual survival must be "transformed" before it can be answered. From the transformation emerges what appears to be a somewhat more encouraging conception of immortality. In his *Outspoken Essays,* he writes:

Spiritual life, we are justified in saying, must have a richness of content; it is, potentially at least, all embracing. But this enhancement of life is exhibited not only in extension but in intensity. Eternal life is no diffusion or dilution of personality, but its consummation. It seems certain that in such a state of existence individuality must be maintained. If every life in this world represents an unique purpose in the Divine mind, and if the end or meaning of soul-life, though striven for in time, has both its source and its achievement in eternity, this, the value and reality of the individual life, must remain as a distinct fact in the spiritual world.[84]

This passage is somewhat ambiguous, involving as it does a confusion between the standpoints of life in time (the soul world) and of eternity (the intelligible world). The nature of the individuality preserved is never described with any real clarity by Inge. Indeed, in the essay from which the above quotation was taken, he seems to have arrived at the idea rather by an interesting turn of reasoning than by any positive conviction on the subject. Having identified value and existence, he merely assumes that if the value realized by the individual soul exists in the eternal world, the soul itself must retain some measure of individuality. The conception of immortality advanced here is a more positive one than is the case in *Personal Idealism and Mysticism,* published eight years earlier. However, it is not easy to conceive of a life which is neither conscious nor unconscious, but above consciousness, or to see how a genuine belief in personal immortality can be reconciled with Inge's rigid monism. Some form of centers of consciousness would seem to be essential for the differentiation of lives which are purely spiritual. Altogether, the pale version of individual immortality pictured in some of Inge's writings is a bit of Christian theology which rests somewhat uneasily in his metaphysical system. Perhaps it results from the demands of his theological training. Perhaps it represents the influence of Plotinus' notion of "transparent" spirits. In a good bit of his writing, Inge ignores it altogether and appears to consider individuality as an aspect of the soul world and, as such, doomed: "My own belief is that whatever is born in time must perish in time, and this must be true of world-systems no less than of individual lives"[85]—no less, and, by implication, no more.

Inge treats any intrusion of the concepts of time, space, or personality in a discussion of ultimate things as a lowering of the ideal to which we should adhere in theology. They may be useful as symbols, but must never be considered as expressing literal truths. The religious man must be content with the expression of faith stated in Inge's work on Plotinus: "The religious faith in immortality is the faith that all true values are valid always and everywhere; that the order of the universe is just, rational, and beautiful; and that those principles which exalt us above ourselves and open heaven to us are the attributes of the Creator in whom we live and move and have our being."[86]

Inge's doctrine, even when it seems to involve personal survival, does not assure us that all souls will be saved or "that all the failures of time will be made good in eternity."[87] He deplores the popular religious optimism which seems to rest on "a good natured idea that no one really deserves to be punished. 'Dieu me pardonnera; c'est son métier.' "[88] Theories of universal salvation usually imply the notion that any failure of a human being is in part a failure of God, a view which Inge regards as pantheistic. He holds, rather, that if a soul is lost, the *being* of God is not affected at all, although we have no way of determining whether the loss affects His happiness. With reference to the question of whether a soul can be entirely lost, Inge's opinions as expressed at different times involve either a contradiction or a change of mind. In *Christian Ethics and Modern Problems,* he writes:

in the sphere of morals Christianity is sterner, more tragic, less optimistic, than Platonism. For the latter, a man may perhaps lose his soul, but not the soul that would have been his if he had not been a bad man. Christianity has a more definite conception of personality, and the person, the Ego, the soul ($\psi\nu\chi\acute{\eta}$) may be finally lost.[89]

Some three years later, he states, "Christianity has consistently taught from the first that a man can finally lose his soul, though not the soul which would have been his if he had not been a bad man."[90] This development provides an instance of the way in which Inge tended in increasing degree to identify as "Christian" views which were in reality Platonic. As a matter of fact, it is rather unexpected to find him admitting as late as 1930 that Christianity has a stable concept of personality in which all the aspects of the soul stand or fall as a unity. Inge's later view is certainly more in accordance with his usual fluid notions about selfhood. The idea that the soul which is evil can in some way be "lost," leaving only the soul which a man admittedly never "had," but which is "real" because it is of value, is hardly derivable from the Christian tradition as such. It is, however, closely related to the rest of Inge's philosophy, particularly to his privative theory of evil.

As a final word on Inge's theory of personal immortality, it may be said that his fundamental conviction, underlying all the modifications and incoherencies in his thought on the subject, is that each person is free to choose which of two worlds he will inhabit. We are temporal in so far as we identify ourselves with earthly things and eternal in so far as we "have our conversation in heaven." Here, as in all the other aspects of Inge's theology, the tendency to start with Platonic thought and fit historic Christianity into it wherever possible is evident. Whether he was, in fact, thoroughly committed to the Christian faith or whether he was above all a Platonist who found himself caught in the impermanent symbols of the transitory life of a portion of the Christian Church is a question not easily answered.

4 CONTEMPORARY CRITIC

It is a curious fact in the career of a man who had been primarily preoccupied with a contemplation of the "spirit of the ages" that his chief fame was won by his trenchant criticisms of the "spirits of the age." In his attitude toward contemporary ideas and events, Inge was frankly a pessimist. However, his discourses, far from being pontifical or melancholy, sparkle with the brand of wit which, despite his refusal to write in a popular or journalistic style, made him one of the most widely read essayists of his day.

The sobriquet "The Gloomy Dean," inflicted on him by the *Daily Mail,* to the extent that it fails to present an accurate picture of a man who was not given to more than ordinary melancholy, was perhaps not too fortunate. Undeniably, however, the persistent tag has contributed much to his reputation with the rather large group of readers who regard "Red" or "Gloomy" deans as more newsworthy than those who can claim no such qualifying adjectives.

Inge's most widely circulated venture into the field of modern criticism is probably his Warburton Lectures, delivered between 1931 and 1933 and later published as

God and the Astronomers, perhaps his best-known book.

The lectures constitute an admission that, even for a Platonist, the formulation of a comprehensive metaphysics necessitates a consideration of the findings of modern science and the theories based on them. The world of the senses is not totally void of reality. Properly viewed, it may point to the nonmaterial truth which underlies it. Nothing is to be gained, however, by attempting to build up a philosophy simply by spiritualizing matter. Radiation is material and has no more to do with spirit than does solid or gas. Thus the attempt to twist modern science to idealistic ends by maintaining that present-day physics has progressively rendered matter less "solid" is, Inge holds, a frivolous one. It is based on a mistaken conception of spirit as "matter in an ultra-gaseous condition."[1] Nor is Berkeleyan idealism helpful in eliminating the apparent dichotomy between matter and spirit. Science must be grounded in realism and cannot be merely mathematical. Eddington's attempt to take refuge in mentalism from the difficulties encountered in a physics which postulates a genuinely physical universe is, for Inge, an illicit step. "From a concrete object to a mental concept," he says, "there is no road. Subjective idealism must not begin with common-sense realism."[2] A panmathematical universe such as Jeans postulated is not a satisfactory substitute for the real universe in which the mechanists believed. The world is not simply our thoughts about it; nor is it merely the thought pattern of a celestial mathematician. It is a creation—not an image of the imagination.

Affirming his own acceptance of the reality of the physical world, Inge says:

I shall have to plead with idealists, whether they are primarily metaphysicians or mathematicians, that there is an ontology of the phenomenal world, and that we can neither regard it as the creation of the human mind nor as a system of symbols with no necessary relation to reality. My own position, I will say at once, is nearer to the realists than to the idealists; but I do not regard the mind as only a mirror of happenings which are independent of it. Reality, as I understand it, is constituted by the unity in duality of the mind and its objects. Mind does not create the intelligible world, nor is the intelligible world independent of the intelligence. The real world is a kingdom of objective "forms," which in the mind of God are the perfect counterpart of His own thought.[3]

This view, though perhaps, as Inge claims, closer to realism than to idealism, seems still a rather far cry from most contemporary forms of realism, and it is clear that any dualism which may be involved in it is essentially phenomenal and ultimately resolvable into an ontological monism in which reality is a fusion of subject and object. Inge's position is further complicated by his acceptance of the notion of degrees of truth and reality, an idea associated with his recognition of the objectivity of values. Inge seems to infer that if values are facts and are susceptible of description in terms of degrees of reality, then facts must be so describable. This, of course, is illicit process, unless it be affirmed, not merely that all values are facts, but that all facts are values. It also involves his acknowledgment of differences of degree in the "reality" of values and not simply in their importance.

The identification of fact with value is, as has already been pointed out, a legitimate consequence of Inge's Platonistic metaphysics. Truth, Goodness, and Beauty are the ultimate realities, and they are both value and fact; indeed, they are the values which are the source of all facts. Existence cannot be understood at all, he holds, "without arranging our experience of things in an order which is frankly valuational or axiological."[4] In affirming that values may be more or less real, Inge implies that the use of words like higher and lower, or better and worse, indicates a recognition of varying degrees of reality. It may be urged, however, that although the differences in quantity or quality of the real values may be readily admitted, it does not follow that values of a higher order need be considered as "more real" than those of a lower, unless the term "real" is arbitrarily made to mean at one time "true" at another "good" and at still another "beautiful." Inge's penetrating mind and basic intellectual honesty led him to see some of the difficulties involved in the application of the "degrees of reality" principle. The "Great Tradition," he says, does not permit a mentalistic interpretation of the universe. The world of common sense is, to be sure, a copy of the world of spirit; but Platonism "does not deny the reality of the phenomenal world, and it does not explain very clearly how there can be degrees of reality within that world, apart from the inadequacy of our construction of it."[5] The concept of degrees of reality is troublesome to Inge and he admits that he finds it particularly difficult in connection with the problem of evil. Evil, he concedes, must be considered as a "terribly real" negative value in the phenomenal world, but it may not wage its battle with good "in the mind of God."[6] Actually, Inge seems to reduce the "degrees of reality" theory to one of degrees of understanding, in which the phenomenal world is interpreted as the real world seen imperfectly. Such a view preserves the usefulness of scientific investigation and renders the physical world a worthy object of philosophical examination.

Having rejected contemporary mentalism and reaffirmed his own Platonic realism, Inge proceeds to an examination of the philosophical and religious implications of the Second Law of Thermodynamics. This law, also known as the Law of [increasing] Entropy, or the Principle of Carnot, states that in any physical process involving the expenditure of thermal energy, a certain portion of that energy will be "lowered" or "degraded." This implies that such processes are irreversible, in that an inversion of the cycle will not permit a return to the initial stage of the process. This law, accepted by most modern physicists as being generally applicable in the material world, remains unreconciled with traditional mechanics, which has regarded all phenomena as reversible. Inge, indeed, regards it as basically irreconcilable with a panmathematical or panmechanical cosmos. All attempts to "rationalize" Carnot's Principle have failed. He objects particularly to the attempt at explanation which has been most widely accepted—that "a given system tends to the configuration offering the maximum probability." This, he feels, postulates an initial state of infinite or almost infinite improbability which, if the law is universal, can hardly have come from one more probable. The annoying principle introduces a rather untidy element into science which cannot reasonably be ignored by the serious metaphysician.

The most serious effects of the Principle of Carnot in philosophy must undoubtedly be felt by those persons who have espoused a doctrine of necessary and universal progress. If the universe is "running down" as the law implies, that type of evolutionary optimism which places all its eggs into the basket of the future must stand appalled before the inexorable process which ultimately will bring its hopes to naught. It is true, Inge says, that our lease on our planet is a long one, but we have no freehold. Ultimately man will die and all his works will vanish. The universe itself will be dissipated in radiation. All human hopes are destined to be thwarted by the slow grinding of the mill of a physical law proceeding inevitably toward a new *Götterdämmerung,* which does not even hold the hope which Norse mythology held out in the unpredictable outcome of the final fight between Odin and the wolf Fenrir. Such a fate for man and nature is not impossible or inconceivable, "but it is, in the judgment of many persons, *intolerable.*"[7] The repugnance which we feel for such a death sentence is greater than that which we feel at the thought of the cessation of our own personal existence or that of our civilization, and it is in no way mitigated by the thought that the race has a great deal of time left to try out anything worth trying.

The Second Law of Thermodynamics, however, is fatal only to those philosophies which Inge condemns as "modernist." The "Great Tradition" is untouched by the ultimate outcome of any series of events occurring within the time series. Spencerian evolution, emergent evolution, and the easy optimism of the nineteenth century are based on the fallacy of mistaking shadow for substance. If the universe is not, as they suppose, evolving, they have no present value structure which they can regard as sufficient to give comfort. Christian Platonism, Inge affirms, faces no such difficulty. It has never held out any hopes of universal progress, nor has it promised a future golden age. It thus regards the destruction of earthly hopes and promises with equanimity.

Inge feels, however, that even a Platonist may be affected by this law in so far as he considers the objectification of values in a universe to be essential to the most complete realization of these values. This world, it is true, may come to an end when entropy is a completed process. God may, after the close of that chapter, express Himself in forms of which we cannot conceive.

Still, it does seem to me to be probable that besides the realm of eternal and absolute values in which the life of God and of beatified spirits has its being "beyond this bourne of time and place," there will always be a created universe which in places is the abode of conscious life. I do not claim that this opinion rests on any evidence. I only say that though God might exist without a world, it is difficult to imagine any reason why He should choose to create a world for a period only, and then destroy it.[8]

Attempts by non-Christians or non-Platonists to incorporate in their philosophies an acceptance of the doom of the physical world stir Inge to disagreement, pity, or ridicule. William James's consoling remark that "the penultimate state might be the millennium" and that at this point the universe would be so perfect and happy that it could not stand it any longer causes Inge to wonder how the father of pragmatism can continue to hold an honored place in the history of philosophy. Russell's defiance of the cosmic process either implies a Job-like faith smuggled into a philosophy where it has no business, or it is like Victor Hugo's "theatrical swagger," presenting man as a critic of the divine conduct, defying where he cannot approve. All such assertions of the unconquerable nature of one's soul, Inge holds, are quite unnecessary, for there is no reason to suppose, if we hold a true conception of our nature and destiny, that the universe is in fact hostile to us. "As a pleasure garden this world is a failure; but it was never meant to be a pleasure garden."[9]

It has been pointed out that Inge objects to the mentalistic position which Eddington adopted in an attempt to overcome the naive deistic assumption implicit in most statements of the law that God at one time "wound up" the physical universe and then "left it to run down."[10] The Dean also points to a considerable amount of confusion in the attempts to reconcile the doctrine of annihilation implied by the theory with the ideas of an expanding universe accepted by many present-day scientists. Both these theories, indeed, bring into question the correctness of the language used by the physicists. "Annihilation" as they employ the term does not really mean annihilation. Their use of the terms "universe" and "space" are equally subject to criticism. A "universe" or a totality of "space" expanding into the void is really neither a universe nor a totality of space, since these terms must include the void as well as ponderable matter. Inge readily admits that if an appeal is made to non-Euclidean geometry, he cannot follow the argument far. But at any rate, he remains "utterly unable" to reconcile the "expanding universe" with "annihilation."[11] He takes comfort in the report that Einstein in 1931 abandoned the idea of an eternal expansion and adopted a cyclical theory of expansion and contraction which Inge finds attractive. "Jeans and Eddington," he remarks triumphantly, "say that it is utterly impossible; but if I may take refuge behind Einstein, I am content."[12]

A position which represents a positive attempt to evade the consequences of the Second Law is that held by some writers such as Brunhes, Haldane, and Lloyd Morgan, who elevate biological law into a position of cosmic significance. Organic evolution, Inge maintains, is not incompatible with Carnot's Principle if we recognize that the former is "a local, sporadic, and temporary phenomenon." However, it is dangerous to give such universal significance to evolution as to make it apply to the whole of the universe. There may be an occasional emergence of higher values and more evolved forms within the cosmic process. There is no evidence that the universe itself is evolving.

The possibility must be considered that entropy may be balanced by another process involving the creation or reactivation of energy. A theory along this line has been advanced by Professor Millikan, who has held that the cosmic rays are infusions into the universe of new energy generated in the reconstruction of matter from radiation. In view of vigorous objections to the theory by other eminent scientists, Inge feels that we have not the right to accept it, no matter how attractive it may be. Several suggestions made by Bavink in *The Anatomy of Modern Science* in an attempt to vitiate Carnot's Principle seem unimpressive to Inge. He particularly objects to the argument that the leveling of energy in an infinitely extended world must take an infinite time. Bavink's curious contention to this effect can hardly be any more self-evident to most critical readers than it is to the Dean.

Bradley and Bosanquet are right, Inge holds, in protesting the modern overemphasis on the reality of time and the insistence that all values must be realized in the future. However, he cannot admit that time has no significance. Time is a limitation of finitude, but all purposes are finite. Time is important for the realization of values by individuals. However, if it were an ultimate reality, the operation of the Second Law of Thermodynamics would mean the ultimate destruction of all value. The preservation of the values actualized by individuals in the historical process rests for Inge on the fact that, once realized, they somehow take their place in the eternal order.

My conclusion, then, is that the philosophy of the Great Tradition may view the prospect of "the new *Götterdämmerung*" without deep concern, just because the fate of its own God is not involved. "Nothing that really is can ever perish"; but it is not in Time that all that has value and true existence on earth is preserved. Nevertheless, though we have no fear that our higher values can ever be destroyed, nor the spirits who are the bearers of them, I prefer to suppose that there will never be a time when there will be no universe. If, as the Platonists assert, Time is in the universe, not the universe in Time, the question answers itself.[13]

The question raised by the last sentence of the above quotation is given an entire chapter in *God and the Astronomers*. The problem of time is one which Inge never solved to his satisfaction. His refusal on the one hand to regard it as ultimately real and, on the other, his insistence on its importance create a tension in his thought which cannot always be harmoniously resolved. Many of the modern thinkers influenced by Bergson have, he maintains, overemphasized the significance of the time series for reality and have, in consequence, misinterpreted early Greek and Neoplatonic views of time. Plato, for example, has been accused of rendering values meaningless in time by placing them in an eternal world. Inge holds that the accusation is unfair. In Plato's philosophy, thought is presented as the agency by which portions of the time flow are united in a "specious present." This is the real meaning, Inge says, of Bergson's *"durée,"* which should not be considered as in time at all, but as transcending the time series. In such a "specious present," as grasped by the mind, past, present, and future vanish, and only "earlier" and "later" are left. This capacity of the mind for transcending time in the process of apprehending it implies for Inge that the intellect is really of a nontemporal nature. In its understanding and interpretation of events which occur in time, it is applying logical categories which have real being in the eternal realm. Temporal sequence corresponds in some measure to real logical relations existing among events as looked at *sub specie aeternitatis;* but time itself is not ultimately real. This conviction of the classical philosophers is not properly subject to the charge made by modern writers that it attempts to freeze or petrify motion. The real meaning of movement lies in the value concepts of potentiality ($\delta\acute{v}\nu\alpha\mu\iota\varsigma$) and actuality ($\acute{e}\nu\acute{e}\rho\gamma\epsilon\iota\alpha$).[14] Inge, however, seems to have had some reservations concerning the implications of an extreme version of this position held by F. H. Bradley, who was of the opinion that there might be beings who live in a reversed time sequence in which "death would come before birth—the wound before the blow." Inge is right in holding that such a view might imply that "we live in a world where nothing ever happens at all."[15] However familiar science-fiction may have made us with some of the more concrete implications of the idea of a reversible time series, that idea remains incredible, and, indeed, almost unintelligible, to many who believe the concept of causality to be a meaningful one. Even Inge, with his reluctance to consider time as an ultimate category of reality, seems unable to regard time as entirely nondirectional, though his actual position with regard to this question seems to be somewhat uncertain. Admitting the difficulties raised by a notion of complete reversibility such as Bradley's, he nevertheless refuses to concede that causation provides an arrow to indicate the direction of time's flow. The conception of causation which is based on force is, he believes, disappearing from modern science. Perhaps philosophy too should abandon it. It may be that earlier events determine later ones no more than later determine earlier.

If earlier and later are reciprocally determinate, the Time-process is not essentially irreversible. The cinema has made it easier for us to imagine movement in the opposite direction. We say that we can alter the future, but that we cannot alter the past. But what does this mean? Of course we cannot make the past other than it was, and it is equally certain that we cannot make the future other than it will be. This is a mere application of the law of contradiction. But there is no absurdity or contradiction in saying that our past would have been different if our present state of mind were different. Our past could, I suppose, be theoretically built up from our present. If I am a necessary consequent, given the atoms, the atoms are a necessary antecedent, given me. . . . The ultimate ground of any event must be sought in all the rest of reality, future as well as past; all is part of an intelligible, coherent system.[16]

It may be urged that the presentation of the position being attacked here is not entirely accurate. The contention

is seldom seriously made, outside of presentations of time
like that of J. W. Dunne, that an existent future can be
"altered." Those who regard the time process as real and
irreversible usually hold that there is as yet nothing in the
future to be altered, but that the present presents a number
of possibilities, each of which may or may not be realized
in a not-yet-existent future. Similarly they would contend
that if the past can be deduced from the present, it is
simply because the present is what the past made it, and in
no way the reverse. The Bradleyan idea might, however,
be quite consistent with Inge's view of an "eternal Now"
in which God lives and through which He perceives the
universe as complete and timeless. There would, thus, be
no difficulty involved in eliminating irreversibility along
with the reality of time if we are willing to maintain that
succession belongs only to the world of the senses and has
no counterpart in the "real" world. Spinoza, Inge believes, would have agreed to the abandonment of any
reference in philosophy to the temporal order and the
substitution of a logical order which really has nothing to
do with sequence.

It is perhaps fortunate for Inge's philosophy in several
respects that he is unwilling to take this final step. Time
and duration are at least "appearances of reality."[17] We
cannot, therefore, ignore whatever they may stand for.
Inge clings tenaciously to the idea of a real meaning for
the terms "earlier" and "later," which he regards as entirely compatible with God's timeless perception of reality.
The translation of these terms into "past" and "future" is
the result of our imperfect apprehension of reality occasioned by our apparent immersion in the time series.

The principal function of time is to provide "the arena in which any purpose is achieved or frustrated."[18] This view must necessarily imply some belief in the reality of the direction of "time's arrow," since it could hardly be meaningfully maintained that the achievement or frustration precedes the purpose or is the cause of it. Time "is as real as the conflict between good and evil."[19] In the higher functioning of our intellectual, and even our moral, activity we conquer time and align ourselves with the eternal.

This position determines the character of Inge's criticisms of views which accord time a greater or a less degree of respect. His disagreement is "complete" with those who identify eternity with endless duration in time. Those who believe that time had a beginning but will have no termination are, he thinks, like a man trying to affirm the existence of a piece of string with only one end. He regards as "deep but cryptic" Hegel's statement that "the whole of reality is quite distinct from Time, but also essentially identical with it."[20] Hegel's desire to eat his cake and have it too with regard to time is in some respects not too different from Inge's wish to hold on to the essential meaning of the temporal process in human life, while at the same time denying its reality in the ultimate world of value. James Ward is criticized for what Inge regards as a misunderstanding of Hegel's view of time and eternity. Regarding existent things as being by their very nature temporal, Ward maintained that anything asserted to be timeless cannot be said to be real and that Augustine's contention that in God's view "futura iam facta sunt" involves "an obvious contradiction."[21] Inge regards Lotze with more favor for holding generally—despite occasional apparent lapses into a view like Ward's—to the Platonic tradition. Opposed to all views which would ascribe ultimate reality to space and time, Inge nevertheless concedes that these two categories "will be the frame of events while there are events, and we cannot even imagine a condition in which there are no events."[22] Ward might feel that in admitting this much Inge had come perilously close to capitulation. But he would be mistaken, for Inge doggedly insists that, imaginable or not, the realm of spaceless and timeless value is the only reality.

Platonism admits the unsolvable nature of the antinomies about space and time and regards them as evidence that the solution of the problem must lie outside the spatial and temporal. Commenting on this, Inge says:

The forms of succession and co-existence belong to a world of origin, purpose, and destiny, in which the eternal counsels of God are actualised on a lower plane than that of the spiritual world, the realm of absolute values. Why and how this lower world was created are questions which, I am convinced, can never be answered. As Bradley says, only the Absolute could answer them. The created world is for us an irreducible given fact; but an ultimate fact it cannot be, for it is not intelligible in itself. This is where we part company from modernist philosophy.[23]

The real parting of company with the modernists here seems to be occasioned by their refusal to admit that, in order for something to be acceptable as an ultimate, it must be "intelligible." Although he uses the phrase "intelligible in itself," Inge must mean that it must be explainable in terms other than itself. One could argue that eternity may be less meaningful without time than time without eternity. Inge agrees, indeed, that just as Plotinus had to speak of "intelligible matter" in his higher world, "so there must be a kind of intelligible Time, χρόνος νοητός, in heaven."[24] The measure of Inge's indecision on this question is shown in this admission as much as anywhere in his writings. It is a curious reversal of ordinary procedure to attempt to explain that which is affirmed to be ultimate by smuggling in an "intelligible" version of that which has previously been denied ultimate reality. Since Inge himself would hardly claim that his treatment of the time problem is totally coherent or consistent, it can only be concluded that his highly fluid presentation represents an effort somehow to include within his philosophy two views which he sensed to be mutually incompatible.

Holding to the supremacy of the ideal world over the realm of the senses, Inge naturally demonstrates somewhat less aversion even to the Eleatic tendency to freeze motion, as shown by philosophers like Bradley, than to tendencies to deify time in the way he accused Bergson and Alexander of doing. Bergson's description of duration as "wholly qualitative multiplicity, an absolute heterogeneity of elements," seems to Inge not to speak of time at all. He regards "absolute heterogeneity," with no element of permanence, as meaningless. In order for change to exist at all, something must be changing, and if this thing is not itself change, it cannot be asserted that all is change. Inge is "grateful" to Bergson, however, for regarding perpetual flux or change as an element of reality. Here again, it seems, we must distinguish between "ultimate" reality and reality as experienced in inadequate fashion on a sensory level. Bergson, of course, would have admitted no such distinction.

His time is ultimately real. As for Alexander, Inge regards
his thought as somewhat related to that of Bergson. Several
of Alexander's remarks about the relation of space to time
are quoted in *God and the Astronomers*. They include the
famous "Time is the soul of Space-Time, with Space for
its body," which Inge presents without elucidation, possibly as much baffled by it as many other readers have been.
Inge's criticism accuses Alexander of materialism, and the
statement upon which he bases the charge—"Mind is a
complex of Space-Time stuff"[25]—seems to justify the conclusion. Interestingly enough, the most telling of Inge's
criticisms of Alexander's views are based, not so much on
the fact that they violate the Platonic subordination of time
to eternity, as on the fact that they do violence to our common-sense apprehension of space and time. Inge shows a
sort of good-natured contempt for the exalted position
which the two categories assume when they cease to be
connected by an "and" and become married by a hyphen.
In a footnote concerning this union, he indulges in an
anecdote:

I recall the election story of how a popular statesman, recently
deceased, put to his audience the question, "What is unearned
increment? Can anybody tell me?" To which came the devastat-
ing answer, "It is just the 'yphen between Joynson and 'icks!"
The unearned increment in the union of Space and Time is
enormous.[26]

Attempts to link the two together in "a Gnostic sygygy"
ignore the obvious differences between them for which our
ordinary perceptions are the guarantee. Inge objects too to
Alexander's conception of a "growing" universe. The idea
of a growth of the totality of existence seems self-

contradictory to the Dean. Science provides nothing to support it, experience gives no basis for assuming it, and entropy negates it. It is provincial to apply laws of growth observed within existence to the whole of the universe. In this connection, Inge quotes with favor Fulton J. Sheen's statement that "there is no more reason for applying biology to God than there is for applying music or chemistry, or even mining engineering."[27] He approves also of Sheen's criticism of Bradley's alleged tendency to make space dependent on time and time on space, a condition which makes them "earn a precarious living by taking in each other's washing."[28] Although pointing out that we admittedly experience space and time in close combination, Inge agrees that Space-Time, apart from the qualities which fill it, cannot be the ultimate answer to the riddle of the universe.

Whitehead and Broad—"and especially Whitehead"— Inge considers so obscure that he attempts no detailed criticism of their views. However, he is sympathetic to Whitehead's insistence on the closeness of the relationship between permanence and flux. As for Broad's conviction that the future is nonexistent for God and man, Inge, of course, rejects the idea immediately and reiterates his view that everything is complete and accomplished in the eyes of God. McTaggart's position on the subject of time is given short shrift as adding little to an understanding of the subject. Like Inge, he denies the reality of time, but his reasons and his conclusions are quite different. The past, he says, is dead, the future is not yet, and the present is a line without thickness separating the two. This, Inge feels, should have made him a pannihilist or acosmist. McTaggart declined

to be one, however, thus drawing down upon his head the
Dean's charge of inconsistency. Inge admires Bosanquet for
his recognition of the fact that morality does not comprise
all the realm of values, and that it is in morality alone that
the reality of the time process is of the utmost importance.
Time thus becomes overvalued through excessive concen-
tration on moral philosophy. Even if it were true, however,
that the other values (Truth and Beauty in Neoplatonic
thought) were not concerned with time, it is difficult to see
how one can render time nonessential simply by pointing
out that only one-third of reality is dependent on it.

It is clear that many of Inge's criticisms of his contemporaries are based on his assumption that time and eternity
are qualitatively dissimilar. Hobhouse recognized the distinction, and is praised for it. Royce, however, by being too
eclectic, became "defective from the standpoint of the *phil-
osophia perennis.*"[29] Inge does not consider it a sufficient
explanation of the eternal quality of God's insight to maintain that it is eternal simply because it knows all of time.
Royce's general belief in the pantemporal character of
God's knowledge seems to involve some features of Platonism of which Inge can approve. His reservation that God
cannot foresee the activities of a free agent is not one of
these.

Friedrich von Hügel is a writer for whom Inge frequently expressed admiration and one who greatly influenced him in the formation of his religious philosophy. In
the German thinker's treatment of time, however, he finds
some features which he cannot altogether accept. Von
Hügel devoted a great deal of attention to the idea of
aevum, which he thought—erroneously, Inge believes—to

be implied in Bergson's concept of *la durée*. *Aevum* is presented as an intermediate state between time and eternity.
Unlike eternity, it involves duration and contains the distinction between earlier and later. It is the final state of
man, who cannot attain the pure eternal state of God, to
whom duration and succession are absent. Inge, though
respectful to von Hügel's presentation, sees no reason why
the important distinction between earlier and later cannot
be attributed to eternity. His criticism that if one attains a
state in which there is no more time, he can hardly still
lead an "essentially durational" life,[30] seems justifiable. He
further holds that von Hügel read a great deal more into
Bergson's philosophy than is really there.

   Eucken, according to Inge a writer of "verbose but excellent books," advances a doctrine of time somewhat similar
to that of von Hügel. Urban, for whom Inge frequently
expressed considerable admiration, is praised for pointing
out that it is a conviction of the axiological unimportance
of time which usually leads to the denial of its reality. Inge
asks whether the eternal values actually necessitate time.
Truth, he decides, requires only timeless logic. Beauty, as
manifested in art, is primarily spatial. (Inge admits that
music is an exception, but the blithe way in which he dismisses this fact as of little significance is an amusing corol-
lary of his avowed distaste for music.) Moral Goodness
seems to be different, for the moral will creates its values in
the temporal realm. However, Inge holds that "every
moral purpose, when fully achieved, passes out of the
plane in which morality itself is active."[31] Time may therefore be dismissed as a mode of the "spiritual life," though
it is necessary to the "soul life."

Inge's final word on the problem of time is an expression of what he believes to be the Christian view:

That events in Time are relevant to the eternal order is the belief of Christianity. Things of lasting moment really happen; souls are saved and lost. Whether the eternal mode of existence can really be deflected in any way by happenings in Time, is a question which I shall not attempt to answer. The philosophical difficulties in the way of an affirmative answer are great; but Christains have always believed that in the personal life the consequences of right and wrong conduct on earth are decisive for the condition of souls in eternity.[32]

On the questions faced by philosophy concerning the relationship between God and human history and God and the created world, Inge's criticisms of contemporary views are again definitely based on his acceptance of the dictates of Christian Platonism. His chief diatribes are reserved for those who would speak of "God as History" rather than "God in History." Though God is, in Inge's opinion, operating through and in the historical process, He is not Himself changing or evolving. The attempt to apply the idea of evolution to the whole of reality and thus to describe God as emerging from or developing in the course of history is symptomatic of the thoughtless way in which the term has been used. The word *evolution* itself is of recent origin. The idea of linear progress and development in man and society is almost wholly absent from Greek and Christian thought. Evolution in these world views is simply individual, and history is catastrophic, not progressive. Evolution of the soul toward God was admitted, and even stressed, by the Neoplatonic philosophers. Why, some thinkers began to demand, should we not assume that the processes of nature and the history of societies show the

same upward striving? Hegel, though somewhat inadvert-
ently, became a prominent precursor of the evolutionary
movement in philosophy. Linnaeus, Buffon, Erasmus Darwin, and Lamarck gave scientific impetus to the idea. Inge
deplores Lamarck's invention of the word biology, "which
ought to mean the science of human society, now described
by the barbarous hybrid 'sociology.' "[33] As for Charles Darwin, Inge holds that, in developing the theory by which all
natural organic processes could be brought under one law,
he had no idea of attempting to extend the philosophic
implications of his theory to the cosmos as a whole. The
misfortune which befell Darwinism was that it became
popular and that the popular mind tended to erect it into a
universal law and at the same time to endow it with a value
theory which was not originally present in Darwin's idea.
According to this theory, that which survives because of its
fitness is necessarily good. Humanity is progressing toward
a goal. Unfortunately, Darwin himself was a victim of the
misunderstanding into which many writers fell through
misinterpretation of the real meaning of his theory and
wrote of the way in which natural selection, working
"solely by and for the good of each being," would insure
that "all corporeal and mental environments will tend to
progress towards perfection." Concerning this lapse, Inge
comments sadly, "How little even the greatest men can rise
above the fixed superstitions of their age!"[34]

Herbert Spencer, "whose philosophy illustrates in a startling fashion the influences of social and political movements on what should be pure thought,"[35] compounded
the error. His assumption that progress as a cosmic law
necessitates the ultimate attainment of perfection by our

places man, not above the rest of nature, as had
optimistic views, but as a specific instance of nature,
evolving according to natural processes. Spencer, Inge feels,
should have followed the idea of the survival of the fittest
through to its logical conclusion and held that might
makes right. This he could not do. "He thought that industrialism is in the line of true development, and militarism in the line of retrogression. That the two may be different forms of the same struggle was an inconvenient truth
on which he preferred not to dwell."[36] Inge also criticizes
Spencer for clinging to the concepts of mechanism and
evolution without admitting that the two are really fundamentally irreconcilable. The fact that he partially recognized the difficulty seems to be indicated to the Dean by
the fact that the "Unknowable" began to be described in
terms not dissimilar to those used by Plotinus and Eckhart
in describing the ultimate source of reality. Spencer could
not consistently regard nature as a closed, uncreated system. His greatest mistake in Inge's eyes, however, was his
adoption of the view that progress is characterized by increasing complexity and a corresponding decrease in homo-
geneity. In addition to the fact that this opinion runs
directly counter to Carnot's Principle, Inge objects to it on
the ground that it is effectively contradicted by many
known facts in biology, technology, and language.

The theory of evolution as such is neither favorable nor
unfavorable to religion. Inge has no quarrel with it as a
scientific theory. Linked to philosophical determinism,
universal relativism, or materialism, however, it arouses his
firm opposition. Its claim that man may be perfectible

gives rise to many laudable secular hopes which religion need not dash. Its substitution of these hopes for the consciousness which individuals need to feel of their citizenship in heaven may properly be deplored. As for the scientific doctrine of organic evolution itself, Inge is fairly unconcerned about arguments as to whether the process operates through the inheritance of acquired characteristics, "mutations" of considerable scope, or the "minimal changes" of Darwin. Nevertheless, with reference to the latter, Inge warns, "We cannot admit the excuse of the girl who palliated the appearance of her baby by saying that it was a very small one."[37] Neither mechanism nor organic evolution is in itself hostile to teleology. However, the notion that everything is evolving toward some remote perfection is derived from a confusion of scientific theory with idealistic metaphysics. The whole of reality cannot be evolving. There is, indeed, no evidence of any single, unitary purpose in the universe. In criticizing the attempt to reconcile mechanism with teleology through the principle of emergence, Inge is unequivocal:

It is an attempt to intercalate the value-scheme into the existential. Values certainly "emerge"—they become visible; I do not think the word has any place in natural science. Professor Lloyd Morgan, who borrows the phrase from Professor Alexander, wishes us to "acknowledge" emergent qualities with "natural piety," an unexpected appeal in a scientific discussion. There is no natural piety in using a word which asserts and denies the reality of change in the same breath. Do the emergents emerge out of what they are not, or are we to take evolution in its earlier and proper sense, of an unpacking of what was potentially there all the time? The advocates of emergent evolution wish to allow for the appearance of something really new, without surrendering to teleology or breaking too sharply with the mechanicists. They have, I am afraid, only succeeded in finding an ambiguous word.[38]

All in all, Inge seems to have believed that emergence, if it is to be accepted at all, must refer to a Creator, who at certain periods of the cosmic process injects something new into it. Creation *ex nihilo* may be thinkable. Emergence under the same conditions—or lack of conditions—is not.

The evolutionists and emergent evolutionists are naturally more concerned with human progress than with evolution in any of its other aspects. The assumption that man is getting better, in addition to being a debatable one, is one which brings into question the whole of the value structure implied in any particular evolutionary view. In what way is the race asserted to be improving? What constitutes improvement? Earlier views held that, considered from any standpoint, man's nature exhibits little in the way of permanent progress, and history was usually interpreted as a static, cyclical, or dramatic affair. It was not until the nineteenth century that the doctrine of universal progress came widely into vogue, and in England, at least, its heyday was short-lived. "It is so manifestly a product of crude anthropomorphism," Inge says, "that even apart from the Law of Entropy one might suppose that it could hardly be defended by an intelligent man."[39] We are permitted to suppose that its incompatibility with intelligence is responsible for the fact that it has virtually disappeared in England. The Italians—perhaps less richly endowed with intelligent men—have revived it in "truly amazing fashion."[40] Croce is the principal villain in the piece. In a quoted selection of his remarks in praise of cosmic progress, Inge sees only "delirious nonsense."[41] Spengler, though certainly no prophet of progress, is treated with little greater respect. His philosophy is an example of "unreasonable pessimism" which "fits historical reality no better than the schemes of Hegel and Comte."[42] Inge feels that all of these views alter facts which cannot be juggled with if we wish to form an intelligible world view. His own view seems to be that we, after all, have a very limited knowledge of the history and future destiny of man. Nor do we know why he is here at all.

If we are asked why God made the earth, sun, and stars, it is best to say simply that we do not know. Disinterested curiosity is a noble passion, but nature has not seen fit to gratify it. We have enough light to walk by, and not much more.[43]

The human race unquestionably has remaining to it on this planet a much longer time than it has already been here. A tremendous amount of progress is possible—although humanity may have serious setbacks; but progress is not inevitable.

As to what progress is, Inge feels that there is no agreement. Many persons say merely that it is "movement in a desirable direction," without specifying the direction or telling why it is desirable.[44] If we use a pleasure-pain criterion, it is hard to tell whether modern man is the product of progression or retrogression. The savage may be happier and more resourceful than the man living in an artificial society, but pleasure is not the criterion which we really use. Inge regards it as obvious that civilization is better than barbarism. In the cultivation of the intellect man has progressed. The same is true with reference to spiritual development, for history records the rise of religion from agrarian ritual to its fullest expression in Christianity. However, we cannot with confidence predict the future on the basis of the past. Our age is exceptional in that in it the idea of progress has itself been changed.

The masses think of further progress mainly as an increase of comfort and amusement, and of leisure in which to enjoy them. In detail, these aspirations are for the most part innocent enough, though not heroic; we shall not be censorious when we remember how much the poorer classes were excluded from the benefits of civilisation a hundred years ago. We are in the middle of a great experiment, which aims at establishing at least a fair measure of comfort and culture embracing the entire nation. It is a question whether such a nation would have as great a survival-value as one organised on a hierarchical scale, with less individual liberty; but the experiment appeals to the generous instincts of almost everybody, and we must all hope that it will succeed.[45]

The passage just quoted reflects Inge's reluctance to admit that current democratic ideals are an unmixed blessing, but it also indicates his refusal to condemn absolutely the spirit which has given rise to many contemporary social movements. Inge has frequently been attacked as an enemy of the common man. He was not that. He merely combined a nostalgia for a more aristocratic age with a vigorously expressed skepticism concerning the effectiveness of modern social amelioration in the production of real values. It is not such social aspirations, however, which furnish the real key to an understanding of our age. That key, according to Inge, is found in the tremendous advance of the natural sciences, which will cause our era to be considered as significant as the great ages of Hellenism and Christianity. But it is only in the form of technology that science has affected the minds of the masses. Only a few persons understand its higher achievements, "and the dysgenic trend of our civilisation is probably making first-class brains fewer in each generation."[46] Although the present rate of discovery must slow down, science will still be the principal determinant of our future. This will produce philosophical and practical dangers which cannot be minimized. Nevertheless, few thinking people would wish to turn back the clock, and, in fact, Inge believes that we have reason for a cautious hopefulness about the future.

The question still remains as to whether Inge sees in history any evidence of divine operation which is especially favorable to man's material progress. Here, it seems, the answer must be in the negative. He admits that the Jews firmly believed that God operates in history, although the Jewish apocalyptic view is certainly not one of universal progress. Christian thought too has stressed the right and the duty to hope, but it "does not bid us to play tricks with our souls in order to produce any results, external or internal."[47] Whether or not it can be said to take an optimistic view of the world of experience depends upon what we think about the relationship between that world and the eternal realm. Inge obviously holds that the only sure refuge for the man who is plagued by troubles and doubts is in the kingdom of the mind and the cultivation of an apprehension of the eternal values. God has given no evidence of any over-all purpose operating in history. His purposes seem rather to be "finite, local, temporal, and for the most part individual."[48] They find their fulfillment, not in this world, but in the "intelligible world." If Christians wish to believe in a day when Christ will reign on earth, it is "an inspiring hope,"[49] but Inge finds little in history or in the Gospels to support it.

As for the relation of God to the world in general, the view which Inge himself would take may readily be inferred from his doctrinal and philosophical views, which have been dealt with at some length elsewhere in this work. However, in *God and the Astronomers,* he considers some of the aspects of his doctrine of Deity which are particularly relevant to a philosophical consideration of science. In so doing, he criticizes implicitly and explicitly certain contemporary views which seem in his opinion to be inadequate concerning the relationship existing between God and his creation. As we have seen, he makes a distinction between the Godhead and the God of religion, who must be considered as epistemologically, if not metaphysically, different.

In considering this idea of God in his role as Creator and Sustainer of the world, Inge contends that the cosmological argument to a Prime Mover is valid only if it is understood in the light of Christian Platonism. The Platonist is under no obligation to trace the whole development of the world back to a Prime Mover and then fall a helpless prey to the question: "Who moved him?" for he believes the universe as a whole to be dependent upon a Creator who exists in His own right. Since the idea of an infinite regress is inconceivable within the physical causal series, we are moved to acquiesce in the proposition that there is "a Mover who is himself outside the series, and distinct from the world."[50] Inge displays a somewhat pained surprise at criticisms of this position like that of Pringle-Pattison, who held that belief in a transcendent Creator-God "carries us back to a primitive state of pictorial thought like that of the Zulus."[51] "Presumed to be a low one," Inge wryly remarks.[52] The cosmological, ontological, moral, and teleological arguments, though not sufficient to establish a genuinely religious view of God, nevertheless seem to Inge to point to some aspects of God as related to the world which modern science cannot reasonably afford to ignore. This is particularly true of the teleological argument. It seems to point to purposes in the mind of God, if not to any single unitary purpose. It can certainly be used effectively against the idea that the world is a product of the fortuitous concourse of atoms. If the Second Law of Thermodynamics is true, the process must have begun from a state of affairs that is almost infinitely improbable. The idea of an accidental shuffling of matter to reach such a state seems to Inge not, indeed, impossible, but "wildly improbable." "Does anyone," he asks, "really think that printer's pie might be shaken up till *Hamlet* emerged complete?"[53] God must be considered as the Creator and Designer of the world, but the relation of this creativity to time is another matter. Inge suggests that, from the standpoint of modern natural science, the Law of Entropy might be considered to involve the proposition that the universe which is now running down must have once been wound up. However, that is a temporal conception, and the Dean urges rather that, in speaking of God as Creator, he should be conceived as an immanent and eternal "world ground" rather than as the agent of a single act of creativity at some time in the past.

The cosmos is dependent upon God, but God's existence

is not bound up with that of the cosmos. The Hegelian theory that the universe is necessary to God is dismissed by Inge with this argument:

> The theory that God is "organic with the world," which is held by the whole Hegelian school, is naturally welcome to the new biologism, which tries to interpret the whole cosmos in accordance with the laws of life. Whether the supporters of this view really escape the fallacies which were fatal to the old vitalism is a question on which Pringle-Pattison has said something, and on which their opponents have said more. When we remember the very small, perhaps even accidental, part which life occupies in the whole universe, it seems rash to make biology the normative science of the cosmos.[54]

If the being of God is inseparable from the world, as some of Inge's opponents claim, we are faced with the sad plight of a Deity who will cease to exist, or at any rate lose all His potency when the universe has become de-energized through the operation of the Second Law of Thermodynamics. Such an inglorious fate for the divine nature is, of course, unthinkable to Platonism and, for that matter, to theism in general. Inge, while admitting God's immanence, invariably insists also upon a recognition of his transcendence, and in this, takes issue not only with the pantheists, but also with those who insist upon smuggling democratic ideas into the Kingdom of Heaven. Persons who attempt to reduce God to the status of "a magnified and non-natural President of the United States" are, in Inge's view, guilty of "profane nonsense."[55]

In a detailed criticism of the idea of the creation of the world in time, Inge is inclined to favor the Augustinian view that it came into existence *with* time rather than in it. This theory was also held by Plotinus, who believed that the soul "entimed itself," a process which was necessary "in order that the will-activities proceeding downwards from the One might be actualised."[56] If time and the universe were born together, the logical conclusion is that, if either perishes, they must perish together:

Time and space are not part of the framework of the real or spiritual world; they are as real as the lives of those who live in them, while they live in them, but they are not—neither of them, nor the two rolled into one—the stuff of which reality is made. If the present world-order had a beginning, "with time, not in time," as Augustine says, it will have an end, "not in time but with time," that is to say, with its own time-framework.[57]

But that does not involve the notion that ours is the only world-order. There may be many worlds quite independent of one another and each with its own framework of time. Such a concept is quite possible if we believe that the creative activity of God is as eternal as God Himself. But Inge confesses that we can neither know nor hope to know whether this is true.

By divorcing creation from the time process, Inge claims that he better establishes the transcendence of God and rules out any pantheistic metaphysic. Nevertheless, he acknowledges God's immanence as well as his transcendence. It is in this connection that he shows particular interest in a teleological interpretation of nature. Beginning with the axiom that matter is never perceived except through the senses, he points out that this indicates some immanence of mind in matter. He proceeds to the observation that men almost universally have a tendency to read divine purpose into living nature. We sense that, although our knowledge is incomplete, we have contact with Him through our apprehension of values, and, indeed, that "we live and move and have our being" in Him. The felt presence of the Logos and the dynamic nature of living things point to an organic teleology. But this is quite a different matter from a teleological interpretation drawn from merely empirical or scientific observation.

Inge regards as "unjustifiable anthropolatry"[58] the view that God created the world solely or primarily for the sake of man. It is entirely conceivable, he holds, that other planets are the homes of corporeally housed souls and that they have been redeemed if they needed redemption. "There is," Inge says, "something derogatory to the Deity in supposing that He made this vast universe for so paltry an end as the production of ourselves and our friends."[59] It is not, however, a matter of unconcern to us whether or not the universe shows some evidence of purpose. Inge accepts a teleology which recognizes the partial truth of both the "organic" and the "mechanistic" views of nature. Ultimately, he feels, it is only a question as to how God works, and the world shows evidences of both types of operation. Inferences based on biological operations alone cannot be carried over into one's thoughts about the vast physical universe, which exhibits different, and in some ways quite alien, characteristics. However, even cosmology may be a source, though a secondary one, of knowledge concerning God's purposes. Naturalism cannot be the truth. Inge continues:

In studying nature, which after all we know very imperfectly, we are learning something of the workings and methods of the divine mind. It is in virtue of our God-given spiritual faculty that we are able to contemplate nature, as it were, from outside,

and to know it in a way which we could never do if we were
ourselves caught in the flux of events. If naturalism were the
truth, we could never know it.[60]

Theism is the only adequate explanation of reality, from
Inge's point of view. God is the source of our philosophical,
as well as our devotional, knowledge. Religion, however, is
not vitally concerned with the fate of the physical universe.
The situation is quite different in philosophy, for, "if entropy is true, some philosophies are in ruins."[61]

In the last chapter of *God and the Astronomers,* Inge
considers the nature of the eternal world. The implications
of much of his discussion are more theological than cosmological, and Inge is certainly less concerned here with criticism of contemporary philosophies than in the remainder
of the work. However, the chapter serves to draw together
some of the threads of his own metaphysics which have
been developed in the course of his critical treatment of
other thinkers. In it he reiterates his identification of his
own philosophy as a form of idealism which is not, however, mentalism. "Reality consists in a trinity in unity of
Spirit ($\nu o\hat{v}s$), Spiritual Perception ($\nu\acute{o}\eta\sigma\iota s$), and the Spiritual World ($\nu o\eta\tau\acute{a}$)."[62] The intelligible world of value is
manifested in the world of time and space, but in the
manifestation the values are "split up and partly disintegrated."[63] Man is tripartite.

Objectively, Body, Soul, and Spirit are respectively the world as
perceived by the senses; the world interpreted by the mind as a
spatial and temporal order; and the spiritual world. The first of
these is apprehended by the five bodily senses; the second by
the discursive reason; the third by the spiritual perception which
alone conveys real knowledge.[64]

This view, lifted bodily from Plotinus' philosophy, is not open, in Inge's opinion, to the charge of being "faculty psychology," for the Platonists do not speak of three separate psychic organs, but rather of the soul, operating in three different ways. Plotinus' philosophy has no "hard lines."[65] "Matter" exists only as the recipient of "Form" acting upon it. The data of sense perception have no independent existence. They cannot be objects of "knowledge," but only of "opinion." The world, as science knows it, "is a mental construction from very defective data."[66] Although material objects have no real being, the thought structures which human beings form about the material realm belong to the intelligible realm. The "laws" of science are thus aspects of reality, and are objective findings rather than arbitrary constructs.

Other questions considered in Inge's final Warburton lecture—such as the nature of the eternal world itself, the problem of human personality, and the survival of the individual after death—are considered elsewhere in the present work. Inge frequently repeats himself in his writings. *God and the Astronomers,* however, remains the most significant of the treatments which the Gloomy Dean made of what are, in his view, contemporary heresies about the nature of the physical world. For him, it would seem that the greatest heresy of all lies in ascribing reality to it.

In 1929 Inge was chairman of an editorial committee supervising the publication of a volume of essays entitled *Science Religion and Reality.* Having first read all the essays written by a distinguished group of contributors, he wrote a Conclusion, in which his comments on the work of his colleagues provide us with some of his most trenchant remarks on modern life and thought.

At the outset he rejects the often-expressed view that science and religion never come into conflict because they never meet. This solution of a very real dispute can, he holds, lead to an armistice, but never to a peace. He continues:

A religion which does not touch science, and a science which does not touch religion, are mutilated and barren. Not that religion can ever be a science, or science a religion; but we may hope for a time when the science of a religious man will be scientific, and the religion of a scientific man religious.[67]

The essays in the book are classified into two groups, one of which is devoted to a historical survey of the fields of religion and science, and the other of which might be termed "philosophical." Inge, in evaluating the two approaches generally, is unable to conceal altogether his distrust and thinly-veiled contempt for the historical method of investigation in the realm of human concepts and institutions. It is more fruitful in religion, to be sure, than in science, for in the latter field, ancient and erroneous ideas are discarded ruthlessly, whereas in religion they are cherished and defended. "Religion," he says, "is a powerful antiseptic, which preserves mummified customs that have long outlasted their usefulness, and otiose dogmas that have long lost their vitality."[68] However, it is an error to treat religion, or any other field of human thought, in terms of its origins, even when the errors of its past are so greatly in evidence in its present. We would not do this in science. "It tells us nothing about Newton to know that he once had a tail."[69] One should concern oneself more with what religion is and can become than with what it has been. This ahistoricism is typical of Inge's approach to religious and philosophical questions, despite an apparent interest on his part in certain aspects of European history. It has brought down upon him the criticisms of some of his associates in the Church of England that he pays inadequate attention to the religious practices which have developed in the continuing life of the Church. Inge would have admitted that an interest in the past of his religion has never been of paramount concern to him, despite his earlier defense of the historicity of Christ. "We are far too much concerned with what happened two thousand years ago," he remarked late in his life. By the same token, however, he held that the more recent history of the Church must not become the sole criterion for the thought of its members.

Inge gives us some reasons for his distrust of the historical method. There is, in the first place, the tendency which it promotes to make an anthropological judgment on every human activity in terms of its origins. The uncertainty of the records in history and anthropology provides a still more serious objection. Civilized men cannot really enter the minds of the savages they study. "Some learned anthropologists have never seen a savage, and would be much alarmed if they met one; others have travelled in barbarous countries, but have failed to master the very complicated native languages, which are not the same in any two tribes."[70] In some cases, he says, the savages have deliberately made sport of the scientists, whose reports are, therefore, correspondingly inaccurate. A third and very important hazard in the historical method is the "superstition" of progress, which often appears explicitly or implicitly in the works of those who rely too much on history. As encountered in works on religion, the fallacy of necessary progress seems to Inge particularly dangerous. It balks at accepting, as the highest revelation yet attained, one which man received some two thousand years ago. Although, as previously mentioned, Inge refuses to base his faith on a particular set of events in the past, he sees no reason for the assumption that religion could not have reached its peak in the great millennium in which Buddhism, Christianity, and Islam were born. If it did, he holds, the subsequent history of religion has been one of deterioration rather than advance. Indeed Inge expresses the strong suspicion that the rise of civilization itself represents a retrograde movement deadly to religion, art, and the higher intellectual processes.

Man the tool-maker has made "inanimate instruments" (as Aristotle says) do his manual work for him; he is now trying to make them do his mental work for him. Nature has no objection—at a price. The price may be the progressive deterioration of our faculties. Our brains may follow our teeth, claws, and fur.[71]

We can find the savage next door, he maintains, without having to seek him in Australia or Africa. We encounter the Stone-Age mind on platform and in pulpit. Superstition, fetish, and tabu abound in modern England and—he would certainly have been willing to add—in America. Progress, Inge says, repeating a favorite theme, is sporadic. It is "a biological episode which other species, such as the bees and ants, traversed long ago."[72] We are more likely to reach a static state like theirs than to advance indefinitely—

"unless," he concludes pessimistically, "our present habits end in mutual extermination."[73]

As for the conflict between science and religion, it is, of course, due, not to any necessary warfare between the two disciplines in their "pure" form, but to the philosophies constructed around science alone and to pseudo-scientific theories which have acquired the force of religious dogma. The conflict is, nevertheless, very real, and Inge recognizes that it cannot be dismissed with pious statements about the ideal harmony that should exist between science and religion. That the schism is so definite and so bitter is, he holds, a historical accident traceable to the Wars of Religion. Religion inevitably becomes coarsened and brutalized when it is the subject about which a war is being fought. Catholics and Protestants in the sixteenth century found it necessary to evolve religions "of a narrow and brutal type" in order to devise and use the sort of war propaganda that would best suit their ends. Unfortunately, the greatest problem ever faced by the Church was forced upon it during that period. In Inge's opinion, this problem, the heliocentric theory of the solar system advanced by Copernicus and Galileo—would, in a happier day, have been met with less bitter opposition, and the Roman Church of the Renaissance would have withdrawn from its untenable Ptolemaic position. No such withdrawal was possible for men of the type of the Inquisitors on the Catholic side and Luther and Calvin on the Protestant. The Copernican Revolution destroyed the three-level picture of the world in which a stable and flat earth sits between heaven and hell "like a dish with a dish-cover above it."[74] The capitulation of the Church, despite the overwhelming evidence against the geocentric theory, has been slow and is not yet complete. The problem remains to this day one which is, according to Inge, more serious than the questions which the scientists have raised concerning time, for the Church has never embraced dogmas which specifically contradict the scientific views about time. It is more serious too than the question of Darwinian theory, for Darwinism disturbs only those Christians who believe in the verbal inspiration of the Scriptures, and Inge—possibly because he underestimated the number and power of the fundamentalists in our society—seems not to have felt called upon to direct advice to them on that subject. The case of the current astronomical picture of the universe, however, is a different one. Christians still cavil at full acceptance of the implications of a theory which seems to make the location of a geographically existent heaven an exceedingly questionable matter.

Inge recognizes no less than three positions among which the Church may choose its position. It may declare that modern astronomical theory is heretical, after the fashion of Catholic and Protestant theologians of the period of the Reformation. Or it may claim that its traditional doctrines are of a higher order than the facts of the natural order, with which science concerns itself, and that they symbolize eternal truths not accessible to the investigations of science. One who holds this opinion will point out that science itself is abstract, symbolic, and imaginative. Such a view in its extreme form may go so far as to deny the reality of the universe. In any case, it permits its proponents to claim that theological formulations are more nearly the truth than are scientific theories. The third position—obviously the one favored by Inge—is to acknowledge that the findings of science in its legitimate sphere are not assailable on religious grounds and that all theological doctrines which depend upon such formulations as the Ptolemaic hypothesis must be revised so as not to conflict with newer conceptions of the universe. According to Inge, this means that "we shall be driven to think of God less anthropomorphically, and of heaven as a state rather than a place—a state, too, which is eternal in a deeper sense than that of unending time-succession."[75] Christianity is held to be strong enough to weather the storm, for as Inge has made abundantly clear in his writings, he does not acknowledge its real involvement with time or space in so far as its ultimate values are concerned.

In his review of an essay by Professor Aliotta, of the University of Naples, Inge considers briefly the problems posed by the growth of various forms of voluntarism and their attendant anti-intellectualism. Here we find a restatement of his earlier views, expressed in *Personal Idealism and Mysticism,* and an anticipation of the position so clearly stated in *God and the Astronomers.* The anti-intellectualist type of thought strikes at both science and religion. In its rejection of the correspondence theory of truth, it is the progenitor of pragmatism, "which disintegrates the whole structure of science, and incidentally bids every superstition which seems to work, to take heart of grace."[76] The newer mathematical theories provide little assistance to philosophy or religion in their attempts to deal with the problem of materialism. Mathematics as such is incapable of making judgments relevant to philosophical ultimates, and Inge expresses a strong suspicion that Einstein's work has been put to uses for which it was never intended. The Dean seems to have identified certain philosophical theories based on this type of mathematical development as essentially in line with the modern revolt against the intellect. He recognizes, however, a necessary distinction between the philosophical revolt and the more justifiable reaction within the sciences against the "tyranny of mathematics and physics."[77] Whereas a man may become an animist or a vitalist without any intention of disparaging science or embracing pragmatism, the philosophical attack on intellectualism leads to skeptical subjectivism. It is a mistake to attack the "doctrine of science" as erroneous, when what is really being attacked is naturalism, a philosophy adopted by many scientists. Furthermore, Inge insists upon a distinction between "true" naturalism and pantheism, which is "generally a conglomerate of animism, poetical fancy, and mysticism."[78] Naturalism in its purer form is an attempt to reduce all reality to quantitative problems in physics and chemistry. Its curious fate, however, is ultimately to reject the reality of the very physical facts which it formally regards as the only ultimate realities. Driven by a passion for simplification, it first eliminates the distinction between mental and physical, organic and inorganic. Then, it must take further steps.

The method of simplification demands an even greater sacrifice. Physics and chemistry are theoretically capable of reduction to the fundamental laws of movement in general; the end of the simplifying process is a statement of the nature of reality in mathematical symbols, which are valid whether there is anything corresponding to them in nature or not. And so the philosophy which professes to be grounded on the solid rock of observed phenomena, severely rejecting all human valuations, ends in pure mentalism, which is independent of the existence of any external world whatever.[79]

The naturalists, Inge concedes, had a right to object to the attempts of theologians to stifle their investigations and discredit their results. The theologians, however, who were not motivated merely by willful blindness to truth, were equally badly treated by their opponents. The suggestion made by many of the earlier naturalists that they appropriate the realm of the knowable and leave the religionists alone in their work with the unknowable was unrealistic and impossible of application, for both sides actually are attempting to interpret the whole of existence. Naturalism is not science, but immature and inconsistent philosophy. It cannot leave religion alone. To the extent that it is successful, it must destroy it.

Intellectual constructions of the universe are attempts to explain all experience in terms of universal law. Exceptions to the laws proposed by a particular construction disprove the authenticity of the construction. Naturalism is not exempt from such testing. If there are phenomena which cannot be explained by its tenets, it is disproved. Biology is pointing out such phenomena, but, Inge maintains, it is really only searching for a broader naturalism. A more fruitful approach may be the investigation of the possibility of a teleological interpretation of nature. We have already seen Inge's interest in the relation of teleology to mechanism. In the essay under discussion, he ends with the conclusion which seems to be his final word on the subject, that purposiveness runs throughout all nature, underlying the inorganic as well as the organic. We get our idea of purpose from observation of our own personalities. We are probably justified, Inge holds, in reasoning by analogy that God must be purposive in the highest degree. We cannot, however, draw a sharp line between the obviously personal and the apparently nonpersonal in our formulation of a teleological doctrine. The classification of things into organic and inorganic categories is an arbitrary one, and, according to Inge, the whole of nature is subject to universal law which exhibits purpose. This being so, we probably cannot expect to see evidences of special purposes operating in specific instances. The laws of an all-powerful and all-knowing God would presumably be regular and uniform. Thus, we need not be surprised that nature acts like a machine. If the machine needed "tinkering," it might, indeed, be considered faulty. It is its regularity which guarantees the supreme competence of its maker. The uniformity of the world favors the conclusion that God as Designer and Builder exists, and at the same time deals a telling blow to polytheism, Manicheism, and all other forms of dualism which would pit God against any other force limiting His omnipotence.

In order properly to evaluate naturalism, though, it is necessary to do more than contradict it. We must understand how it developed. "Ism's" are always movements in opposition to something, and it behooves us to consider the nature of the world-view which naturalism opposed. Inge cites with approval Professor Wallace's view that it was originally a protest, not against the supernatural, but against the view of the supernatural as arbitrary and capricious—"the idle profanity which thinks it has explained an event when it has said that it is the work of God, as if anything were not the work of God."[80] Quite correctly, however, Inge points out that Wallace does not refer to a consistent naturalism when he concludes that the world of law desired by idealism and that sought by the naturalists are not different. Wallace wrote: "To assault Naturalism and Rationalism is to strike at Nature and Reason; it is to support supernaturalism and the materialism of authority." Inge saw more clearly than Wallace that the goal implied by naturalism is not the recognition of a kingdom of spiritual law, but just what it appears to be—the reduction of the things of the spirit to the quantitative terms of a mechanistic and materialistic world view. In this, he holds, the naturalists have failed.

Science cannot, however, abandon the attempt to fit the universe into one system of laws. Inge believes that since it has had no success in explaining spirit materialistically, science must perforce resort to explaining matter spiritually. He points to evidences of a movement in this direction in the panpsychism suggested by writers like Professor J. S. Haldane and Professor Carveth Read. Such a movement might, he holds, lead to a revival of the philosophy of Fechner, with its contention that even planets and stars have spirits which are themselves manifestations of the one all-embracing Spirit, God. However absurd this view may seem in its details, it would, in Inge's view, provide a significant antidote to materialistic determinism and a boon to a teleological interpretation of the world. "What we call mechanism," he writes, "may be the teleology of the inorganic world."[81] Considerations of this sort may, he maintains, be leading to a spiritualistic monism which could do much to reconcile the conflict between science and religion in that it will provide a genuinely religious view of reality which will also satisfy the requirements of science.

As for the religious view of reality manifested in the life of modern Europe, Inge points out that it contains many corruptions and distortions which prevent us from ac-knowledging it as religion at its best, just as science may be subject to distortions which have nothing to do with its basic tenets and techniques. Just as a mentally diseased individual will first show the symptoms of decay in the exercise of his highest mental faculties, so a decadent race or individual will exhibit decadent religion. In trenchant terms, obviously directed at the religion of our own time, Inge describes the decadence:

> The close connection between religion and morals is loosened; the religious conscience, except in relation to some tradition of the elders which has no real ethical sanction, becomes blunter than that of the respectable man of the world. The happy and joyous temper, which characterises a fresh and confident faith, degenerates into moroseness, or into the vapid hilarity of the seminary. Religion relapses into mere cultus, which is the husk of religion; its genial symbolism petrifies, and offers a stolid op-position to the best-established secular knowledge. In order to retain the allegiance of the masses, it stoops to fraud and decep-tion, and endeavors either to impede education or to control it. A decadent religion does far more harm than good in the na-tional life.[82]

Furthermore, religion is never found in a pure state. Its doctrines always infringe to some extent upon the domains of natural science. It is more difficult for mistakes to be corrected in religion than in science because of the sacra-mental or emotional significance which they have for many worshipers. The result is that fragments of exploded scientific belief, "imprisoned like a fly in amber in the solid mass of a religious creed, may have become the casket in which the soul keeps her most valued treasures."[83] Even the higher religions have so much archaic content that the contention of men like Comte and Croce that religion is only "half-baked" philosophy has some plausibility. Nevertheless, religion cannot, as these men anticipated, disappear, for it holds a place in human life which science and philosophy cannot fill. It presents the only way in which man can recognize and deal with the "antithetic consciousness of alienation from, and of communion with, the unseen power which surrounds us."[84] It is in these feelings that the origins of religion are found and from them that the sacrifice of self-will and the process of prayer develop. These find their highest expression in the mystical consummation of communion with God and in the final resolution of the feeling of estrangement. Inge finds another antithesis between the expansion of the self and the "sinking deeper into" the self[85]—an antithesis also resolved by religion in the "loss" and "gain" of the soul in interests larger than the isolated self.

Religion is concerned with values, and the ultimate values in Inge's catalogue are, of course, Goodness, Truth, and Beauty. These are "the attributes of ultimate reality,"[86] and we cannot go beyond them in thought. Science is, in reality, no more nonvaluational than religion. The scientist isolates certain values—coherence, uniformity, and commensurability—and presents an abstract picture of the world without reference to the equally real values of Goodness and Beauty. It follows that in devoting its attention to all three of the fundamental values, religion is concerned with objective facts and not merely with subjective mental states or pure feeling. Feeling is in itself no guarantee of the objective truth of religion. It really has nothing to do with truth or falsity. Religious feeling, to be sure, is never aroused except by ideas of truth and value, but it must be noted that the ideas generate the feeling and not the other way around. Violent emotions are dangerous to the spiritual life. "The fruits of emotional revivalism, if they are permanent, are chiefly bad."[87]

Even the concept of "the Holy," presented by Otto as the essential element in religion, is an object of Inge's suspicion. Admitting that the feeling of "awe, dread, and fascination" suggested by the term is a necessary part of religion, Inge holds, none the less, that the feeling is usually accompanied by a good deal of superstition. Ignoring his own attacks on the historical method, he complains that the history of the idea of holiness "is not edifying." "The holiness of Jehovah," he remarks, "as exemplified by the death of Uzzah for touching the ark, was much more like electricity than any moral quality."[88] As for those movements which make faith a matter of will, they represent, according to Inge, a philosophy of skeptical empiricism. They are at the root of pragmatism and Roman Catholic Modernism—both views with which the Dean locked horns at some time during his career. Persons addicted to the voluntaristic approach to religion tend to disparage "intellectualism." The intellectual approach to religion at which they level their criticisms generally emphasizes intellect at the expense of will and feeling. Inge admits that there is a considerable amount of justification for such intellectualism, and, in this essay as elsewhere, he asserts his confidence that the ontological, cosmological, teleological, and moral arguments for the existence of God are, if not actually cases of demonstration, at least "closely interwoven with the texture of rational experience."[89] There is a sort of intellectualism which he disparages manifested in pantheistic naturalism or subjective idealism. However, these philosophies, inadequate though they undoubtedly are, do not, according to Inge, constitute justification for a blanket condemnation of positions which place their main reliance on the intellect. Skepticism, pragmatism, and anti-intellectualism cannot keep men from using their intellects or from relying on human reason. The pragmatist's violent objection to "absolutism" Inge finds entirely unjustified. If we abandon our concept of a systematic unity in reality, we abandon philosophy and science. He continues his criticism of pragmatism with an attack on William James. "If the world is 'wild,' as William James thinks," he remarks, "only wild men, whom we do not permit to be at large, would be at home in it."[90] James and his followers are further described as "constructing the universe of enigmatical atoms dignified by the name of persons, and rushing into polytheism."[91] Laws must be regarded as being just as objective as the particular facts which they regulate. The search for the Absolute is an intellectual necessity, for even the relativist regards the principle of relativity as having the force of universal law. Intellectualism is thus justified in seeing the universe as a structure of laws which can be apprehended by the intelligence. Inge maintains that the objections against intellectualism are justifiable only if the intellect is considered as a separate department of the mind, as was done by the old faculty psychology. If the term is used in the Platonic sense of "the whole personality become self-conscious and self-directing,"[92] there can be no valid objection to emphasizing its importance.

The emphasis on an intellectual search for truth is especially important in view of the "widespread frivolity" apparent in many contemporary religious practices.

In Southern Europe, especially, religion is largely a social diversion, a spectacular performance, an artistic enjoyment. The attitude of our own public towards popular superstitions, half belief and half make-belief, is too common among church-goers. The scientific man cannot understand the playfulness where matters of the highest moment are at stake. Nothing repels him more from the worship of the churches. It is difficult for a student of science to realise how weak the love of truth is in the majority, and how widespread the mistrust of reason. The real sceptic does not write books on agnosticism; he never thinks at all, which is the only way to be perfectly orthodox.[93]

The realm with which the intellect is concerned in religion is the world of permanent value. Those who recognize the power of the mind to apprehend real value refuse to regard it as an epiphenomenon which must, with respect to its reality, give precedence to "Nature" considered from a nonmental standpoint. Without mind and its free and creative activity, there could not even be any naturalism. Science itself and the world as we know it are, in the last analysis, created by the spirit.

Inge's remarks on the last essay in the book—one by Professor C. C. J. Webb—concern the position of Christianity as a religion among other religions. The religion of Christ must be considered apart from its institutional aspects. "It is even possible," Inge writes, "to speculate (though I should not go so far myself) whether the reli-

f Christ might not be a greater power in the world
professional custodians were removed."[94] Historically
considered, Christianity has been a religion for white Europeans, and its conquests among Asiatics and, indeed,
among all brown, yellow, or black peoples have been something less than outstanding. The "arrogant, domineering,
and rapacious" European nations have not recommended
Christianity to Asiatics and Africans, and attempts to force
Western Church organization on the East are unlikely to
succeed. We may hope, Inge says, for a day in which religious persons in all nations will recognize the Gospel of
Christ. We may not entertain much hope of a universal
institutional Church. Furthermore, we may not credit all
the good features of European civilization to organized
Christianity.

European civilization has been, like Hellenism, a permanent enrichment of humanity, and the religion of Europe has borne
many exquisite flowers. But unless, like the Roman Catholic
Modernists, we assume that every transformation which helped
the Church to survive and prosper was a legitimate development of the original design, we shall not find it easy to affiliate
Hildebrand, Oliver Cromwell, and Cardinal Manning to the
Gospel as it was preached to the fishermen of Galilee. Organized
religion is not, in modern times, one of the strongest forces in
human affairs. As compared with patriotism and revolutionary
aims, it has shown itself lamentably weak. The strength of
Christianity is in transforming the lives of individuals—of a
small minority, certainly, as Christ clearly predicted, but a large
number in the aggregate. To rescue a little flock, here and there,
from materialism, selfishness, and hatred, is the task of the
Church of Christ in all ages alike, and there is no likelihood
that it will ever be otherwise.[95]

The hope for a reconciliation between science and religion lies in those persons who find it possible to accept the

findings of science and at the same time to follow Christ. Inge agrees with Bacon that, whereas a little knowledge may lead a man away from religion, a deeper knowledge will bring him back. However, he points out that the religion which the enlightened man arrives at is not the one he abandoned.

The two works just discussed give as good a key as any to the criticisms which Inge habitually leveled at contemporary thought. His other critical writings are expressions of the same point of view, though aimed at a variety of targets.

For example, his Paddock Lectures of 1906, later published under the title *Personal Idealism and Mysticism,* are, in large measure, an attack on the pragmatic assumptions implicit in much nineteenth- and early twentieth-century American philosophy. Inge felt that many of the undesirable aspects of the pragmatic world-view were embodied in "Personal Idealism" as a movement opposed to naturalism and absolutism. No disciple of naturalism himself, Inge nevertheless found himself more in sympathy with that philosophy than with Personal Idealism. Absolutism, of course, was precisely what Inge was most concerned to defend.

Contending that Personal Idealism tends to abstract man artificially from nature, Inge maintains that when we point out the lack of mercy and justice in nature, we are ignoring the fact that they are often present in that part of nature in which they are understood. Man is a part of nature, and, in the last analysis, nature includes the best of men—Jesus Christ. We have no right, therefore, to anathematize nature as something devilish which can only be respected when referred to the categories of the "will world." Such a course, according to Inge, is the exercise of a right which "leads to disaster even in the 'will world,' and which is not recognized in the world of reason—the right to be wilful."[96] We do not have the right to use our own narrow criteria to determine what the world ought to be. The laws of the universe may be superior to our notions of morality. Tyrrell, the Roman Catholic Modernist, in Inge's opinion, is guilty of deism in his denial that God's presence in the world of his creation is evident and of Manicheism in his apparent readiness "to hand over the natural order to the devil."[97] Inge also criticizes a similar view expressed by Huxley in his Romanes Lectures that moral ideals and the processes of nature are irreconcilably at odds—a position which, in Inge's opinion, postulates two Gods or one with a dual and inconsistent nature. A similar objection applies to the theory that the world of nature has no independent reality, but consists of "instruments" for the use of personal spirits. Inge deplores the dualism implied in all these approaches. "Science and sound philosophy," he says, "teach us that all nature is of one piece, animated in various degrees by one and the self-same spirit and obeying the self-same laws."[98]

He attributes much of this dualistic philosophy to Lotze, who, despite his attempts to be a monist, concluded that God could not be approached through the beauty of nature. Repudiating the idea that only like can know like, the German denied that there is any identity between mind and its objects. Nature has no symbolic value. Whatever suggestions it may have to offer concerning conduct are not moral ones. Inge takes exception to this, as to the more formally dualistic theories. He writes:

I agree with Scotus Erigena that "every visible and invisible creature is a theophany," and with Charles Kingsley that "all symmetrical natural objects are types of some spiritual truth and existence." I hold no brief for the so-called "mysticism" which arouses the ire of writers like Max Nordau. I have already disclaimed any sympathy with fanciful symbolism, as being above all else alien to the true spirit of mysticism. We must treat fact with the utmost reverence, and merely subjective interpretations of fact with a wholesome scepticism. But the approach to God through beauty, whether in nature or art, is not in any way hampered by this caution. For though the ideals of truth and beauty may seem like rivals, as being alike universal in their claims, and demanding a wholly disinterested mind in their respective worshippers, they clash with each other singularly little, less than either of them does with the moral ideal, and they help each other in many ways. I believe, then, that the moral consciousness is not the only faculty by which we apprehend God, but that the laws of nature and the beauty of the external world are also revelations of His being and character.[99]

Inge maintains that the Christian Platonism which constitutes his philosophy can serve as a corrective to the modern views. It upholds an acceptable version of the reality of the universe rather than making it dependent on the imaginations of personal centers of consciousness. More important, for Inge, it does not accept the view of "persons" as separate substantial entities which he regards as so offensive. Having made clear his distaste for the pragmatic and personalistic doctrines which seemed to him to dominate American thinking, he devoted the greater part of his Romanes Lectures to a presentation to his New York audience of his own system as a substantial alternative.

In a number of his collected essays and sermons, he performs the role of critic of the contemporary scene, but in all of them, as in the works just discussed, his point of view exhibits something of the Olympian character which comes from a conviction that the world of change is comprehensible only when looked at *sub specie aeternitatis.*

5 MODERN MORALIST

It was with some reluctance that Inge embarked on a systematic treatment of contemporary ethical problems. His interests were for many years mainly in the fields of the classics and systematic theology, and it was really only after he became Dean of St. Paul's that he admitted to himself that it would be necessary to pay some attention to specific moral problems of the day.

In the preface to his *Christian Ethics and Modern Problems,* published in 1930, he remarks that he has been forced, almost unwillingly, "to leave the *templa serena* of divine philosophy, in order to take part in the turmoil of the street and the market-place."[1] He then proceeds to a searching examination of the role of Christianity in the solution of twentieth-century problems.

Admitting the diversities of Christian theory and practice, which make it impossible to formulate a legalistic system of Christian ethics applicable to varying cultural situations, Inge maintains that the term "Christian Ethics" is, nevertheless, a meaningful one.

I shall try to find, not a system, but a fountain of life which has never ceased to flow from its source in the life and teaching of the Founder. The river of Christianity (as Clement of Alexandria said) has received many affluents; the tree of Christianity has many branches, bearing diverse fruits of its own as well as many that are *non sua poma;* but beneath all diversities of type we can recognise, I think, manifestations of one and the self-same Spirit, dividing to every man severally as He will.[2]

The Church has not, he holds, been supernaturally protected against error. The Spirit of Christ has always to some extent been present in it, but the record of the Church is "very largely a history of decline and perversion."[3] The climax of centuries of disruption and discord came when the Christian churches found themselves face to face with the technological advances and social upheaval of the age of industrialism and were quite unable to meet the ethical problems posed by these changes. The Roman Catholic Church, he contends, has been set at odds with modern civilization by the very institutionalism which enables it to maintain its pretensions to dogmatic authority in matters of morals. The Protestant organizations, by their very nature, cannot lay claim to such authority. However, Inge finds in the Protestant tradition greater hope for constructive moral influence than is possible in the Roman Church because, in his view, Protestant countries provide conditions under which the moral principles of Christianity have some influence on elements of the population who have no concern with the Church. In Catholic countries, on the other hand, there is a deep-seated hatred of the ecclesiastical order on the part of the unchurched, who, in consequence, identify Christ with the visible Church and, in rejecting it, reject Him.

To take our own country as an example [he writes], Christianity as a leaven has a great though indefinable influence upon the character and moral ideals of the English people. In Catholic countries the people are, in common speech, either "devout" or "free-thinkers," and the free-thinker is usually untouched by any moral influences proceeding from Christianity. It seems to me that the political power of a highly organised Church is too dearly purchased at this price, and that our Lord's parables indicate that He meant His message to mould society in a very different manner. Only when it is recognised that the Church has no interests except the moral and spiritual welfare of the whole society in which it is placed; only when the Church is content to be the conscience of the nation, holding up, as a shining light, the standard of values which Christ came to earth to reveal, can the Church discharge the duty which it ought to perform. It is not enough that the individual should be willing to sacrifice himself for the institution; the institution also ought to be willing to sacrifice its tangible interests for the society which, in the name of its Master, it exists to elevate and redeem.[4]

By the term "Ethics of Christianity," Inge explicitly means the ethics of the New Testament, and particularly of the Gospels. But in going back to the Gospels for authority, we must, he holds, avoid the dangers inherent in certain attitudes prevalent in our own time.

In the first place, we must not, as liberal Protestant theologians of the nineteenth century did, remove Christ from his first-century historical setting and present the details of His life as a suitable model for direct imitation by a modern European. The universality of His teaching can be arrived at only by understanding Him in relation to His time. The same procedure must be followed in dealing with the other books of the New Testament, such as the writings of St. Paul. Such a process is tremendously difficult in the case of the Synoptic Gospels, and the difficulty is enhanced with the Fourth Gospel, which represents a type of literature with which we are not familiar and seems to refer to a movement within Christianity of which we now know nothing except what is included in the work itself.

Some forms of Biblical criticism accomplish nothing in arriving at the universal principles on which a Christian ethic may properly be based. The theory that Christ never existed at all is quite properly rejected by Inge, in less than a sentence, as absurd. He devotes more attention to eschatological theories such as those of Schweitzer, already dealt with in a previous chapter. His criticism of Schweitzer's theory from an ethical point of view is the obvious one that a man enmeshed in the toils of eschatological delusion would propound an ethic which could have no more than temporary significance, even if we could get an accurate historical picture of him. Although this difficulty would presumably drive the Christian into a form of mysticism in which his attention would be centered on the eternal Christ rather than the historical Jesus, Inge does not regard the prospect with favor. If the Christian ethic is to be based on the New Testament, we must accept the picture of the man portrayed by the Gospels as essentially a correct one and must regard that man as sane.

This sanity is not incompatible with a hope that God would soon intervene with power and establish a reign of righteousness on earth. But it is wholly incompatible with a delusion that He had been commissioned to predict a stupendous miracle, and to warn His contemporaries to prepare passively for it. The real question is whether a pure delusion generated the mission, or whether in the glow of their enthusiasm the disciples, and possibly the Master Himself, threw their ideals into the near future, and foreshortened the vision of their fulfilment, as idealists are always prone to do. The theory of Schweitzer makes Christ a psychological monster, and His character an insoluble enigma. And yet His character in the Synoptic Gospels comes out clearly, not only His profoundly religious and spiritual nature, but His deep wisdom, balance, and breadth of mind, even His irony and humour. These are not the characteristics of a half-crazy visionary.[5]

Jesus, Inge maintains, was a teacher of righteousness, who rightly regarded Himself as having a place in the line of Jewish prophets.

We cannot, however, envision Christ merely as another prophet and certainly not as a lawgiver like Moses. Nor must we regard Him simply as a human model for our emulation. "As the consciousness of Christ was the life of God in the soul of a human being, so the inspiration of the Christian is the mind of Christ, now operating as the Holy Spirit, in his soul."[6] This presence within us, presumably as ordered and guided by our historical knowledge of Jesus, is the source of the Christian's moral enlightenment.

The importance of the continued presence of Christ in the lives of individual persons can hardly be overestimated in Inge's thought. A recognition of the contemporaneity of the living Christ saves us from a slavish following of tradition and authority. "There is no excuse for refusing to apply the principles of the Gospel to circumstances very unlike those which came within the purview of the human Christ, or for denying the competence of the Spirit of truth to teach humanity many truths which believers in the first century were 'unable to bear.' "[7] This same idea is central in *Things New and Old,* where Inge states his conviction "that Christianity is a living and therefore a changing thing, a way of walking, not a way of talking, a divine life, not a divine science, and that in times of upheaval like this it must take new forms and learn a new language."[8]

The religion of Christ is, without reservation, an ethical one, but it is not merely an ethical system. Its only external authority is the New Testament record of Christ's life and teaching. "And this," Inge adds, "is hardly external, for it is accepted and interpreted by the *testimonium Spiritus Sancti* declaring itself in the Christian society and in the individual conscience."

An important consideration concerning Christian ethics is that Christianity regards the universe as friendly to the real needs and aspirations of man. The attitudes of men like Huxley, Hugo, and Russell, expressed in a heroic defiance of a hostile cosmic process, can hardly be saved by their literary genius from "toppling over into absurdity."[9] The Christian ethical view for Inge must recognize the nature of the universe as that of God, Who is the Being in Whom the ultimate values of Truth, Goodness, and Beauty are eternally realized.

As is the case with many philosophical systems which emphasize eternal values as the ultimate goal of human endeavor, Inge's system does not lend itself readily to an explanation of how these eternal values are related to particular ethical activity. Specific moral duties are not easily ascertained merely by contemplating the ultimate value of Goodness. In fact, it is not from his version of the Platonic value system as such that Inge derives the particulars of his moral philosophy, but from his conclusions concerning the character of Jesus applied in the particular social context in which a specific ethical problem occurs. His appeal is not so much to the teachings of Jesus as to the picture of His personality given by the Gospels.

So strong was the conviction that the revelation consisted not in word but in act and power, that the first believers made no attempt to draw up a manual of conduct from His reported sayings; the Synoptic Gospels give us a standard of values and an example—these and little more. To this restraint we owe it that so little in the Gospels is of merely local and temporary importance, and also that a constant reference may be made to "the mind of Christ" as shown in action.[10]

In a sense, it may be accepted that the ethic of Inge remains based on the apprehension of an ideal system, but it is an ideal system as seen in the life of a man Who is regarded as capable of realizing perfectly within His own character the relation of ideal and circumstance which is involved in moral action.

Although Christ is the source of Christian morality, Christian ethics does not, Inge holds, involve a direct attempt to imitate His life in any detail. The difficulty is not that His character is unworthy of imitation or that we lack a clear picture of Him. We have in the Gospels a portrait far removed from the gentle, somewhat effeminate Christ of tradition. We are, on the contrary, shown a man of commanding personality moved by strong human emotions. Power, rather than gentle good nature, seems to have been the most noticeable feature of His personality. His appeal is more to the moral will than to emotion. He demonstrates a "royal independence" of the accepted authority of His day.[11] Far from being "a fanatic, an anarchist, a socialist, a dreamer, or an Essene ascetic," He displays in His teachings, "not only perfect sanity and balance, but (if one may say so without presumption) great intellectual power."[12] We see in His teachings, in a degree perhaps greater than was visible to His reporters, irony, playfulness, and great prophetic vision. A man of prayer and meditation, He lived always in close communion with God. All these characteristics are, in a sense, imitable, but mere imitation would lose an essential characteristic of the Christian ethics, which is its inwardness.

The same difficulty would obtain in any attempt to obey His precepts by interpreting them as a code of conduct in the usual sense of the word. In place of such a code, we find "an outlook, a manner of thinking and acting, a standard of values, which necessarily penetrate every corner of the personality."[13]

At the root of Christian Ethics lies what Harnack has called a transvaluation of all values in the light of our divine sonship and heavenly citizenship. To the man who boasts of his possessions He says, "Thou fool." He can even say, "He that hateth his life in this world shall keep it unto life eternal." (The difference between the two lives in such utterances is clearly qualitative, not durational.) In proclaiming the reality of this higher realm of values, he raises immeasurably the status of the human soul, which can breathe in this region.[14]

Some clues to the basis for Inge's approach to social problems are to be found in his interpretation of the character of Christ's ethical teachings. One lies in his emphasis on the inwardness of the Christian ethic. Christ attacks diseases, Inge holds, rather than symptoms, and is thus concerned more with the inner character of a man than with his outward actions. He is unconcerned with labels and ignores barriers. No human being is beyond His concern for being "a sinner, a foreigner, or a heretic."[15] His fundamental motive for conduct is love—love of God and love of one's neighbor.

It is in his interpretation of this last characteristic that Inge reveals much of his attitude toward Christian action related to the material evils of society. Acknowledging that the recognition of the brotherhood of man in Christ demands that a man should invariably seek the good of his neighbor as he would his own, he assails the view which regards this duty as substantially satisfied by those "who think that they are fulfilling the command of love by showing themselves merely soft-hearted and compassionate in relieving the wants of others, while aiming at a very different standard for themselves."[16] Works of mercy and charity are our moral duty, but Christianity does not assume that these are in every case accomplished by acts of direct relief. Admitting that Christianity involves social duties and that these duties relate to the bodily needs of men, Inge nevertheless seems to lay more emphasis on "individualism," not so much in the economic sense as in the mystical. He holds that the Gospels also provide an ethic of simplification and that this outlook is fundamentally optimistic, though in no sense lacking in a recognition of the seriousness of evil in the temporal world. The Christian ethic, recognizing that man cannot be made invulnerable, "accepts the Cross."[17] In this connection, Inge writes:

The doctrine of the Atonement perhaps hardly belongs to a book on Christian Ethics; but it may be worth while to distinguish between vicarious punishment, which is immoral, and vicarious suffering, which love is willing to endure. It is most important to realise that the Christian keeps no *meum* and *tuum* account with his Maker. He makes no claim to individual justice, remembering what treatment his Master received. We shall receive justice at God's hands, no doubt, but not what the unregenerate and unloving would call justice. Only those who are willing to lose their soul ($\psi\nu\chi\acute{\eta}$) for Christ's sake shall find it unto life eternal.[18]

Inge defines Christian humility as "pure receptivity" rather than lowliness of spirit.[19] Joy, as a Christian virtue, means not only freedom from anxiety, but the positive attitude which comes from the consciousness of the love of God and the mutual affection and good will which should obtain among the children of God. Other elements of the good life mentioned in the Gospels are love, peace, faith, and hope. The sins which Christ chiefly condemned are hypocrisy, hard-heartedness, and worldliness. Hypocrisy is described as "acting a part, where no pretence or concealment should be necessary."[20] Hard-heartedness appears often in Calvinism, manifesting itself in a lack of sympathy for others and in overseverity of moral judgment. "God's mercy is justice," Inge remarks; "man's justice should often be mercy."[21] Worldliness produces "calculating ambition"[22] and a mistaking of means for ends.

The worldling is devoted to some of the instruments of a good and happy life, as if they were ends in themselves. Christ found the most salient instance of this error in the love of accumulation, which He called the service of Mammon. What He had in His mind was mere hoarding, not profitable trade, of which He speaks without censure in His parables; but we must not eviscerate His warnings of their plain meaning. Worldliness, and the covetousness which is a common form of it, indicate a radically wrong estimate of values, an irrational worship of mere instruments, without thought either of their intrinsic worth, or of the injustice of appropriating selfishly what has really been created by the whole society in which we live. Such a radical error can hardly coexist with the service of God.[23]

In considering some of the objections that have been leveled against the ethic of Christ by His critics, Inge first rejects the notion that the Gospel fails to take account of the ethical value of natural beauty and art. He finds in the character of Jesus an attitude toward nature resembling that of Wordsworth and quotes with approval Eucken's judgment that "Christ effected an artistic transformation of human existence."[24] He appears to have felt that the apparent disparagement of family ties to be found in Christ's teaching has been overestimated. The language of the popular teachings is frequently hyperbolical and may not be taken literally. Furthermore, there may be in the case of some of the ethical teachings a trace of the *Interimsethik* which Inge refuses to see as a general characteristic of Christianity. At any rate, the Dean concludes, a great many evils have sprung from some forms of family loyalty, and Christ had ample reason for denouncing these evils. "Quite apart from the higher call which Christ addressed to His apostles, some loosening of a bond which had been drawn too tight was desirable, and perhaps still is so."[25]

Nietzsche's "master-morality" is rejected on the obvious ground of its incompatibility with certain fundamental Christian principles. Inge approves his insistence that the race should be improved and his objections to "an emasculated morality," but holds that he is striking at Christ as well as organized Christianity in rejecting mercy and pity.[26] Furthermore, the Nietzschean ethic is attacked as unrealistic. "The romantic 'hero,' who hacks his way through all obstacles, is a figment of armchair historians,"[27] Inge comments. The most serious objection, however, is its failure to recognize with Christianity that society must be organized on a broader basis than the relation of master and slave.

The tendency of social reformers in our day to claim Christ as the authority for their particular forms of social and economic order caused Inge to devote some attention to the apparent attitude of Jesus Himself toward economic matters.

Characteristically, he first assails Marxian Socialism as being at odds with Christianity. The disagreement is frankly admitted by the Marxians themselves, but some Socialists raise a greater problem for Christian ethics by claiming that Christ Himself was of their number. This claim cannot survive a thorough examination of the Gospels, Inge holds, although he admits some justification for finding in Luke a friend of the poor and an enemy of the rich. Even Luke, however, did not, as some seem to suppose, suggest that the worth of a man is in direct proportion to the scantiness of his goods, and it is Luke who includes the story of Christ's refusal to judge a property dispute and His warning to beware of covetousness. Inge writes:

It is not really doubtful how our Lord regarded these questions. He had His own standard of values, and among these values He ranked wealth very low indeed. He complained, not that wealth was badly distributed, but that it was grossly over-valued. His attitude was one of gentle detachment, touched with irony. He consorted mainly with the common people, that is to say, with the self-respecting and fairly well educated peasantry who belonged to His own class; but He neither avoided the society of the rich nor showed any repugnance to their way of living, except when their wealth was dishonestly come by or selfishly spent. In this tolerance He differed from some of the Old Testament prophets, who denounced the rich as such, and still more from the Jewish writers of His time, who cultivated "a genius for hatred" of the rich. . . . But Christ thinks so little of money that He feels only an amused contempt for the avaricious, and honestly thinks that the "poor," who in Northern Palestine were not very poor, have the best of it. Nevertheless, He does not spiritualise life so far as to preach indifference to temporal misfortunes. Sickness for Him is sickness, and want is want. He would have had no patience with those who on the plea of being above such sordid interests do nothing to relieve those who are in distress. This combination of indifference to comfort and luxury with a readiness to help physical misery is very characteristic of Christianity, where it has been faithfully accepted. Sometimes, as I have said, Christians have shown a degree of mental confusion by excessive pity for troubles which they could bear easily themselves; but even this is better than Stoic apathy.[28]

Christ, says Inge, would undoubtedly have opposed the "externalism" of modern civilization as well as that of those movements which would reform it. The Socialists fail to realize that it is the inside of the cup which must first be cleaned, and Inge seems, interestingly enough, to have felt that the eugenists come closer to truth in this respect than those who would reorganize society by legislation. In criticism of Inge's position, it may, of course, be questioned whether, in the Christian sense, genes are any more "inside" the cup than rickets or slums; but it must be remembered that here we are dealing with one of the particular concerns of the Dean, who for many years gave active support to eugenic causes. At any rate, he admits, Christ had something to say about the service of Mammon, and the picture of the good life given by Him "was very different from that of a successful man of business."

It is probable, according to Inge, that the key to Christ's attitude toward economic matters lay in His conception of service. Economic evils stem from the tendency of society to measure success in terms of one's ability to take from society more than is justified by one's service or one's need. "Where the main object of business is not to give people what they want, but to strip them of what they have, it falls under the censure of Christ."[29]

To those who, in their allegiance to "The Social Gospel," think that Christianity cannot be reconciled with the possession of capital on the ground that such ownership involves anxiety, Inge asks, "Has not the man *without* capital much more temptation to be anxious?"[30] While the question may seem a trifle beside the point, in view of the fact that the men whom Inge is criticizing generally advocate some reorganization of society to reduce or eliminate the occasion for anxiety, the Dean comes closer to the mark when he accuses them of giving inadequate attention to the tremendous differences between modern and ancient societies. "The problems of capital and labour," he says, "certainly cannot be solved by the mere citation of verses from the Gospels."[31]

His advice to those who wish to apply the spirit of Christianity to social questions is well summarized in words spoken to Cambridge students. After expressing his conviction that technology is itself solving the problem of poverty without the necessity for radical alterations in the political and economic structure, he concludes:

I am therefore convinced that the path for you lies not through political revolution, but through moral, spiritual, and cultural reform. Your task, in short, is to make better men and women; to make society less selfish, less acquisitive, less given over to frivolity and dissipation; more ready to co-operate in social service, more able and willing to make a worthy use of the larger leisure which may be at their disposal, better citizens and better Christians.[32]

The objection sometimes made to Christian ethics that it has a negative rather than a positive character, is, in Inge's opinion, directed more against certain developments in the history of the Church than against the original ethic of the Gospel, which does not enjoin a flight from normal human life. As for the criticism that the standard of morality set by Christ is impracticable because it is too high for a human being in normal society, Inge recognizes that it is indeed so. Rejecting the solution of the Roman Church, which admits a dual standard of conduct in which those who wish to be "perfect" may try and others may compromise with society, he simply hints that the standard of perfection is applicable to everyone as an ideal which every man is obligated to try to attain in society in so far as possible. "The standard in the Gospels is heroic and perfectionist; it is not, as we cannot remind ourselves too often, a code of permissible conduct for a large community."[33]

Finally, he deals with the objection that the Gospel ethic is too much concerned with reward and punishment and too little with virtue for its own sake. Here again, Inge admits that this emphasis has occasionally been a fault of the historic Church when it has used cajolery and terror to attempt to keep people under control. He does not, however, admit that selfish hope of heaven or fear of hell has been an important ethical motive for people in general, particularly in our own time. The desire to save our souls is a legitimate one, he maintains, and little distinction can be drawn between this motive and the love of God and Goodness. The good man is never too much concerned with externally administered reward and punishment. "The appropriate punishment of an evil life is not to be baked in an oven; it is to become incapable of seeing God, here or hereafter."[34]

The Epistles of St. Paul, once they are liberated from the accretions of Paulinism, throw much light on Christian ethics, Inge holds, for we know more of St. Paul than of any other person of antiquity except, possibly, Cicero. Jewish apocalypticism and Logos Christology existed not only successively, but side by side, in his thought and both influenced his character. A zealot and a mystic, he found those qualities which he already possessed transformed by his vision of Christ, and, in Inge's words, "This intimate relationship with the Spirit-Christ is unquestionably the core of his religion."[35] He defends the Apostle vigorously against the charge of accepting a magical and, to Inge, unethical view of the Christian sacraments. Elements of this sort, he maintains, were entirely foreign to Paul's thought. The religion of Paul, as of others of the apostolic age, was a religion of the spirit. Justification, sanctification, redemption, and similar concepts, were not, as Paul used them, arid legalistic matters, but simply ways of expressing what is meant by being "in Christ Jesus."

Characteristically, Inge's admiration for St. Paul is based on the Platonic elements which he finds in Pauline thought. These elements are strong, he maintains, in passages such as "The things that are seen are temporal, but the things that are not seen are eternal," and "We all with unveiled face reflecting like mirrors the glory of the Lord are transformed into the same image from glory to glory."[36] He acknowledges several ways, however, in which Platonism and Pauline ethics differ in philosophical theory and moral practice.

The principal difference rests in the conceptions held by the two schools of the relation of the higher and lower parts of human nature. The Platonists distinguished strongly between the "real" life of the soul in the eternal world and the "unreal" life of the body in the world of matter. Paul, on the other hand, though he disparages "the flesh," does not identify "the body" with "the flesh." The unity of body and spirit is retained in the eternal realm, where a "spiritual body" is to be prepared for the redeemed. Inge admits that this willingness to recognize the sanctity of the body is essential to the doctrine of the Incarnation if Docetism—the theory that the human nature of Christ was merely an appearance—is to be avoided.

The other ethical differences between Platonism and Paulinism stem from this fundamental one. Paul placed more emphasis on sins which defile the body, simply because he considered the body more important than did the Platonists. His often-criticized views on marriage and related subjects were conditioned by his view of the seriousness of sexual offenses. As for the Apostle's view on the status of women, Inge does not find so logical an answer, and merely comments:

It is not a subject on which he could be expected to anticipate the modern movement for sex-emancipation; his task was merely to issue recommendations for the little society which looked to him for advice. His regulation that women must cover their heads at public worship was no doubt based on a strange superstition; we cannot cut demonology out of St. Paul's Epistles.[37]

Inge finds little in the other books of the New Testament which would alter his main impressions of Christian

ethics based on the Gospels and the Pauline writings. As
for the life of the early Church, Inge holds that it was
probably at its moral best in the second century. The picture given by Pater in *Marius the Epicurean* is, he thinks,
substantially true, and he regards as probable the substantial accuracy of the picture of a Christian community in
the reign of Antoninus Pius in the *Apology* of Aristides,
which he summarizes in the following words:

> The Christians, we are told, live in the hope and expectation of
> the world to come. They do not commit adultery nor fornica-
> tion; they do not bear false witness; they are honest in business.
> Their women are pure; they call their slaves, whom they have
> persuaded to accept the faith, brethren without discrimination.
> They love one another, and are charitable to all who are in need.
> But they try to conceal their good deeds from the public eye.[38]

Inge devotes a chapter of his book on Christian ethics to
an evaluation of asceticism as it appears in the Scriptures
and in the history of the Church. In the Scriptures, it obviously occupies a greater place in the writings of St. Paul
than in the teachings of Jesus, and it became more prominent in the second and third centuries than in the first.
Taking issue with those who regard all historical development in a religion as a retrogression, Inge indicates his
unreadiness "to condemn asceticism as simply the disease
of a moribund civilisation."[39] Defining asceticism, or *asce-
sis,* as a course of training, he further proceeds to character-
ize the religious ascetic as "the athlete of religion," who
" 'strives for mastery' in a field where most people are content if they can pass muster."[40] He does not regard the deliberate maltreatment of the body as essential to asceticism.
Those saints of the Church who resorted to such practices

have their forerunners in the Cynics rather than the Platonists, and Inge regards all the asceticism that can be attributed to Christ or the central tradition in Christianity as
Platonic in character. This type emphasizes the necessity of
detachment from material concerns. The more exaggerated varieties of asceticism found in such creeds as
Gnosticism were never characteristic of Christianity as a
whole, though they were sometimes practiced in monas-
teries in Catholic Christianity and, in some sects outside
the Roman Catholic Church, have been demanded of all the
communicants.

Recognizing that asceticism seems to run counter to ordinary human impulses, Inge asks why people adopt a way
of life which complicates it by deliberately diminishing
their comfort. One reason, he suggests, is the desire to
escape one's surroundings. The monastic life and the disciplines of hermits provide a way of detachment which may
in many cases provide for the development of the capacity
for genuine mystical experience. A second reason is found
in the effort to avoid occasions of sin. Here the ascetic life
meets with less success, and Inge shows little respect for
the motive. "We do not think that we were sent into the
world to avoid venial sins," he says. "The talents committed to us are not to be wrapped up in a napkin, but to be
put out to interest for the benefit of our fellows. We should
ask not whether a man is good, but what he is good for."[41]
A third motive in some forms of asceticism is the desire for
self-punishment, a desire which, during the long and
varied history of religion, has led to many curious excesses.
Closely related to the preceding motives, but not, according

to Inge, identical with any of them, is the urge to purify the spirit from the contamination of sense and matter by the thorough subjugation of the flesh.

A motive which Inge appears to have regarded as somewhat higher than the others is the desire to induce the mystic trance. But though the motive is high, the method is wrong. The vision of the Absolute, says Inge, is the result of long spiritual and intellectual discipline based on rational philosophy. It cannot properly be hastened by violent ascetic disciplines. "Attempts to force on artificially these very abnormal mental states," Inge writes, "inevitably lead to severe nervous reactions, in which the depression, wretchedness, and fear of being abandoned by God are quite as violent as the joys of the mystical state."[42]

The methods of asceticism are greatly varied. Among them are efforts to crush sexual desire, silence, abstention from food and drink, the deliberate cultivation of a condition of filthiness, self torture, and even subjugation of the intellect. This last particularly shocked Inge, who in attacking the views of two of his favorite opponents, writes:

Unhappily, the passion for mortification was not confined to the body. The sacrifice of the intellect to authority was also commended as a gift acceptable to God. Hence in part came that horrible blasphemy against the divine endowment of reason, which makes it so fatally easy for a priesthood to nip in the bud any revolt against the absurdities which the disciple is required to accept. "What must be the face-to-face antagonist," asks Cardinal Newman, "by which to withstand and baffle the all-corroding, all-dissolving energy of the intellect? . . . What is intellect but a fruit of the Fall, not found in paradise or Heaven, more than in little children, and at the utmost but tolerated by the Church, and only not incompatible with the regenerate mind." It seems almost incredible that this obscurantism should have been echoed by a secular philosopher, Henri Bergson, who writes, *'L'intelligence est caracterisée par une incompréhension naturelle de la vie.'*[43]

The institutional churches have greatly modified asceticism in practice from the standpoint of their several attitudes toward the things of the world. In general, among the Catholics, it is mild and symbolic for the many, designed to provide easily performed acts of obedience to the Church. For the few, more rigorous disciplines are available. The Jesuits, Inge holds, use asceticism as a method of training members of their order to be submissive, not in order to be able to retreat from the world, but to conquer it.

Luther objected to this double standard and maintained that the demand for self-denial and submission applies to all Christians. "And yet," Inge comments, "the principle on which this attitude rested was so undefined that Lutheranism has, on the whole, been found consistent with a hearty acceptance of the good things of the present life."[44]

The Calvinist believes in temperance and is sparing concerning pleasures which cannot be shown to be necessary or useful. The typical Calvinist shows "a vigorous political interest, but not for the sake of the State; a steady diligence in labour, but not for the sake of riches; a careful, often intrusive social organisation, but not for the sake of increasing human happiness; a zeal for productivity without any great interest in the objects of production."[45] The result is that in Calvinism, "on the one side, almost for the first time the dignity of work as work is upheld, and on the other, since the value of work is not measured with reference to any ulterior motive, there is sometimes a strange blindness to the maladjustments of industrial society."[46] A Calvinistic civilization "is characterised by an intense but rather unintelligent activity."[47]

Traditional forms of asceticism have not been wholly absent from the Protestant churches, but in recent years they have not been widespread. In their place, we have a number of the "queer, almost arbitrary rules and prohibitions" characteristic of "sect-type" religions.[48]

Some of these relate to Sunday observance as conditioned by Puritan Sabbatarianism. Inge is not sure that, despite the many absurdities connected with it, the old-fashioned English Sunday was not better than what was once called the Continental Sunday. In any event, he remarks, in view of the fact that workers demand one day in the week for rest, "The Sunday is therefore secure, whether God is remembered on that day or not."[49]

Whatever may have been the more legitimate reasons for taboos on card-playing, theatre-going, and attendance at race-meetings, Inge contends that a good portion of the motive behind their condemnation by Evangelicals lay in the distrust of pleasure as such.

Some of Inge's bitterest criticism is directed against those Protestants who engage in militant campaigns against tobacco and alcohol. The following passage is indicative of his own attitude toward these sources of pleasure:

We may grant that excess in alcoholic drinks is very common, and that many lives have been ruined by it. But a moderate consumption of alcohol could not be called sinful by any reasonable man. Nevertheless, it is treated as if it were a deadly sin by the fanatics of "temperance," who have even induced one great nation to attempt to abolish it altogether. The same set of fanatics are now trying to forbid cigarette-smoking, and perhaps all use of tobacco. It is very significant that these "fads," and the attempt to enforce them on everybody, are hardly known in Catholic countries. They are chiefly Anglo-Saxon, and specially characteristic of those who in England are called noncomformists. We have already found that it is a mark of the sect-type to allow no secondary Christian morality—no pass-examination for the weaker brethren. What is right for some is right for all. This view does not make for liberty and toleration. It cannot be doubted that, for some occult reason, far more indignation is aroused by the transgression of an artificial rule, some tradition of the elders, than by laxity in keeping the weightier matters of the law. The most harmless action may acquire by association a symbolical guilt, which makes the performance of it distressing to the beholder. The anti-tobacconist, whose favourite text is "Worship the Lord with clean lips," may feel actually sick at the smell of a cigar, just as some of the monks and hermits experienced physical digust at the sight of a woman.[50]

Inge concludes that asceticism, with the exceptions noted, has almost disappeared from Christianity. There is much in this fact that is not to be regretted. Certainly, Inge holds, there is no reason to think that it means that we are no longer Christian. The particular forms of asceticism which he criticizes were themselves far in spirit from the religion of Christ and the Apostles. "There is not the slightest reason to think that Christ would have commended Simeon Stylites, or Henry Suso, or the Flagellants," Inge says. "He would probably have laughed heartily at the American prohibitionists, when they begged Him to reverse His miracle at Cana in Galilee."[51]

Returning to problems of eugenics, Inge comments that the decline of asceticism has enabled us to lose that "horror of procreation" which for a long time made it impossible for the Christian Church to consider the importance of systematic preparation for the future in terms of future births.

Despite the regained freedom of thought which has accompanied the rise of a nonascetic ethic, Inge maintains that the discarded ideal contains important truths which it is dangerous for us to neglect. Religion demands that pleasure and comfort on occasion be sacrificed. There is, moreover, a real place for the "specialist" in the field—the man who devotes himself to the saintly life. In a larger sense, we need to apply some of the principles of the ascetic ideal to our own lives. The emphasis which has frequently been placed in our society on the unwisdom of "repression" as a source of disharmony within the personality has all too frequently led to the assumption that unrepressed human nature is normally harmonious and that if we simply permit ourselves to be ruled by impulse, we can attain the good life. Inge quite rightly disputes this. "The disorderly mob of desires," he says, "must be controlled by the central authority of what the Stoics called the ruling principle— the dedicated conscience."[52] This process may initially involve real repression of those instincts which are in rebellion. Asceticism, in the sense of a renunciation of what is superfluous and unhelpful in gaining the higher ends of life, has much to commend it. "The idea of getting and spending at high pressure, which in America is sometimes called 'consumptionism,' is barbarous and unchristian,"[53] he writes, and in another context he tells us:

. . . I am strongly in favour of a simpler mode of living, and of that constant though not severe self-discipline which even William James recommends. "Do something every day for no other

reason than because you don't want to do it." Our Lord set a
very small value on the accessories of life. The Western nations value them far too much.[54]

With reference to the degree and kind of asceticism
which should be practiced, Inge asks and attempts to answer a twofold question: "What are the proper limits of
specialisation?" and "How far are what we call the lower
experiences a help, and how far are they a hindrance, to
the higher life?"[55] Overspecialization is, he acknowledges,
one of the major problems of our century. Few personalities are developed harmoniously because of the demands
of our society which force men to pursue one line of work
until the rest of their personalities are damaged beyond
repair. Does not the same objection apply to specialization
in the saintly life? Inge holds first that it is true that the
price of specialization is a degree of mental impoverishment. The evil is, however, exaggerated, for he holds that
work which is done well attains a quality of universality.
"A broad mind is not much cramped by a narrow
sphere."[56] This is particularly true, he holds, of the true
saint, who is usually "a man of warm sympathies and a
shrewd judge of human nature."[57]

As for the second question, Inge admits that even Plato
was not consistent in his view of the extent to which the
lower experiences can be utilized in attaining the higher.
He maintains, however, that we must not fall into a dualism which would attribute malignant independence to
matter, which is actually "only an instrument for the ac-
tualising of spiritual values."[58] For the rest, each man must
decide on the degree of pleasure he can permit himself

without damage to his spiritual life. Every man, however, should include in his mode of living such disciplines as will enable him to attain self-mastery.

One of the things about which Inge is most insistent is his contention that Christian morality cannot properly be legislated by an authoritative ecclesiastical structure. The argument that the Church, in adapting itself to its environment, had to become a strong political organization does not justify the assumption that it therefore speaks with the authority of Christ or that it is consistent with His teachings. Inge asks:

Are we justified in assuming, as the Catholic Church has usually assumed, that the Spirit of Christ has permanently incarnated Himself in an institution, inspiring the institution with infallible wisdom, and dispensing the grace of God through the medium of its officers, who enjoy a monopoly of this privilege? Is this privileged position indefectible, whatever abuses may arise in the administration? Is the possibility that a Church, like an individual, may gain the whole world and lose its own soul, excluded? Are we not permitted to apply to an ecclesiastical corporation the one test which the Sermon on the Mount seems to sanction as of universal validity? "A good tree cannot bring forth evil fruit, neither can a corrupt tree bring forth good fruit. Therefore by their fruits ye shall know them."[59]

The evils of what Inge calls "theocratic imperialism" are admittedly not confined to the Roman Catholics, although the conquest of their Church by the Empire started the process which led to "the most imposing of all political anachronisms, in the palace of the pontifex maximus on the Vatican."[60] It is true that the Dean regards Protestant churches as much freer of the taint than the Church of Rome, but, rather self-consciously, he announces his intention of being fair by finding some things to criticize in

Protestantism and by exempting from his criticism of Rome "the gentle and truly Christian piety which has sheltered itself so loyally and gratefully under that banner."[61]

Inge's objection to the Church of Rome from an ethical standpoint is based on his rejection of its claim to despotic authority, embodied in such conceptions of itself as that expressed by Bellarmine in the statement: "The Church is an organized social body, as visible and palpable as the Roman people."[62] Belloc, Inge points out, goes so far as to state categorically that the Church inherited the lawful sovereignty of the Empire and that the Protestants of the Reformation were barbarians in revolt against lawful authority. The increasing claim to temporal as well as spiritual authority became greater and greater in the Church of Rome, until in 1493 the Pope felt himself qualified to give the whole new world to Ferdinand and Isabella in the following words:

Acting on our own initiative, from pure generosity and certain knowledge, and with the plenitude of our apostolic power, we make over all the islands and continental lands which have been discovered or may hereafter be discovered, towards the West and South, by drawing a line from the North Pole to the South Pole, whether these continental lands already discovered and hereafter to be discovered are towards India or towards any other part of the world; this line is to be drawn a hundred leagues west and south of the Azores and Cape de Verde Islands, provided that the said lands were not in the actual possession of any other Christian king or prince on Christmas Day of last year, by the authority of Almighty God, granted to us in the person of St. Peter, and as vicar of Jesus Christ, which authority we exercise on earth, to be held by you, your heirs and successors for ever, with all and every right of sovereignty thereto pertaining, in accordance with these presents.[63]

Despite the excessive power and the abuses of the Church, Inge admits that, in preserving some order and civilization in the midst of the barbarism of the Dark Ages, it insured that not all contact with classical civilization was lost. It also tried to enforce some decency in a period characterized by atrocious standards of morality. The heavy price paid for its services, however, was the opportunity it had to enlarge the area in which it claimed authority and exercised power. One of the greatest sources of corruption in a strong institutional church is the costliness of its operations. This, in the absence of taxation by force, necessitated, in the case of the Roman Church, a resort "to barefaced threats and promises, to shameless frauds and pretended miracles, to corrupt intrigues with secular powers, to the cruelties of the Inquisition, which . . . was even more anxious to confiscate property than to burn heretics, to the sale of indulgences, and to other methods of deceit and distortion."[64] These practices, together with the fact that an international political organization, faced with a growing nationalism, had inevitably to devote more and more of its energies to its own survival and aggrandizement, are greatly responsible, Inge maintains, for the Roman Church as it exists today. "Its usefulness as an institution," he writes, "belongs to the time when it was educating the barbarians. From the time of the Renaissance downwards it has been an obstacle to civilisation and progress."[65] It finally consolidated its centralization of power when in 1870 it made its bishops agree to accept the contention that the doctrine of Papal infallibility was the historic position of the Church. "The submission of the vast majority of the bishops is very significant," Inge comments. "It resembles the abject retractations of prominent Russian Communists when threatened with excommunication by Stalin."[66]

The most serious ethical fault of Roman Catholicism, however, is one which, according to Inge, began long before the Renaissance. Its monopolistic and ritualistic character necessitated the perpetration of "a monstrous conception of the character of God," bearing more resemblance to the picture of Him in the most primitive portions of the Old Testament than to that given by Christ. The distinction between the elect and the lost on the basis of membership in a body and participation in certain rites is, Inge protests, "absolutely unethical, and revoltingly unjust."[67] It results in a situation in which "religion is almost completely de-ethicised, and the standard of right and wrong is likely to be much lower than among high-minded persons who care little for religion, but act according to their instinctive notions of what is just, decent, and honourable."[68] The worst forms of the Catholic notion of hell are used to frighten people into submission to the only institution which allegedly can save them from its torments. With no conditions admitted between complete salvation and complete damnation, no real gradations in morality can be posited, and a totally unrealistic picture of ethics results. The history of the Church demonstrates the fact that its view of morality as allegiance to the institution leads to intolerance, persecution, and a lowering of genuine moral feeling. Inge cites the case of a suspect brought before the Inquisition about 1233, who, to defend himself against a charge of heresy, declared: "Hear me, my lords! I am no heretic. I have a wife, and cohabit with her, and have children; and I eat flesh and lie and swear and am a faithful Christian."[69] The threats of hell and the torments and murders of the Inquisition were used against those who threatened the authority of the Church, and concern with genuine goodness was either irrelevant or subsidiary to that issue.

Inge refuses to admit that the Protestant churches have had an attitude or a history in this regard in any way comparable to the Church of Rome. That in its earlier forms the Protestant movement was intolerant he admits, and he cites the persecution of Anabaptists and Quakers, the burning of Servetus by Calvin, and the witchcraft trials and executions in Europe and America as instances of that intolerance. Such persecutions, however, he regards as uncharacteristic of Protestantism. In his opinion, they existed only because the early reformers themselves were products of the Middle Ages and did not understand thoroughly the implications of their own position. That the Protestant churches have irrevocably abandoned persecution he regards as more obvious than may actually be the case. That the Roman Church would return to the enforcement of its still unrepudiated persecutory edicts if it had the opportunity seems to him most likely.

The situation with reference to the moral degeneration attributable to "theocratic Imperialism" seems to Inge to be well explained in Lecky's *History of Rationalism*. Lecky's interpretation of the doctrine of *extra ecclesiam nulla salus* is of questionable accuracy, but Inge quotes it with approval:

Persuade men that when they are ascribing to the Deity justice and mercy they are speaking of qualities generically different from those which exist among mankind—qualities which we are altogether unable to conceive, and which may be compatible with acts that men would term grossly unjust and unmerciful; tell them that guilt may be entirely unconnected with a personal act, that millions of infants may be called into existence for a moment to be precipitated into a place of torment, that vast nations may live and die, and then be raised again to suffer a never-ending punishment, because they did not believe in a religion of which they had never heard, or because a crime was committed thousands of years before they were in existence: convince them that all this is part of a transcendently righteous and moral scheme, and there is no imaginable abyss to which such a doctrine will not lead. You will have blotted out those fundamental notions of right and wrong which the Creator has engraven upon every heart; you will have extinguished the light of conscience; you will have taught men to stifle the inner voice as a lying witness, and to esteem it virtuous to disobey it.[70]

Inge quite properly draws a distinction between the suppression of opinions and the forbidding of overt acts of an immoral nature committed in the name of religion. He maintains that even on utilitarian grounds, the former course must not be taken, whereas the latter is obligatory for the preservation of society. The impracticability of persecution to root out opinions rests in the fact that in practice "we have to choose between tolerating what we think error and suppressing all intellectual activity over a very broad area." A tyranny which attempts to stamp out some opinion of which it disapproves must track down any forms of thought which might lead in the direction of the forbidden idea. All thinking must, therefore, come under the scrutiny of the state, with the result that original thought and intellectual progress must be destroyed. The hatred engendered against the institution that attempts to exercise control of this sort over its citizens almost inevitably results in the ruin of the corporate structure.

The suppression of acts committed in the name of religion which offend the general moral sense of mankind is another thing altogether. "The alleged command of a god ought not to shelter such institutions as human sacrifice, widow-burning, and religious prostitution," Inge holds. "Those who wish to practise such atrocious acts cannot be allowed to take refuge behind an invisible accomplice."[71] It is when we persecute people of unquestioned moral character for holding unorthodox opinions or refusing to belong to some corporate structure that we are guilty of tyranny.

To the objection that the punishment of heretics by the Church is no less justifiable than the punishment by the state of people who evade conscription in time of war, Inge answers that a man has no proper and natural citizenship in a theocratic empire operating in the name of a Founder who never intended for such a structure to develop. He holds that the Roman Church, in its political character, has little relation to Christianity. Indeed, the only real virtue he sees in that structure is the strength with which it has been able to stand up against "the spirit of the age."[72] In this respect, however, he allows himself almost a paean of praise about the Church of Rome, which he describes as standing "like an impregnable fortress amid the welter of half-civilised barbarism, like a rock surrounded by raging seas."[73] In its recognition of the fact that the fundamental truths of human society do not change, the Church can regard all revolutions as merely surface phenomena. "In comparison with other religious bodies," he continues, "the Roman Church shows a great courage; it

is not afraid to rebuke and condemn fashionable enthusiasms, and to appeal to an older and deeper wisdom. This
stability gives it a wonderful dignity, and supports the im-
measurable pride with which it confronts the modern
world."[74] Its political structure is superbly designed to support its position, and far from being an anachronism as it
appeared in the nineteenth century, the papacy looks, in a
century of dictatorships and democracies, like a structure
which "may even compel admiration as the best of all attempts to solve an insoluble problem—that of devising a
form of government which shall not be a nuisance or a
laughing-stock."[75]

Though the Roman Church is a formidable organization, which cannot be despised by an intelligent man, Inge
maintains that it must, from the Christian standpoint, be
regarded as "a complete apostasy," in so far as its institutional structure is concerned.[76] Furthermore, by its very nature, it cannot permit any real reform which would
threaten its structure, for to permit such changes would be
to renounce its ambitions. And yet, these ambitions are
doomed to failure, because Rome cannot, like the Protestant churches, permit a flexibility of doctrine which could
serve as a basis for "a morality which is based not on tradition but on the broad principles of the Gospel applied to
modern problems."[77] The Church of Rome, if it has served
a purpose, can no longer serve it by perpetuating and en-
hancing its imperialistic structure. "The one object of a
good educator," says Inge, "is to make himself unnecessary."[78]

The structure of Christian ethics, however, is in no way
tied up with the mistakes of a church.

If it be said that in regarding nearly the whole of Church history as an aberration from the intentions of the Founder I am surrendering the Citadel, I cannot agree. Two thousand years are a very short time in the history of humanity. Circumstances favoured the growth of a political Church; other circumstances may promote its decay. But the revelation of Christ is a permanent enrichment of the human race, which is very far from having yet exhausted all that the revelation potentially contains. A thousand years hence, when the idea of Rome as the world's capital will evoke only a smile, mankind will still be wrestling to draw out temporal meanings from the eternal Gospel, and they will still be sitting at the feet of Jesus Christ. Beyond Pheidias, said Rodin, art can never go. Beyond Jesus of Nazareth, we may add, the moral stature of humanity can never go.[79]

In his consideration of matters related to social ethics, Inge shows on one side the essential conservatism of temperament which characterized his economic outlook, combined with a willingness rather startling in an Anglican clergyman of his stature to advocate new solutions for problems related to the limitation of population and the like.

He was much concerned with the impact of the scientific outlook on contemporary ethical problems. We have already seen that his writings do not indicate any agreement with the optimism of those men of science who thought that evolution necessarily involves universal progress. So unjustifiable does he judge such a view to be in the light of any real scientific knowledge that he expresses surprise that any men of genuine scientific stature should ever have been taken in by it. The twentieth century has dealt serious blows to the optimism prevalent in the nineteenth, with results which may be anticipated whenever a world outlook having the emotional force of a religion begins to crumble. "A successful religion (real Christianity has never been successful)," he comments, "is a superstition which has enslaved a philosophy, and the philosophy which was supposed to guarantee automatic progress, attractive as it is, labours under the disadvantage of being almost the only philosophy which can be definitely disproved."[80] On the whole, the decline of the delusion has had beneficial effects, he holds, for a feeling of pessimism about the fate of the material order may be actually conducive to a greater willingness to recognize a kingdom of values outside that order. However, Inge views with some alarm the attendant tendency in our time to revolt against the fundamental postulate of science—the belief in uniformity of sequence.

It is in this connection that his distaste for miracle is most clearly evidenced. However, he recognizes the difficulty of maintaining a belief in "the moral miracle of conversion" if we deny the possibility of supernatural intervention in the regular order of nature. His answer is in terms of a real distinction between the material and the spiritual world, which is never quite reconciled with the insistence on lawfulness in the realm of spirit on which his objection to miracle really seems to be based. Admitting that we cannot explain the freedom of spirit which experience guarantees, he nevertheless asserts that it exists, and he repudiates moral and spiritual determinism. Even this assertion of freedom, however, leaves no place for an imputation of caprice or magic to the higher realm.

The scientific conscience has its protests to make against certain theological doctrines. Forgiveness without change of heart—grace imputed but not imparted—a change of status towards

God effected by sacerdotal magic—these are theories of the relation between man and God which the conscience of our age,
supported by the scientific hypothesis of unbroken continuity,
rejects. And it will be seen that they are all unethical theories.
Whatever power we may assign to grace, whatever indulgence
we may hope for from a merciful Judge, it must remain true
that "whatsoever a man soweth, that shall he reap."[81]

On the ethical side, the dominance of the natural sciences in our society has resulted in the development of two
different trends in philosophy. One is atheism, with its
attendant denial of the reality of absolute values. The other
is pantheism, which in sanctifying nature, tends toward an
ethic of kindliness without real human warmth. The majority of persons in our day do not accept either of these
views as a systematic philosophy, but rather "a jumble of
pantheism and Naturalism, combined with other elements
taken over from other traditions."[82]

Inge describes the nineteenth-century English scientists
as Victorian upholders of traditional morality, despite their
theories about the natural world. The real effects of the
revolution in thought for which they were responsible are
evident in the views of younger men not reared in the
solid traditions of their predecessors. Along with the
ethics of the older traditions, these men rejected the sort of
psychological and ethical hedonism promulgated by Ben-
tham. In its place, they substituted the goal of the full
healthy development of the human being. Seeing in Christian morality a good deal of mere taboo, they were willing
to set aside accepted standards of behavior. They rejected
asceticism and repudiated the traditional Church-sanc-
tioned standards of sexual morality. They stressed the positive character of morals and insisted that virtue be pursued

for its own sake rather than from fear of punishment or hope of reward. All moral goals, however, are here and now, and censure is reserved almost exclusively for anti-social conduct. Those most thoroughly conditioned by the scientific temper of the age have little respect for old-fashioned humanitarianism, democracy, or the sort of delicacy which governed relations between the sexes before their day.

The ethics of the new scientism is, in short, secular in character, though not all the secularism in our culture stems from science. Claiming to be all-embracing in its scope, secularism concentrates with fanatical zeal and conspicuous success on immediate, empirically ascertainable ends, and it can be as cruel and persecutory as any religion. Religions try to make terms with the secular spirit to their own detriment, for it is bound by its nature to regard their claims as untenable.

The vulgar type of secularism, however, can hardly be laid to the door of science. Philosophy based on science to the exclusion of other disciplines is wrong, but pragmatic materialism, rather than stemming from an intellectual system, is, in Inge's view, a product of man's corrupt nature. On the whole, he hails the moral influence of modern scientific knowledge as a good thing. It has been responsible for a greater regard for veracity and evidence in many disciplines. It has redeemed the virtue of curiosity from the monkish condemnation of it as *turpis* and promoted the search for truth. It has shifted the emphasis in morals from authority to individual reason and conscience, though in this respect Inge holds that a great deal of caution is called for. It has, though agnostic about the reality of a personal

God, been useful in destroying many unworthy notions of God. In this connection, Inge writes:

> God, if there is a God, is not a capricious Oriental sultan, nor a magnified schoolmaster, nor the head of the clerical profession. Seeley was quite right in saying that Science reveres a worthier God than the average churchgoer. The God of traditional Catholicism and Calvinism, though not lustful like Jupiter, was far more cruel and unjust. Nothing so revolting as the damnation of unbaptised children, of all Jews, Turks, infidels, and heretics, or of those who without fault of their own were predestined to reprobation, was ever taught by Paganism. Mill's well-known refusal to call any Being good who is not what we mean by good when we apply the word to our fellow-creatures is in accordance with the conscience of our time. "Shall not the Judge of all the earth do right?" Abraham's question is now asked confidently; and an affirmative answer sweeps away a mass of iniquity which ought never to have been attributed to the Father of our Lord Jesus Christ. False, not to say blasphemous, beliefs about the character of God and His dealings with men, have been responsible for a large proportion of the crimes and frauds which have stained the history of the Church, and for the rejection of the Christianity in which they were brought up by many high-minded men and women.[83]

The tendency of modern thought to inquire "what a man is good for" rather than what he is bad for, to attack diseases rather than symptoms, and to prefer prevention to cure he regards as quite in accordance with genuine Christianity. The insights that men are a part of the natural order and that through "rational self-determination" they can improve themselves and their environment are good, according to Inge, as is the recognition of the greatly extended horizon provided by science.

There is, he maintains, even an idealistic element in modern secularism.

When purged from its superstitions and apocalyptic accessories, it may restore for us some of the enthusiasm with which the early Christians awaited the second coming of Christ. It would not be fanciful to find some analogy between the joyous trust of Christ in the Father in heaven who makes his sun to rise on the evil and on the good, and without whom no sparrow falls to the ground, and the reverent spirit in which the man of science accepts whatever facts his studies reveal to him, confident that "the universe is friendly" to him who devotes himself to the discovery of truth.[84]

The first factor in the development of modern civilization was science; the second was industrialism. The two are clearly interrelated in that, without the former, the latter would have been impossible. When the awakening of the West brought about the "decisive triumph of Europe over Asia in material power and prestige,"[85] Europe became complacent. It was regarded as beyond question that God was on the side of the white man, Christianity, and, in many countries, Protestantism.

No attempt was made to trace the connection of the Protestant religion with the possession of the best coalfields and of the geographical position most favorable for trade. A kind of Deuteronomic religion was popular in Britain; because we were a righteous and Christian nation, our trade increased, our debt diminished, and our children possessed the earth. The rivals of Christianity were no longer formidable; even the tribesmen of Jenghiz Khan, by adopting Buddhism, had become harmless and peaceful, unlike Mohammedans or Christians. But this complacent Christianity was a secularized religion. The modern man laboured religiously when he knew that evolution was on his side; he rested his faith on progress—that is, on that form of advance which can be measured by statistics. Christianity became what it had never been before, a rather vulgar this-world religion. The middle ages had made religion a business; the nineteenth century made business a religion.[86]

The industrial revolution was without question successful in producing a high standard of living. Could it be
maintained under collective ownership? Inge thought not,
long before the question of public *vs.* private ownership
reached its present crucial state. He feared that under
Socialism there would be an increase in unemployment
and a fall in the aggregate income available for distribution. The elimination of poverty is, of course, a Christian
and humane goal; but as an alternative to collectivism or
Communism, he suggests standardized large-scale production and use of improved machinery. This method has, in
the United States, he says, diminished drudgery and increased the prosperity of the working man to an unprecedented degree. On the basis of this achievement, he
ventures a prediction that "it is in this direction, rather
than by the confiscation of all private capital, that the nations of the West are likely to move."[87]

He attacks at some length the question whether Socialism is "in the true line of development of Christian
Ethics." Early experiments with voluntary communism in
monastaries do not alter the fact that early Christians were
indifferent to social organization as such and did not consider the monastic pattern applicable to society in general.
Inge himself goes further and maintains that it has been
proved by history that "Communism is possible only under
two conditions—a religious basis and celibacy."[88]

He recognizes the socialistic tendencies of fourth-cen-
tury Christian homiletics and cites the denunciation of
riches by Ambrose. However, he dismisses these as "flowers of oratory" rather than "prophetic warnings uttered in
deadly earnest." Whereas the Stoics considered the original

Law of Nature to be communistic, early Christians, even when influenced strongly by Stoical ethical doctrine, recognized that it must be accommodated to circumstances.

As for the Middle Ages, the Schoolmen, in going back to Aristotle, admitted a relative Law of Nature which applies to man in a state of sin. To the question as to how the unchanging Law of God can be altered by circumstances, Thomas Aquinas had no facile answer, but said merely that utility, or expediency, has quite legitimately modified the Natural Law. Private ownership, then, while not permissible to man in a state of innocence, is appropriate to man in his fallen state—a state in which the communism appropriate to Eden is actually wrong because impracticable.

Inge holds that Catholic political theory could conceivably take a revolutionary turn on the basis of the contentions of medieval writers concerning the right of revolt against bad government. Even Thomas Aquinas says that "in the court of conscience there is no obligation to obey an unjust law."[89] However, this recognition implied no acceptance of any Christian idea of general social reform. Social stratification was accepted as the realization of the Natural Law in society. Thomas was a believer in the doctrine of the divine right of kings, though in no debased form. Only in heaven can distributive justice be dispensed fairly to all. The ancient church had rejected social reform as too difficult to realize. The medieval church, idealizing the social order and identifying it with the order of nature, considered a doctrine of social reform unnecessary.

Nominalism and Protestantism undermined the Thomistic society, but furnished little basis for a Christian socialism. For Luther, morality was personal. ". . . you may rightly call polity (political institutions) the Kingdom of sin," he wrote.[90] He was essentially conservative. Himself one of the causes of the peasant uprising, he could not support it because of his exaggerated respect for authority, and so he encouraged the princes to wipe out the rebels. "This," Inge maintains, "was not only an indelible blot on the character of Luther. It estranged the official Reformation in Germany from democratic sympathies and ideas. Henceforward, Lutheranism was in the main a middle-class movement; the artisans of the towns were the chief supporters of the Anabaptists."[91]

Luther, Inge points out, defended inequality in man's earthly state. "His social Ethics," the Dean comments, "are patriarchal and medieval, not modern, and when the patriarchal system passed away, and an era of absolutism succeeded, Lutheranism had no more any valuable social message."[92]

Calvinism he regards as tending toward a conservative democracy, characterized by no notion of equality, but by strong feelings of individuality and initiative. Calvin and Knox were both conservative men, and Calvin regarded Christianity as quite compatible with trade and industrialism. His followers could view capitalism as a virtuous system, and their tendency to do so was strengthened by the fact that large numbers of Calvinists, denied participation in public life in many countries, took to trade and became successful at it.

Inge succinctly describes the ethical result:

So we can understand how Calvinism created that curious product, the modern business man, who works like a slave in accumulating money which his tastes and principles forbid him to enjoy, and about the value of which to himself and others he asks no questions. No system was ever devised so effectual in promoting that kind of progress which is measured by statistics. If a nation can be convinced that steady industry in profitable enterprise is eminently pleasing to God, but that almost all unproductive ways of spending superfluous wealth are wrong, that nation will become very rich.[93]

In America, deterioration has set in, for, Inge admits, "if the American millionaire still sometimes leads a very austere life, his wife squanders enough for two."[94] The asceticism necessary to maintain a Calvinistic social structure is, therefore, threatened from the distaff side.

He regards the "modern" period as having had a profoundly disturbing effect on Christian teachings, characterized by an unprecedented secularization of the Gospel and a revolt against religion as a source of ethical standards. Jean Jacques Rousseau is named as the chief villain in this process.

The influence of this sentimental rhetorician has perhaps been more pernicious than that of any other man who has ever lived. . . . He is the founder of sentimental humanitarianism, that mawkish travesty of Christianity which transforms morality by basing it solely on pity, and transfers guilt from the individual to the State under which he lives.[95]

Inge even theorizes that had it not been for Rousseau, the world might have been spared Karl Marx and the Bolshevist revolt. The state of twentieth-century Russia he cites as evidence to support his thesis that sentimentalism "ends in tyranny and homicidal mania."[96] Admitting that there is need for social reform, he nevertheless denies that it can properly be effected by an indiscriminate attack on existent social institutions. "If it were not for our orators," he comments with some bitterness, "many who are now cursing their fellow-men for the faults of our social system would be praising God that we have any social system at all."[97]

Theoretic Socialism, though still eliciting enthusiasm from those who hold it as an ideal, has declined as a program from the peak of its importance at the end of the nineteenth century. The reason for this he finds in the practical results stemming from attempts to put socialistic plans into effect.

The radical divergence and incompatibility between State Socialism, in which the State is everything, and Syndicalism, in which the State is nothing, have become glaringly apparent. The ugly brat, Communism, seems likely to destroy its parents, and the attempt to carry out the theories of Marx in Russia has condemned the second largest empire in the world to a prolonged crucifixion. Communists have repudiated any alliance with democracy and liberalism, and trust only to propaganda, coercion, and terrorism. The olive-branch tendered by some earnest Christians to the revolution has been rejected with scorn and hatred.[98]

Whether Socialism is, or is not, a live issue at the present time, it could not, at any rate, properly be a program of the Church, according to Inge. For that matter, he holds that it is not within the province of the Church to deal with practical questions of social economics and that it must confine itself to attacking obvious moral evils. If it attempts to gain political power, it sacrifices its moral influence and to that extent abandons its proper Christian function.

At any rate, he does not admit that the economic problem is so great—at least in England—as to justify any general radical alteration. He cites statistical evidence to attempt to demonstrate that employed artisans receive a just share of the national income. The inequities are so arranged, he contends, that if all the income of persons receiving greatly more than their share could be divided up, the workers would find their wages increased by very little.

Needless to say, this argument was hardly sufficient to convince those engaged in battles for social reform in the nineteen-thirties that their services were unneeded, and Inge found himself branded as an arch-conservative defending the *status quo*. It must be admitted that, in most respects, he was out of sympathy with the men of the left. "Political agitators," he complains, "have much to answer for, with their silly talk about 'wage-slaves,' as if a slave were not by definition a worker who gets no wages, and as if the essence of the wage system were not that under it a man may sell his labour without selling himself."[99] Here the Dean may have been semantically more accurate than his opponents, but arguments of this kind are not apt to demonstrate satisfactorily to an underpaid and overworked Welsh coal miner that his situation is one which calls for no change. It is, perhaps, in the area of social and economic justice that Inge, however sympathetic he may have been toward the poor, shows his greatest incomprehension of the issues really involved.

In effect, he dismisses the whole problem of inequities in the distribution of world goods and turns to that of

260   THE GLOOMY DEAN

consumption. In this connection he issues a challenge not
untinged with that Calvinism of which he is sometimes
a severe critic.

Who is it that ordains that the whole labour of myriads of men
shall be wasted—devoted to producing things that nobody ought
to want? Not the capitalist, but the consumer. The demand creates the supply, and in all the richer countries a large portion of
the demand is vulgar, senseless, and selfish. The amount of
money wasted on champagne, women's dress, cosmetics, sweetmeats, betting, and other barbarous indulgences, would amply
suffice to put an end to poverty and to restore the financial credit
of the war-stricken nations. It seems to me that though the New
Testament has a very little to say about distribution, it has a great
deal to say about consumption, and that the homely maxim,
"Waste not, want not," may be what society most needs today.
On the whole, this is an argument for indirect taxation, applied
to the luxuries of rich and poor alike.[100]

An *argumentum ad hominem* might without too great
injustice be leveled against the Dean at this point.
Though temperate, the Dean was not Spartan in his way
of life. Champagne, women's dress, cosmetics, sweetmeats,
and betting may have had little appeal for him, but he
permitted himself a number of luxuries which better
suited his taste.

A more serious objection may be leveled against the concept of equity implied in his taxation proposal, for in
taxation "applied to the luxuries of rich and poor alike,"
a government may be prohibiting luxuries to the poor
while inflicting at most a minor annoyance on the rich.

Inge devoted more serious attention to what he called
"the population question" than to any other social problem. The present humanitarian concepts of government
have operated, he maintains, to prevent natural selection

in human heredity, thus necessitating some consideration of methods whereby the quantity of a population can
be rationally controlled and its quality improved. For obvious reasons, however, serious attention is seldom given to
the matter.

The importance of the problem would seem to be sufficiently obvious. But politicians know that the subject is unpopular. The
unborn have no votes. Employers like a surplus of labour, which
can be drawn upon when trade is good. Militarists want as
much food for powder as they can get. Revolutionists instinc-
tively oppose any real remedy for social evils; they know that
every unwanted child is a potential insurgent. All three can appeal to a quasi-religious prejudice, resting apparently on the
ancient theory of natural rights, which were supposed to include
the right of unlimited procreation. This objection is now chiefly
urged by celibate or childless priests; but it is held with such
fanatical vehemence that the fear of losing the votes which
they control is a welcome excuse for the baser sort of politician
to shelve the subject as inopportune. The Socialist calculation is
probably erroneous; for experience has shown that it is aspiration, not desperation, that makes revolutions.[101]

Some sort of eugenic control is, he maintains, necessary,
if the upper classes and the families which provide the
greatest supply of professional men are to survive. For
them not to survive would be calamitous, and yet they
are threatened by their own low birth rate as contrasted
with the high one of the lower classes.

Inge insists with almost startling emphasis that Christianity itself is the source of modern eugenic doctrines.

Sir Frances Galton used to say that eugenics ought to be a religion. It is a religion, and its name is Christianity. The Gospels
contain the most uncompromising eugenic utterances. "Do men
gather grapes of thorns, or figs of thistles?" "A good tree cannot

bring forth evil fruit, neither can a corrupt tree bring forth good fruit." "Every tree that bringeth not forth good fruit is hewn down and cast into the fire." In this, as in several other matters, the new morality can appeal to the Founder of Christianity across long ages in which His followers have distorted His precepts or failed to understand them.[102]

One of the chief influences which militates against rational social ethics, according to Inge, is humanitarianism. This movement must be recognized as quite distinct from a proper and legitimate concern for humanity, and a confusion of the terms humanity and humanitarianism is a fault of the movement. Admittedly, humanitarianism has many reforms to its credit, but its championing of these reforms is based on no standards higher than sentiment, and sentimentalism, "usually kind only to be cruel,"[103] has no standard beyond pity.

Inge sets himself squarely against humanitarianism in its opposition to capital punishment, which he defends as a quite appropriate penalty, not only for murder, but also for arson and rape. "In parts of America," he remarks, "the penalty for rape is burning alive, but only if the offender has a black skin."[104] He even approves the extension of the death penalty to incorrigible minor offenders such as thieves, who, he writes, if they cannot be reformed, should be quietly executed with a minimum of publicity. "They have been officially pronounced to be thoroughly bad citizens," he writes coldly, "and they may be removed by the same right which a gardener has to pull up weeds from his flower-beds."[105]

The Dean praises humanitarianism for the improvements it has brought about in our treatment of animals, an area of ethics in which the Christian position has never been entirely clear. The Roman Catholic Church has never properly recognized that the lower animals have any rights, and the treatment of beasts in Catholic countries has generally been deficient by English standards. However, the kindness which the English show for animals has usually been demonstrated most toward those domestic species used as pets. Others, as he recognizes, are with considerable license enslaved, killed, eaten, cut open, hunted, and shot, and he asks whether or not we have the right to do so. Here his answer is admittedly less definite than those which he customarily gives to ethical questions involving only human beings.

My own attitude may be inconsistent [he writes]; I cannot help that. We have, I think, a right to make the animals supply our needs, on condition of treating them kindly; we have a right to kill and eat them, for creatures which are not useful for food will not long be suffered to exist at all; we have a right to vivisect them under anaesthetics, but only if there is no other way of acquiring medical knowledge, and if no unnecessary pain is inflicted; but to take a pleasure in killing our helpless cousins in fur and feathers seems to me a disgusting relic of barbarism. Personally, I have never killed anything larger than a wasp, and that was in self-defence. It is not necessary or possible to draw hard and fast lines; what is necessary is that we should recognise that the animals have as good a right on the earth as we have; that "our heavenly Father feedeth them," and wishes them to have such happiness as they are capable of; and that they are, in fact and not in metaphor, our own kith and kin.[106]

Inge's attitude toward the emancipation of women is a combination of his recognition that Christianity brooks no discrimination between the sexes with his equally strong conviction that modern developments in the position of women have endangered the home and the Christian structure of society. The most important statement made by Paul on the subject, he says, is the remark that "in Christ there is neither male nor female."[107] Most of our laws of inheritance violate this spirit and defy clear biological fact in being based on the "strange physiological blunder" that "the father alone is the active agent in procreation."[108] On the other hand, we live in a period in which married women, in their new status of political and social equality, frequently refuse to have children or neglect their duty to them for self-regarding pleasures. The possession of wealth only compounds the problem.

The wives and daughters of the rich, most numerous in America but well represented at home, are the largest and most irresponsible leisured class that the world has seen. Their insatiable thirst for pleasure, their vulgar ostentation and extravagance, make them a peculiarly pernicious influence in the society in which they live. In America their every whim is indulged, and often nearly the whole of the monstrous fortunes which the law allows Americans to accumulate is wasted year by year by their women on the senseless rivalry of profligate expenditure. As Havelock Ellis says, "It is impossible for anyone under these conditions to lead a reasonable and wholesome human life."[109]

Toward one of the greatest problems confronting Christian moralists—that of war—he takes an essentially optimistic view at striking variance with the "gloom" which is popularly supposed to pervade his outlook on temporal matters. "Human institutions arise when they are inevitable, and neither common sense nor moral indignation can destroy them while they are inevitable," he writes. "There is reason to think that war has not always been inevitable; that during the greater part of human history it has been inevitable; and that a time is approaching when it will no longer be inevitable."[110]

Its causes, he maintains, are psychological, political, and economic, but the three are by no means easily differentiated. Inge sees evidence of the psychological predisposition of the human race toward war in the forms of play engaged in by modern man. Hunting, fishing, shooting, dancing, and competitive sports are all based on warlike instincts.

> But we sometimes crave for the real thing, hot and strong. It is quite as irrational as the harmless substitutes which we have found for it; for apart from the horrible misery which it causes, the armies have no real reason to hate each other, and the prizes of victory are illusory.[111]

Self-preservation, pugnacity, hatred, social solidarity, boredom, ignorance, and fear are all designated as psychological causes of war. Closely allied with these are the political causes, under which Inge includes desire for national security, racialism, étatisme, as a perversion of patriotism, and the military preparedness which cultivates a doctrine of preventive war. For his economic causes, he cites Lord Stamp's three conditions: economic penetration, economic inequality, and differential population. To these, Inge adds the claim for Lebensraum, which may result in the deportation or massacre of entire populations to make room for colonization.

War in the fullest sense, he holds, began with the discovery of metals. It may be ended by a wave of disgust like that which abolished cannibalism. Starting with tribal raids, human armed conflict gradually developed into wars of conquest and then into miscellaneous wars over a variety of disputes. During the modern period, European struggles have generally stemmed from the desire of some power to extend its dominion over the entire Continent.

"In the earlier part of the modern period," he comments, "men massacred each other in the name of what they called religion; in the latter part the chief appeal has been chauvinism or jingoism, miscalled patriotism."[112]

The Christian Church has never universally condemned war. Its uncertain attitude toward the problem has expressed itself in the ways in which it has temporized when confronted with the question whether or not the clergy may fight. Inge cites the quite literal interpretation given by the Church in the Middle Ages to the prohibition against the "shedding of blood," so that "martial prelates . . . went into battle with heavy maces, with which they could pound their enemies into pulp without breaking the skin."[113] A twentieth-century recognition of the same warlike spirit among Christians is found in the remark of an English officer in the Burmese War: "These fellows would have given us a lot of trouble if they had been Christians instead of Buddhists."[114] Inge holds that, for the most part, a double standard for clergy and laity is not reasonable, but he offers no very definite way of settling the question. The best advice he seems to be able to offer the clergy is that "in the numerous cases where the question of right or wrong is not quite clear, it may be better for ministers of religion to abstain from actual fighting, if the State allows them the choice. The question, in fact, is by no means easy to settle."[115]

On the ground that conscientious objection ignores the responsibility of the individual to the corporate structure of which he is a part, Inge maintains that it cannot be a generally acceptable course of action. In the event of a threat to the existence of the state, he holds, "those pacifists decided rightly who determined to throw in their lot with their fellow-citizens, and share their sacrifices for a common cause."[116]

At best, however, war is a terrible curse, primarily, in Inge's view, because it is dysgenic, killing off the best rather than the worst of the population. Furthermore, its modern forms are appallingly inhumane, contrasting sharply in this respect with the relatively limited conflicts of the eighteenth century.

Modern war means ruin and bankruptcy for both sides, and if territory is annexed, unwilling subjects are a weakness, not a strength. The old saying, *vae victis,* is as true as ever. But *vae victoribus* is equally true. The conquered start again from scratch, unencumbered; the victors are loaded with self-imposed burdens and live in fear of *la revanche.* France and Germany have belaboured each other like a pair of flagellant monks, and each time the flogged has had his revenge on the flogger.[117]

If war should prove to be inevitable, Inge holds that it must be humanized as much as possible.

He makes it clear that, in deploring the mental attitudes which produce war, he is not minimizing the value of patriotism. Under the present circumstances of the human race, it is "the noblest emotion on which men are likely to act together."[118] However, it does not appear as often as might be desired in a form which would justify its being described in those terms. Too frequently it "consists of a vulgar and ignorant contempt for foreigners, of

absurd pride, of sheer pugnacity and acquisitiveness."[119] As
such, it is the perversion of a noble feeling. "Patriotism,"
he declares, "when purged of its dross, is love of our country as we wish it to be, of the England 'the type of which
is laid up in heaven,' as Socrates said."

From social problems, Inge turns to a consideration of
"personal ethics," and in this area too, he sees the twentieth century as a period of radical upheaval. There can
be no question of a return to the pattern of Latin Catholicism, which is medieval rather than primitive or modern.
Far from showing any tendency to revert to a reliance
on institutional authority, the modern spirit has for centuries been characterized by a progressive emancipation
from authority, culminating in the giving of citizenship
to women—a move which Inge gloomily indicts as a major factor in breaking up the home.

The modern concept of ethics has been correct in its
insight that "unremitting drudgery" is not a duty, but has
produced in its place the philosophy of "consumptionism,"
which Inge appears to have regarded as just as bad. "To
multiply wants—" he says, "wants of a highly standardised
type, in order to keep trade humming, is to barbarise leisure and diminish happiness."[120] In personal as in social
ethics, Inge characterizes modern man as humanitarian
and secular. In this connection, he discusses with approval
an article in the *Hibbert Journal* for April 1905, by Mr.
W. H. Garrod, afterwards Professor of Poetry at Oxford.
In this article, entitled "Christian, Greek, or Goth," Garrod maintained that, whereas we usually consider our
moral code as a Hebraic one, tinged with Hellenism, it is
in actuality the code of the "Goth." Inge apparently agrees

with him and presents a picture of the "Goth" which, if it does not identify him with all the varied elements of modern society, is, at least, a successful portrait of an English gentleman of the late nineteenth or early twentieth century.

Now the "Goth" [he writes] does not really like either the saint or the *phronimos*. He is tolerant of several acts which the Church regards as deadly sins; but there is one sin which in his eyes has no forgiveness—the sin of being a cad, failure in the idea of chivalry and the idea of honour. Neither the Jew nor the Greek came up to this standard. (Inspired by this article, I once preached on the character of David, as exhibited by his conduct to Saul, Michal, Abner, Uriah, Shimei, and others. My parishioners were so little pleased that I decided to avoid Old Testament characters for the future.) The "Goth" finds that the man after God's own heart was no gentleman. He also finds Achilles a violent and sulky savage, and Ulysses, the jolly sailor, who had a wife in every port and a lie for every emergency, an amusing rascal. The Goth would not ask any of the three to dinner.[121]

It is on the matter of the relationship between Christian ethics and the Gothic ideal that Inge takes issue with Garrod. As against Garrod's contention that chivalry and honor are virtues of "natural man," constituting "an undefined and instinctive protest against Christianity," which preaches "an unnatural, pusillanimous, and impossible" morality, Inge holds that the Gothic ethic expressed in the code of an English gentleman and the Christian ideal are not incompatible. If he had found them to be so, it may be wondered which Inge would have elected to support, for he has at least as much praise as Garrod for the more secular ethical code.

The idea of a gentleman is the fine flower of our national character. Stripped of its adventitious connexion with heraldry and property in land, and with the close morality which brought it into disrepute when England was under an oligarchy, it is the finest ideal which a nation has ever set before itself. To it we owe most of the things in our history of which we may be reasonably proud. To it we owe our incorruptible magistrates, our habitual fairness, our instinct to help the weak and to hurry to the post of danger, our respect for speaking the truth, our dislike for tortuous and underhand procedures. We do not always live up to our convictions, and of course many Englishmen do not even try to live up to them; but for all the world the English gentleman stands for a recognisable type. It is, beyond question, the national ideal, and Mr. Garrod is quite right in saying that there is no forgiveness among us for those who conspicuously fail to approach it.[122]

The Dean maintains that although reconciliation of the two ideals is possible, it has not been effected by the Roman Catholic Church, which is preoccupied with sin rather than caddishness. Something of the Catholic attitude must be retained in Christianity, he concedes, if it is to keep its identity, and the loss of the consciousness of sin by modern man is dangerous. Even within the framework of Christianity, liberal and modern Protestant thought has vitiated the concept of sin to a dangerous degree. "Religion without tears" is not Christianity, he says, and the fear of the Lord is still the beginning, though not the end, of wisdom.

One of the areas in which traditional standards of personal conduct are most seriously challenged in the present century is that of sex. Inge describes the ancient position of Christianity on this subject as involving a demand for monogamy, fidelity, and abstention from homosexual practices. Although many scandals existed in the Church during the Middle Ages, even among religious persons sworn to chastity, the demands of Christian morality were unambiguous and the misconduct was recognized as violation of a generally accepted ideal.

It is the ideal itself which has in the present day been brought into question, and Inge, deploring the modern tendency, seeks to account for its origin, particularly in his own country. As a good Englishman, he could not believe "the sympathetic condonation of adultery" to be an indigenous phenomenon, and so he sought the cause where Englishmen have traditionally been prone to search for the origins of disease or sin.

This aberration of the moral sense seems to have come to this country from the Continent, and expecially from France, where the combined influence of *mariages de convenance* and of the absolute prohibition of divorce, under the old *régime* produced a tolerant attitude towards a sin which under healthy conditions should surely be most strongly condemned.[123]

He expresses wholehearted support of the general proposition that the body, as the temple of the Holy Spirit, should be kept "in sanctification and honour."[124] Although the accuracy of many of the surveys attempting to provide statistical data on sexual conduct may be seriously open to question, Inge recognized the widespread nature of the movement for sexual freedom among adults. Many of the arguments advanced in support of near-promiscuity rest, he maintains, on the illicit assumption "that men and women cannot be close friends without carnal connexion."[125] The reverse is true, he argues. It is the maintenance of high standards of sexual morality which makes it possible for innocent friendships between men and women to exist, and irregular relationships undermine the desirable freedom which makes such friendships possible.

As for homosexuality, Inge regards as somewhat ominous the tendency to regard all aberrations in this category from a medical rather than a moral viewpoint. He writes:

The large majority of pederasts, I believe, are psychically quite normal; their offence is a sin, not a disease. I suspect that the rebellion against sexual taboos will be extended to this vice, and that increasing vigilance will be needed to protect the young, who will be in most danger from it.[126]

With reference to the question of divorce, the problem for Christians is partly a result of the circumstance that it has been possible to conduct an argument on the basis of specific passages from the Gospels. A careful study of Christ's teaching indicates that, if the "adultery" passage in Matthew is not interpolated, He certainly permitted divorce under certain conditions with the privilege of remarriage. The question is, however, complicated by the fact that the reservation in question has been widely held to be an interpolation. If, as Inge believes, this is probably the case, the prohibition against divorce is apparently absolute.

Nevertheless, Inge was not content to resolve the problem by a literal adherence to the word of the Scripture. He urges that "we cannot close the inquiry without asking whether it was not our Lord's method to make statements in an unguarded form, leaving it to the common sense of His hearers to make the necessary qualifications."[127]

The principle—the permanent character of a real marriage—is clear. The specific restrictions which should be placed on divorce and remarriage must depend on a number of circumstances. Inge holds, for example, that the Christian conscience can support a law forbidding the marriage of one guilty of adultery to his or her paramour. He maintains, however, that the injured party in a divorce based on adultery should not be forced to remain single, though it may be "nobler" to do so. A Christian state may permit divorce, not merely for adultery, but also for such causes as desertion, brutality, habitual intoxication, venereal diseases, the conviction of either party of a felony, or concealment by either party of physical or mental defects. Inge suggests that the Church, in order to express its general disapproval of divorce, might impose a period of discipline upon divorcees, with temporary exclusion from communion. It is, however, somewhat difficult to see how this would be justifiable in the case of the innocent party if, indeed, divorce is not in itself morally culpable.

More deeply, he holds, two conceptions of marriage are really involved—the contractual, which may be temporary, and the sacramental, which is permanent. The state should, he contends, recognize both sorts, with the former being regarded, presumably, as something less than marriage but as "something better than mere concubinage."

"Whether those who have married without the religious ceremony should be allowed to be members of the Church is a rather difficult question of discipline,"[128] the Dean says. He apparently found it so knotty a problem, in fact, that he made no further attempt to solve it.

With reference to the ethical implications of suicide, Inge takes issue with the traditional Christian position. The prohibition against self-destruction should be relaxed, he maintains, sufficiently to permit the voluntary ending of torture by persons suffering from incurable diseases. God did not intend for the soul of the sufferer to be benefited by such methods, nor is there any indication that suicide for other reasons must necessarily be judged as severely as is the practice among Christians. "At the same time," he admits, "I hope, inconsistently perhaps, that if I were attacked by a painful illness I should have patience to wait for the end, and I do not think I should wish anyone near and dear to me to act otherwise."[129]

Holding as he does that Goodness and Beauty are facets of one eternal reality, it is not surprising to find Inge treating one's attitude toward the arts as a specific concern of Christian ethics. Historic Christianity has some faults to answer for on this count, he admits. The early Church forgot the beauty of the human body and did not recover its aesthetic attitude toward it until the time of the Renaissance. However, architecture flourished during the Middle Ages and there was no cult of ugliness. Inge holds that the works of men all over Europe were beautiful until the Industrial Revolution spread its blight over England and the Continent. The modern period has since then been characterized by indifference to the aesthetic and unprecedented bad taste. Symptomatic of the deterioration of standards is the present state of masculine dress, with its drab utilitarian uniformity.

One of the arts which has suffered most is painting. In that discipline as much as in any of the others there has been a failure to recover the feeling which makes the production of aesthetic values possible. He writes:

In painting, indeed, there are now signs of a lower degradation than has ever been known. Anyone who has paid several visits to the unique collection of Italian paintings exhibited in London

in the early part of this year (1930), and who has gone away almost intoxicated with the splendour of Italian genius in the
time of the Renaissance, must feel a kind of horror and stupe-
faction at the revolting productions of the modernist school,
which resemble now the work of a very unpleasant child, now
the first efforts of an African savage, and now the delirious hal-
lucinations of an incurable lunatic.[130]

Despite his general pessimism concerning attitudes toward beauty, he notes hopefully the beginning of a revival
in architecture, particularly in the United States and Swe-
den. The beauty of the human form is also beginning to be
appreciated again on the Continent, and there is some hope
that Christians may once more come to realize that the
body is the temple of the spirit.

The service of Beauty is the service of God, if we know what
Beauty means [he says]. We must prepare hopefully for the next
flowering-time of the arts, and make up our minds that
when the radiance of the divine loveliness once more shines
upon the minds of man, we will not leave this precious gift to
be snatched by the world, the flesh, or the devil.[131]

Inge's final word in his book on Christian ethics is a fit-
ting summary of his view concerning the way in which
principles which he regards as eternal are related to changing circumstances.

Civilisation . . . is actually passing into a new phase. The
Church, like a wise householder, must bring out of her treasure
things new and old—not so much some things that are new and
others that are old, as new things that are the legitimate interpretation of the original Gospel for a state of society of which
the first Christians never dreamed, and old things upon which
the illuminating Spirit has passed with quickening breath and
revealing light. It will be long before European civilisation

reaches a state of stable equilibrium. We may see strange experiments in practical Ethics, and the authority of Christ may be more widely rejected than it is to-day. But I have no fear that the candle lighted in Palestine nearly two thousand years ago will ever be put out. "Lord, to whom shall we go? Thou hast the words of eternal life."[132]

NOTES

CHAPTER I

1 p *5* W. R. Inge, *Vale* (London: Longmans, Green & Co., 1934), p. 5.
2 p *6 Ibid.,* p. 7.
3 p *10* Maurice Nédoncelle, *La Philosophie Religieuse en Grande-Bretagne de 1850 à Nos Jours* (Librairie Bloud & Gay), p. 175.
4 p *11* Inge, *Vale*, p. 26.
5 p *12 Ibid.,* p. 27.
6 p *13 Ibid.,* p. 29.
7 p *13* W. R. Inge, *Diary of a Dean* (London: Hutchinson & Co., 1949), p. 34.
8 p *13 Vale*, p. 30.
9 p *14 Ibid.,* p. 31.
10 p *14 Ibid.*
11 p *15 Ibid.,* pp. 31–32.
12 p *17* W. R. Inge, *The Platonic Tradition in English Religious Thought* (London: Longmans, Green & Co., 1926), p. v.
13 p *17 Vale*, p. 34.
14 p *18 Ibid.,* p. 39.
15 p *19* W. R. Inge, *Christian Mysticism* (London: Methuen & Co., Second Edition, 1912), p. vi.
16 p *19 Ibid.,* p. vii.
17 p *20 Ibid.,* p. ix.
18 p *21* W. R. Inge, *Mysticism in Religion* (London: Hutchinson's University Library, 1947), p. 120.
19 p *24* W. R. Inge, *Faith and Knowledge* (Edinburgh: T. & T. Clark, Second Edition, 1905, pp. 287–88.
20 p *24* W. R. Inge, *Studies of English Mystics* (London: John Murray, 1906), p. 238.
21 p *25 Vale*, p. 64.
22 p *29 Ibid.,* p. 68.
23 p *30 Ibid.,* p. 69.
24 p *30 Ibid.*
25 p *30 Ibid.,* p. 70.
26 p *31 Diary of a Dean*, pp. 17–18.

27   p *32 Vale*, p. 72.
28   p *34 Ibid.*, p. 75.
29   p *34 Ibid.*, p. 76.
30   p *35 Ibid.*, p. 81.
31   p *37 Diary of a Dean*, p. 12.
32   p *39 Vale*, p. 88.
33   p *39 Ibid.*, p. 89.
34   p *41 Diary of a Dean*, p. 42.
35   p *41 Ibid.*
36   p *42 Vale*, p. 47.
37   p *43* W. R. Inge, *Personal Religion and the Life of Devotion* (London: Longmans, Green & Co., 1912), p. 90.
38   p *43 Ibid.*, p. 91.
39   p *43 Ibid.*, p. 92.
40   p *43 Ibid.*, p. 93.
41   p *43 Ibid.*, p. 92.
42   p *44 Vale*, pp. 84–85.
43   p *44 Diary of a Dean*, p. 101.
44   p *44 Ibid.*, pp. 102–3.
45   p *45 Ibid.*, p. 109.
46   p *45 Vale*, p. 92.
47   p *46 Ibid.*, p. 104.
48   p *48* W. R. Inge, *Things New and Old* (London: Longmans, Green & Co., 1933), pp. 1–2.
49   p *48 Diary of a Dean*, p. 112.
50   p *49 Ibid.*, p. 180.
51   p *53* "End of the Gloomy Dean," *Newsweek*, XCIII, No. 10, March 8, 1954, p. 73.
52   p *53 Ibid.*
53   p *54 The Christian Century*, LXXI, No. 11, March 17, 1954, p. 327. Copyright 1954 Christian Century Foundation. Reprinted by permission from *The Christian Century*.

CHAPTER II

1   p *55* W. R. Inge, *The Philosophy of Plotinus* (London: Longmans, Green & Co., 1929) I, 74.
2   p *57 Ibid.*, p. 116.
3   p *57 Ibid.*, p. 120.

4 p 57 *Ibid.*
5 p 58 *Ibid.*, p. 115.
6 p 58 *Ibid.*, p. 121.
7 p 58 *Ibid.*, p. 3.
8 p 59 *Ibid.*, p. 2.
9 p 59 *Ibid.*, p. 3.
10 p 59 *Ibid.*, pp. 3–4.
11 p 60 W. R. Inge, *Personal Idealism and Mysticism* (London: Longmans, Green & Co., 1907), p. 9.
12 p 60 *Ibid.*
13 p 61 *The Philosophy of Plotinus,* I, 22.
14 p 61 *Ibid.*, p. 23.
15 p 61 *Ibid.*
16 p 62 *Ibid.*, p. 123.
17 p 63 W. R. Inge, *God and the Astronomers* (London: Longmans, Green & Co., 1934), p. 264.
18 p 64 *The Philosophy of Plotinus,* I, 125–26.
19 p 64 *Ibid.*, p. 126.
20 p 64 *Ibid.*
21 p 66 *Ibid.*, pp. 129–30.
22 p 66 *Ibid.*, p. 131.
23 p 66 *Ibid.*
24 p 67 *Ibid.*, p. 133.
25 p 67 *Ibid.*, p. 134.
26 p 67 *Ibid.*
27 p 67 *Ibid.*, p. 135.
28 p 67 *Ibid.*, p. 137.
29 p 67 *Ibid.*, p. 139.
30 p 68 *Ibid.*
31 p 68 *Ibid.*, p. 140.
32 p 68 *Ibid.*
33 p 68 *Ibid.*, p. 143.
34 p 68 *Ibid.*, p. 147.
35 p 69 *Ibid.*, p. 150.
36 p 70 *Ibid.*, p. 168.
37 p 70 *Ibid.*, p. 169.
38 p 70 *Ibid.*, p. 170.
39 p 70 *Ibid.*, p. 171.
40 p 70 *Ibid.*, pp. 171–72.
41 p 70 *Ibid.*, p. 172.

42   p 71 *Ibid.*, p. 173.
43   p 71 *Ibid.*, p. 186.
44   p 72 *God and the Astronomers*, p. 265.
45   p 72 *The Philosophy of Plotinus*, I, 195.
46   p 73 *Ibid.*, pp. 202–3.
47   p 73 *Ibid.*, p. 203.
48   p 73 *Ibid.*, p. 204.
49   p 74 *Ibid.*, p. 209.
50   p 74 *Ibid.*, p. 211.
51   p 75 *Ibid.*, p. 213.
52   p 75 *Ibid.*, p. 214.
53   p 75 *Ibid.*
54   p 75 *Ibid.*
55   p 75 *Ibid.*, p. 217.
56   p 75 *Ibid.*, pp. 247–48.
57   p 76 *Ibid.*, p. 250.
58   p 76 *Ibid.*, p. 254.
59   p 76 *Ibid.*
60   p 77 *Ibid.*, p. 262.
61   p 77 *Ibid.*, pp. 263–64.
62   p 78 *Ibid.*, p. 264.
63   p 78 *Ibid.*, II, 39.
64   p 78 *Ibid.*, pp. 38–39.
65   p 78 *Ibid.*, p. 39.
66   p 78 *Ibid.*, p. 40.
67   p 79 *Ibid.*
68   p 79 *Ibid.*, p. 41.
69   p 79 *Ibid.*, p. 42.
70   p 80 *Ibid.*, pp. 43–44 (quoting from the Fifth Ennead).
71   p 80 *Ibid.*, p. 48.
72   p 81 *Ibid.*, p. 53, note.
73   p 81 *Ibid.*, p. 55.
74   p 82 *Ibid.*, p. 56.
75   p 82 *Ibid.*, p. 58.
76   p 82 *Ibid.*
77   p 82 *Ibid.*, pp. 59–60.
78   p 82 *Ibid.*, p. 60.
79   p 83 *Ibid.*, pp. 61–62.
80   p 84 *Ibid.*, p. 66.
81   p 85 *Ibid.*, p. 71.

82   p *85 Ibid.*, p. 74.
83   p *86 Ibid.*, p. 75.
84   p *86 Ibid.*
85   p *86 Ibid.*
86   p *86 Ibid.*, p. 76.
87   p *87 Ibid.*, p. 77.
88   p *88 Ibid.*, p. 78.
89   p *88 Ibid.*, p. 79.
90   p *88 Ibid.*, p. 80.
91   p *89 Ibid.*, p. 82.
92   p *89 Ibid.*, p. 83.
93   p *90 Ibid.*, p. 92.
94   p *90 Ibid.*, pp. 94–95.
95   p *90 Ibid.*, p. 98.
96   p *90 Ibid.*, p. 102.
97   p *91 Ibid.*, p. 104.
98   p *91 Ibid.*
99   p *91 Ibid.*, p. 108.
100 p *91 Ibid.*
101 p *91 Ibid.*, p. 109; cf. *God and the Astronomers*, p. 259.
102 p *92 Ibid.*, p. 116.
103 p *92 God and the Astronomers*, pp. 258–59.
104 p *93 The Philosophy of Plotinus*, II, 109–10.
105 p *93 Ibid.*, pp. 113–14.
106 p *93 Ibid.*, p. 115.
107 p *93 Ibid.*
108 p *94 Ibid.*, pp. 115–16.
109 p *94 Ibid.*, p. 118.
110 p *95 Ibid.*
111 p *96 God and the Astronomers*, p. 261.
112 p *96 Ibid.*, p. 266.
113 p *97 Personal Idealism and Mysticism*, pp. 12–13.
114 p *98 Ibid.*, p. 16.
115 p *98 The Philosophy of Plotinus*, II, 122–25.
116 p *99 Ibid.*, p. 125.
117 p *99 Ibid.*, p. 126.
118 p *100 God and the Astronomers*, pp. 90–91.
119 p *101 Ibid.*, p. 208.
120 p *101 Ibid.*, 209.
121 p *101 Ibid.*, p. 210.

122   p *102* *The Philosophy of Plotinus*, II, 134–35.
123   p *102* *Ibid.*, p. 135.
124   p *103* *Ibid.*, p. 136.
125   p *103* *Ibid.*
126   p *103* *Ibid.*, p. 137.
127   p *103* *Ibid.*, p. 138.
128   p *104* *Ibid.*, pp. 138–39.
129   p *104* *Ibid.*
130   p *104* *Ibid.*, pp. 140–41.
131   p *105* *Ibid.*, pp. 142–43.
132   p *105* *Ibid.*, p. 127.
133   p *106* *Ibid.*, p. 132.
134   p *106* *Ibid.*, p. 133.
135   p *106* *Ibid.*, pp. 161–62.
136   p *107* *Ibid.*, p. 163.
137   p *108* *Ibid.*, p. 189.
138   p *108* *Ibid.*, p. 192.
139   p *109* *Ibid.*, p. 203.
140   p *110* *Ibid.*, p. 216.
141   p *110* *Ibid.*, p. 241.

CHAPTER III

1   p *113* *Faith and Knowledge,* pp. 8, 9.
2   p *114* *Ibid.*, p. 175.
3   p *114* W. R. Inge, *Faith and Its Psychology* (London: Duckworth & Co., 1919), p. 1.
4   p *114* *Ibid.*, p. 2.
5   p *115* W. R. Inge, "Roman Catholic Modernism," *Outspoken Essays (First Series)* (London: Longmans, Green & Co., New Impression, 1927), pp. 169–70.
6   p *115* *God and the Astronomers*, p. 264.
7   p *116* *Faith and Knowledge*, p. 34.
8   p *118* *Christian Mysticism*, p. 5.
9   p *118* *Faith and Its Psychology*, pp. 42–43.
10   p *119* *Faith and Knowledge*, pp. 179–80.
11   p *119* *Ibid.*, p. 179.
12   p *119* *Faith and Its Psychology*, p. 67.
13   p *120* *Ibid.*, p. 69.
14   p *122* *Ibid.*, p. 184.

15 p *122 Ibid.*, p. 198.
16 p *123 Ibid.*
17 p *123 Ibid.*, p. 197.
18 p *124* Rudolf Metz, *A Hundred Years of British Philosophy* (London: George Allen & Unwin, 1938), p. 787.
19 p *124* Inge, *Christian Mysticism*, pp. 6–8.
20 p *124 Personal Idealism and Mysticism*, p. 4.
21 p *125 Ibid.*, p. 5.
22 p *126 Christian Mysticism*, p. 10.
23 p *126 Ibid.*, pp. 10–11.
24 p *126 Ibid.*, p. 12, and *Personal Idealism and Mysticism*, pp. 15–16.
25 p *126 Christian Mysticism*, p. 12.
26 p *127 Ibid.*
27 p *127 Personal Idealism and Mysticism*, p. 12.
28 p *127 Ibid.*
29 p *128 Ibid.*, p. 13.
30 p *129* W. R. Inge, *Christian Ethics and Modern Problems* (5th ed.; London: Hodder & Stoughton, 1932), p. 203.
31 p *129 Ibid.*, p. 204.
32 p *129* W. R. Inge, "Conclusion," in *Science Religion and Reality,* ed. Joseph Needham (London: The Sheldon Press, 1925), p. 383.
33 p *130 Ibid.*, p. 384.
34 p *131 Ibid.*, p. 386.
35 p *131* Metz, *A Hundred Years of British Philosophy*, p. 790.
36 p *132* W. R. Inge, *The Eternal Values* (London: Oxford University Press, 1933), p. 23.
37 p *132 Personal Idealism and Mysticism*, p. 110.
38 p *132 Faith and Its Psychology*, p. 151.
39 p *133 Personal Idealism and Mysticism*, p. 51.
40 p *133 Ibid.*
41 p *134* W. R. Inge, "The Person of Christ," in *Contentio Veritatis* (London: John Murray, 1907), p. 64.
42 p *134 Ibid.*, p. 70.
43 p *135 Ibid.*, pp. 76–77.
44 p *135 Ibid.*, p. 81.
45 p *136 Ibid.*, p. 99.
46 p *138* W. R. Inge, *The Gate of Life* (London: Longmans, Green & Co., 1935), p. 14.

47   p *139* *Personal Idealism and Mysticism*, p. 63.
48   p *139* *Ibid.*
49   p *139* Raymond Bernard Blakney, *Meister Eckhart, A Modern Translation* (New York: Harper & Bros., 1941), p. 267.
50   p *140* Inge, *Personal Idealism and Mysticism*, p. 82.
51   p *141* *Ibid.*, p. 85.
52   p *141* *Ibid.*
53   p *141* *Ibid.*, p. 90.
54   p *141* *Ibid.*, p. 94.
55   p *142* *Ibid.*
56   p *144* *Ibid.*, p. 103.
57   p *144* *Ibid.*, p. 99.
58   p *144* *Ibid.*, p. 109.
59   p *145* *Ibid.*, pp. 119–20.
60   p *145* *Ibid.*, p. 120.
61   p *145* *Ibid.*, p. 116.
62   p *146* *Ibid.*, p. 102.
63   p *147* *Ibid.*, pp. 102–3.
64   p *147* *Ibid.*, p. 101.
65   p *147* *Ibid.*, pp. 105–6.
66   p *148* *God and the Astronomers*, p. 271.
67   p *148* *Ibid.*, p. 269.
68   p *148* *Ibid.*
69   p *149* *Personal Idealism and Mysticism*, p. 121.
70   p *149* *Ibid.*, p. 144.
71   p *149* *Ibid.*, p. 120.
72   p *151* W. R. Inge, *All Saints' Sermons* (London: Macmillan & Co., 1907), p. 128.
73   p *151* *God and the Astronomers*, p. 95.
74   p *151* *Ibid.*, p. 245.
75   p *152* *Faith and Knowledge*, p. 187.
76   p *152* W. R. Inge, "Survival and Immortality," *Outspoken Essays (First Series)*, p. 270. See Pringle-Pattison, *The Idea of God*, pp. 113–14.
77   p *152* *Ibid.*, p. 272.
78   p *153* *Ibid.*
79   p *153* *Ibid.*, p. 273.
80   p *153* *Faith and Knowledge*, p. 193.
81   p *153* "Survival and Immortality," *Outspoken Essays (First Series)*, p. 273.

82   p *154* *Ibid.*, p. 275.
83   p *155* *The Philosophy of Plotinus*, II, 23.
84   p *156* "Survival and Immortality," *Outspoken Essays (First Series)*, p. 276.
85   p *157* *God and the Astronomers*, p. 246.
86   p *157* *The Philosophy of Plotinus*, II, 28.
87   p *157* *God and the Astronomers*, p. 207.
88   p *158* *Ibid.*
89   p *158* *Christian Ethics and Modern Problems*, p. 57.
90   p *158* *God and the Astronomers*, p. 207.

CHAPTER IV

1   p *161* *God and the Astronomers*, p. viii.
2   p *161* *Ibid.*, p. 42.
3   p *162* *Ibid.*, pp. 6–7.
4   p *163* *Ibid.*, p. 185.
5   p *163* *Ibid.*, p. 186.
6   p *163* *Ibid.*, p. 187.
7   p *165* *Ibid.*, p. 25.
8   p *166* *Ibid.*, p. 29.
9   p *167* *Ibid.*, pp. 32–33.
10   p *167* *Ibid.*, p. 34.
11   p *167* *Ibid.*, pp. 49–50.
12   p *168* *Ibid.*, p. 50.
13   p *169* *Ibid.*, pp. 69–70.
14   p *170* Ibid., p. 78.
15   p *170* *Ibid.*, p. 79.
16   p *171* *Ibid.*, p. 88.
17   p *172* *Ibid.*, p. 89.
18   p *173* *Ibid.*, p. 90.
19   p *173* *Ibid.*, p. 91.
20   p *173* *Ibid.*, p. 96.
21   p *173* *Ibid.*, p. 97.
22   p *174* *Ibid.*, p. 101.
23   p *174* *Ibid.*, pp. 101–2.
24   p *175* *Ibid.*, p. 103.
25   p *176* *Ibid.*, p. 111.
26   p *176* *Ibid.*, p. 112, note.
27   p *177* *Ibid.*, p. 113.

28 p *177* *Ibid.*, p. 115.
29 p *178* *Ibid.*, p. 120.
30 p *179* *Ibid.*, p. 282.
31 p *179* *Ibid.*, p. 122.
32 p *180* *Ibid.*, p. 124.
33 p *181* *Ibid.*, p. 131.
34 p *181* *Ibid.*, p. 133.
35 p *181* *Ibid.*
36 p *182* *Ibid.*, p. 134.
37 p *183* *Ibid.*, pp. 137–38.
38 p *184* *Ibid.*, p. 140.
39 p *184* *Ibid.*, 153.
40 p *184* *Ibid.*
41 p *185* *Ibid.*, p. 154.
42 p *185* *Ibid.*
43 p *185* *Ibid.*, p. 156.
44 p *185* *Ibid.*, p. 160.
45 p *186* *Ibid.*, p. 164.
46 p *187* *Ibid.*, p. 165.
47 p *187* *Ibid.*, p. 170.
48 p *187* *Ibid.*, p. 172.
49 p *188* *Ibid.*, p. 173.
50 p *188* *Ibid.*, p. 234.
51 p *189* *Ibid.*, p. 233.
52 p *189* *Ibid.*, p. 234.
53 p *189* *Ibid.*, p. 227.
54 p *190* *Ibid.*, p. 234.
55 p *190* *Ibid.*, pp. 231–32.
56 p *191* *Ibid.*, pp. 238–42.
57 p *191* *Ibid.*, p. 246.
58 p *192* *Ibid.*, p. 248.
59 p *192* *Ibid.*, p. 249.
60 p *193* *Ibid.*, p. 254.
61 p *193* *Ibid.*, p. 256.
62 p *193* *Ibid.*, p. 260.
63 p *193* *Ibid.*, p. 262.
64 p *193* *Ibid.*, p. 264.
65 p *194* *Ibid.*, p. 264, note.
66 p *194* *Ibid.*, pp. 265–66.
67 p *195* "Conclusion," *Science Religion and Reality*, p. 348.

68 p *195 Ibid.*, p. 349.
69 p *196 Ibid.*, p. 350.
70 p *196 Ibid.*
71 p *197 Ibid.*, p. 351.
72 p *197 Ibid.*, p. 352.
73 p *198 Ibid.*
74 p *198 Ibid.*, p. 357.
75 p *200 Ibid.*, p. 360.
76 p *200 Ibid.*, p. 361.
77 p *201 Ibid.*, p. 362.
78 p *201 Ibid.*, p. 364.
79 p *202 Ibid.*, p. 365.
80 p *203 Ibid.*, p. 370.
81 p *204 Ibid.*, p. 372.
82 p *205 Ibid.*, p. 373.
83 p *206 Ibid.*, p. 374.
84 p *206 Ibid.*
85 p *206 Ibid.*, p. 375.
86 p *206 Ibid.*, p. 376.
87 p *207 Ibid.*, p. 378.
88 p *207 Ibid.*
89 p *208 Ibid.*, p. 379.
90 p *208 Ibid.*, p. 380.
91 p *208 Ibid.*
92 p *209 Ibid.*
93 p *209 Ibid.*, p. 381.
94 p *210 Ibid.*, p. 387.
95 p *210 Ibid.*, p. 388.
96 p *212 Personal Idealism and Mysticism*, p. 23.
97 p *212 Ibid.*
98 p *212 Ibid.*, p. 24.
99 p *213 Ibid.*, pp. 25–26.

CHAPTER V

1 p *215 Christian Ethics and Modern Problems*, p. 11.
2 p *216 Ibid.*, pp. 18–19.
3 p *216 Ibid.*, p. 19.
4 p *217 Ibid.*, pp. 22–23.
5 p *219 Ibid.*, p. 26.

6   p *219 Ibid.*, p. 30.
7   p *219 Ibid.*, p. 31.
8   p *220 Things New and Old*, p. 2.
9   p *220 Christian Ethics and Modern Problems*, p. 36.
10 p *221 Ibid.*, p. 47.
11 p *221 Ibid.*, p. 50.
12 p *222 Ibid.*
13 p *222 Ibid.*, p. 51.
14 p *222 Ibid.*
15 p *222 Ibid.*
16 p *223 Ibid.*, p. 52.
17 p *223 Ibid.*, p. 54.
18 p *224 Ibid.*, pp. 54–55.
19 p *224 Ibid.*, p. 55.
20 p *224 Ibid.*, p. 54. Cf. p. 59.
21 p *224 Ibid.*, p. 60.
22 p *224 Ibid.*, p. 59.
23 p *225 Ibid.*, p. 61.
24 p *225 Ibid.*, p. 62.
25 p *225 Ibid.*, p. 63.
26 p *225 Ibid.*, p. 65.
27 p *225 Ibid.*
28 p *227 Ibid.*, pp. 68–69.
29 p *228 Ibid.*, p. 70.
30 p *228 Ibid.*, p. 71.
31 p *228 Ibid.*
32 p *229 Things New and Old*, p. 11.
33 p *229 Christian Ethics and Modern Problems*, p. 73.
34 p *230 Ibid.*, p. 75.
35 p *230 Ibid.*, p. 79.
36 p *230 Ibid.*, p. 84.
37 p *231 Ibid.*, p. 87.
38 p *232 Ibid.*, p. 90.
39 p *232 Ibid.*, p. 95.
40 p *232 Ibid.*, p. 96.
41 p *233 Ibid.*, p. 113.
42 p *234 Ibid.*, p. 116.
43 p *235 Ibid.*, p. 126.
44 p *235 Ibid.*, p. 129.
45 p *235 Ibid.*, pp. 129–30.

46 p *236 Ibid.*, p. 130.
47 p *236 Ibid.*
48 p *236 Ibid.*, p. 132.
49 p *236 Ibid.*, p. 133.
50 p *237 Ibid.*, pp. 133–34.
51 p *237 Ibid.*, p. 135.
52 p *238 Ibid.*, p. 137.
53 p *238 Ibid.*, p. 138.
54 p *239* W. R. Inge, *The End of an Age* (London: Readers Union with Putnam & Co., 1949), p. 77.
55 p *239 Christian Ethics and Modern Problems*, p. 138.
56 p *239 Ibid.*, p. 139.
57 p *239 Ibid.*
58 p *239 Ibid.*, p. 140.
59 p *240 Ibid.*, p. 143.
60 p *240 Ibid., p. 145.*
61 p *241 Ibid.*
62 p *241 Ibid.*, p. 160.
63 p *241 Ibid.*, p. 166.
64 p *242 Ibid.*, p. 170.
65 p *242 Ibid.*, p. 172.
66 p *243 Ibid.*, p. 173.
67 p *243 Ibid.*
68 p *243 Ibid.*, p. 174.
69 p *244 Ibid.*, p. 181.
70 p *245 Ibid.*, p. 189, quoted from Lecky, *History of Rationalism*, I, 386.
71 p *246 Ibid.*, p. 192.
72 p *246 Ibid.*, p. 193.
73 p *246 Ibid.*
74 p *247 Ibid.*
75 p *247 Ibid.*, p. 194.
76 p *247 Ibid.*
77 p *247 Ibid.*, p. 195.
78 p *247 Ibid.*, p. 196.
79 p *248 Ibid.*, p. 197.
80 p *249 Ibid.*, p. 201.
81 p *250 Ibid.*, p. 205.
82 p *250 Ibid.*, p. 207.
83 p *252 Ibid.*, pp. 212–13.

84   p *253 Ibid.*, p. 214.
85   p *253 Ibid.*
86   p *253 Ibid.*, p. 215.
87   p *254 Ibid.*, p. 217.
88   p *254 Ibid.*, p. 219.
89   p *255 Ibid.*, p. 225.
90   p *256 Ibid.*, p. 232.
91   p *256 Ibid.*, p. 234.
92   p *256 Ibid.*, p. 235.
93   p *257 Ibid.*, p. 240.
94   p *257 Ibid.*
95   p *257 Ibid.*, p. 243.
96   p *257 Ibid.*, p. 244.
97   p *258 Ibid.*, p. 246.
98   p *258 Ibid.*, p. 247.
99   p *259 Ibid.*, p. 253.
100   p *260 Ibid.*, pp. 254–55.
101   p *261 Ibid.*, p. 258.
102   p *262 Ibid.*, p. 277.
103   p *262 Ibid.*, pp. 279–80.
104   p *262 Ibid.*, p. 283.
105   p *262 Ibid.*
106   p *263 Ibid.*, p. 286.
107   p *264 Ibid.*, p. 287.
108   p *264 Ibid.*
109   p *264 Ibid.*, p. 290.
110   p *265 Ibid.*, p. 293.
111   p *265 The End of an Age*, pp. 121–22.
112   p *266 Christian Ethics and Modern Problems*, p. 299.
113   p *266 Ibid.*, p. 309.
114   p *266 Things New and Old*, p. 27.
115   p *266 Christian Ethics and Modern Problems*, pp. 309–10.
116   p *267 Ibid.*, p. 311.
117   p *267 The End of an Age*, p. 122.
118   p *267 Christian Ethics and Modern Problems*, p. 331.
119   p *268 Ibid.*, p. 332.
120   p *268 Ibid.*, p. 340.
121   p *269 Ibid.*, pp. 342–43.
122   p *270 Ibid.*, pp. 343–44.
123   p *271 Ibid.*, pp. 349–50.

124 p *271 Ibid.*, p. 354.
125 p *271 Ibid.*, p. 365.
126 p *272 Ibid.*, p. 367.
127 p *272 Ibid.*, p. 370.
128 p *273 Ibid.*, p. 374.
129 p *274 Ibid.*, p. 379.
130 p *275 Ibid.*, p. 381.
131 p *275 Ibid.*, p. 382.
132 p *276 Ibid.*, pp. 399–400.

ACKNOWLEDGMENTS

The various publishers of Dean Inge's works have been most cooperative in granting permissions to quote, as have those from whom biographical information or critical comment has been drawn.

The author wishes to express his grateful acknowledgment to the following for the various permissions granted:

To David McKay Company, Inc., for numerous quotations from the following works, all by Dean Inge himself: *Vale, The Platonic Tradition in English Religious Thought, Personal Religion and the Life of Devotion, Things New and Old, The Philosophy of Plotinus* (2 vols.), *Personal Idealism and Mysticism, God and the Astronomers, Outspoken Essays (First Series), The Gate of Life.*

To Methuen & Co., Ltd., for several quotations from W. R. Inge, *Christian Mysticism.*

To Hutchinson & Co. (Publishers) Ltd., for a brief quotation from W. R. Inge, *Mysticism in Religion,* and various quotations from W. R. Inge, *Diary of a Dean.*

To T. & T. Clark for several passages from W. R. Inge, *Faith and Knowledge,* Second Edition, 1905.

To John Murray for a brief passage from W. R. Inge, *Studies of English Mystics,* and for various quotations from Dean Inge's essay, "The Person of Christ," in *Contentio Veritatis,* a symposium.

To Gerald Duckworth & Co., Ltd., for several passages from W. R. Inge, *Faith and Its Psychology,* in Duckworth's *Studies in Theology,* a series.

To George Allen & Unwin, Ltd., for two brief passages

from Rudolph Metz, *A Hundred Years of British Philosophy*.

To Hodder & Stoughton, Ltd., for various passages from W. R. Inge, *Christian Ethics and Modern Problems*.

To The Society for Promoting Christian Knowledge for several passages from Dean Inge's "Conclusion" to Joseph Needham (ed.), *Science Religion and Reality*, a symposium.

To Oxford University Press for a brief passage from W. R. Inge, *The Eternal Values*, published under the auspices of Durham University.

To Harper & Brothers for a brief passage from Raymond Bernard Blakney, *Meister Eckhart, A Modern Translation*, Torchbook #8.

To Macmillan & Co., Ltd., for a brief passage from W. R. Inge, *All Saints Sermons*.

To Putnam & Co., Ltd., for brief passages from W. R. Inge, *End of an Age*.

To *The Christian Century* for a passage from "Last Great Victorian," in its issue of November 14, 1961.

To *Newsweek* for brief passages from "End of the Gloomy Dean," in its issue of March 8, 1954.

A LIST OF BOOKS BY W. R. INGE

All Saints Sermons. London: Macmillan & Co., 1907.

Assessments and Anticipations. London: Cassell & Co., 1929. Published also as *Labels and Libels*. New York and London: Harper & Bros., 1929.

Authority and the Inner Light. Liverpool: J. A. Thompson, 1912.

The Awakening of the Soul: An Introduction to Christian Mysticism, ed. A. F. Judd. London: A. R. Mowbray & Co., 1959.

The Bible and How to Read It: Being the Introduction to Every Man's Bible. London, New York, etc.: Longmans, Green & Co., 1935.

Christian Ethics and Modern Problems. London: Hodder & Stoughton, 1930; New York and London: G. P. Putnam's Sons, 1930.

Christian Mysticism, Considered in Eight Lectures Delivered before the University of Oxford. London: Methuen & Co., 1899, 1912, 1933, 1956; New York: Charles Scribner's Sons, 1899; New York: Meridian Books, 1956.

The Church and the Age. London, New York, etc.: Longmans, Green & Co., 1912.

The Church in the World: Collected Essays by William Ralph Inge. London: Longmans, Green & Co., 1927.

Diary of a Dean. London: Hutchinson & Co., 1949; New York: Macmillan Co., 1950.

The End of an Age and Other Essays. London: Readers Union with Putnam & Co., 1949; New York: Macmillan Co., 1949.

England. New York: Charles Scribner's Sons, 1926, 1927, 1933; London: Ernest Benn, 1953; New York: McGraw-Hill Book Co., 1953.

The Eternal Values: Delivered before the University of Durham at Armstrong College, Newcastle-on-Tyne, on November 23rd and and 24th, 1932. London: Oxford University Press, 1933.

Every Man's Bible. London: Longmans, Green & Co., 1931, 1935.

Faith and Its Psychology. London: Duckworth & Co., 1909, 1910, 1919; New York: Charles Scribner's Sons, 1910.

Faith and Knowledge. Edinburgh: T. & T. Clark, 1905.

The Fall of the Idols. London: Putnam & Co., 1940.

Freedom, Love, and Truth. London, New York, etc.: Longmans, Green & Co., 1936.

The Gate of Life. London, New York, etc.: Longmans, Green & Co., 1935.

God and the Astronomers: Containing the Warburton Lectures, 1931–1933. London, New York, etc.: Longmans, Green & Co., 1933, 1934.

Greeks and Barbarians: Presidential Address Delivered to the Classical Association at St. Paul's School, 4th January, 1934. London: John Murray, 1934.

Hebrews: A Little Library of Exposition, with New Studies, by W. R. Inge and H. L. Goudge, illustrated by T. Noyes-Lewis. London, etc.: Cassell & Co., 1926.

The Idea of Progress. Oxford: The Clarendon Press, 1920.

Lay Thoughts of a Dean. New York and London: G. P. Putnam's Sons, 1926; Garden City, New York: Garden City Publishing Co., 1926.

Liberty and Natural Rights. Oxford: The Clarendon Press, 1934.

Light, Life and Love: Selections from the German Mystics of the Middle Ages. London: Methuen & Co., 1904, 1920, 1935.

Modernism in Literature. London: Oxford University Press, 1937.

More Lay Thoughts of a Dean. London and New York: Putnam & Co., 1931, 1932.

Mysticism in Religion. London and New York: Hutchinson's University Library, 1947; Chicago: University of Chicago Press, 1948; London: Hutchinson & Co., 1959.

Origen. London: G. Cumberlege, 1946.

Our Present Discontents. London: Putnam & Co., 1938.

Outspoken Essays (First Series). London, New York, etc.: Longmans, Green & Co., 1921, 1927.

Outspoken Essays (Second Series). London, New York, etc.: Longmans, Green & Co., 1922.

A Pacifist in Trouble. London: Putnam & Co., 1939.

Personal Idealism and Mysticism: The Paddock Lectures for 1906, Delivered at the General Seminary, New York. New York, London, etc.: Longmans, Green & Co., 1907.

Personal Religion and the Life of Devotion. London: Longmans, Green & Co., 1924.

The Philosophy of Plotinus: The Gifford Lectures at St. Andrews, 1916–1918. 2 vols. London, New York, etc.: Longmans, Green & Co., 1918, 1929.

The Platonic Tradition in English Religious Thought: The Hulsean Lectures at Cambridge, 1925–1926. London, New York, etc.: Longmans, Green & Co., 1926.

Plotinus. London: H. Milford, 1929.

Possible Recovery? London: The Individualist Bookshop, 1941; London: The Society of Individualists, 1943.

Protestantism. London: Ernest Benn, 1927; Garden City, New York: Doubleday, Doran & Co., 1928.

A Rustic Moralist. London: Putnam & Co., 1937.

Science and Ultimate Truth: Fison Memorial Lecture, 1926, Delivered at Guy's Hospital Medical School, March 25, 1926. New York, London, etc.: Longmans, Green & Co., 1926.

The Social Teaching of the Church. New York, Cincinnati, etc.: The Abingdon Press, 1930; London: published for the Social Service Lecture Trust, The Epworth Press, 1930.

Society in Rome under the Caesars. New York: Charles Scribner's Sons, 1888.

Speculum Animae: Four Devotional Addresses Given in the Chapel of Corpus Christi College, Cambridge, to Public-School Masters and College Tutors, on Jan. 14 and 15, 1911. London, New York, etc.: Longmans, Green & Co., 1911, 1920.

Studies of English Mystics: St. Margaret's Lectures, 1905. London: John Murray, 1906.

Talks in a Free Country. London: Putnam & Co., 1943.

Things New and Old: Sermons and Addresses in Great St. Mary's, Cambridge, January 28th to February 5th, 1933. London, New York, etc.: Longmans, Green & Co., 1933.

The Things That Remain. New York: Harper & Bros., 1958; Published in England under the title *Goodness and Truth.* London: A. R. Mowbray & Co., 1958.

Truth and Falsehood in Religion: Six Lectures Delivered at Cambridge to Undergraduates in the Lent Term, 1906. New York: E. P. Dutton & Co., 1907.

Types of Christian Saintliness. London, New York, etc.: Longmans, Green & Co., 1915.

Ultimate Values. London: The Society of Individualists and National League for Freedom, 1945.

Vale. London, New York, etc.: Longmans, Green & Co., 1934.
The Victorian Age: The Rede Lecture for 1922. Cambridge: The
University Press, 1922.
*Wit and Wisdom of Dean Inge: Selected and Arranged by Sir
James Marchant, with a Preface by William Ralph Inge*. London,
New York, etc.: Longmans, Green & Co., 1927.

INDEX

6²

✓6

14 DAY BOOK

656869

B   INGE

HELM

GLOOMY DEAN

✓**656869**

B   INGE

HELM

GLOOMY TROTTER